A WOMAN OF SUBSTANCE

Lilliet Garrison

A WOMAN OF SUBSTANCE

Copyright © 2012 by Lilliet Garrison
Printed in the United States of America
Published by: Wisdom Brings Freedom Ministries

All rights reserved, including the right to reproduce this book or portions thereof in any form whatsoever without permission, except for brief quotations in books and critical reviews.

All Scripture quotations, unless indicated are taken from the Holy Bible, New International Version, (NIV) copyright © 1973, 1978, 1984 by International Bible Society. Used by permission of Zondervan Publishing House. All rights reserved.

(Bold and italicized words in Scripture quotations reflect the author's emphasis.)

ACKNOWLEDGEMENTS

A huge thank you to my editor Donna Huisjen.

As always your attention to detail and knowledge of the Word, as well as your patience and excellence is appreciated beyond words.

And immense thanks to my husband Rick, for your constant encouragement and support.

LILLIET'S OTHER BOOKS ON AMAZON

http://www.amazon.com/Lilliet-Garrison/e/B004H28MCU

Saying Goodbye to Discouragement-100 Bible Verses About Discouragement
How to Test the Spirits to See if They Are from God-61 Scriptures About Testing the Spirits
Binding the Strongman-How to Keep Satan from Stealing What is Rightfully Yours
How to Know if You Belong to God-54 Scriptures About Knowing God Personally
19 Ways We Grieve the Holy Spirit–100 Scriptures About Grieving the Holy Spirit
How to Resist the Devil-100 Scriptures on Resisting the Devil
Victory without Trying-100 Scriptures About God's Grace
Practicing the Presence of Jesus– 24 Scriptures on the Presence of Jesus
El Shaddai-The God Who is Enough- 67 B.V. on God is Always Enough
How to Die to Self…and receive the life Jesus died to give you
10 Reasons Why the Bible is the Word of God-100 Bible Verses About the Word of God
Recognizing the Antichrist: Bible Signs of the End Times-65 B.V. About the Antichrist
Deliverance from Bondage-100 Bible Verses About Deliverance from Evil
How to be Ready for the Rapture-100 Bible Verses About the Rapture
All of God's Promises are Yes and Amen -65 Bible Verses About Answered Prayers
I Will Not Leave You Comfortless-49 Bible Verses About the Comforter
Satan Wants Your Mind- 85 B.V About Satan & Our Mind -47 B.V. About Having a Sound Mind
How to Pray for the Lost, 100 Bible Verses About Praying for the Lost
Defeating Satan and Evil Spirits-100 Bible Verses About Satan, 58 Bible Verses About Evil Spirits
Don't Let Your Heart Harden- 40 Bible Verses About a Hard Heart
The Most Important Question -7 Benefits to Making the Right Decision about Jesus
How to Have Daily Family Devotions -91 Bible Verses About the Family

How God Guides Us – 96 Bible Verses About God's Guidance
Because Your Heart Was Tender-You Will Not See Evil-100 Scriptures. on the Tender Hearted-98 About Gentleness
A Much-Needed Heart Change- 100 Bible Verses About the Heart
Our Faithful Promiser-100 B.V. About the Promises of God - 67 B.V. About the Faithfulness of God
How to Overcome Sin-100 Bible Verses About Sin
Prayer Puts God to Work – 100 Bible Verses About Prayer
Spiritual Warfare-A Practical & Real Path to Victory over Temptation
Be Filled with the Holy Spirit-Living the Spirit Filled Life
A Faith that Saves-What is Believing Faith?
Choosing to Live One Day at a Time
Nothing Can Separate You from the Love of God
What Does the Bible Say About Satan and the Origin of Evil? 100 Bible Verses About Satan
Satan's Twisted Counterfeits – 100 Bible Verses About Satan
Is Heaven Real? – 100 Bible Verses About Heaven
What God's Love Teaches Us – 100 Bible Verses About God's Love
What Does the Bible Say About God's Mercy and Grace-85 Verses About God's Grace–88 About God's Mercy
What Does the Bible Say About Not Being Fearful–57 Verses About "Do Not Fear"–100 About Fear
What Does the Bible Say About Marriage? – 100 Bible Verses of God's Counsel for a Thriving, God-Centered Marriage
Will God Forgive Me? 100 Bible Verses About God's Forgiveness
What Does the Bible Say About Life After Death – 91 Bibles Verses from God to You
100 Bible Verses About Eternal Life
100 Bible Verses About Money: What God Says About Wealth & Poverty
Scriptures of God's Unfailing Love for You–God's Promises to Love You Forever
100 Bible Verses of God's Healing Power
40 Healing Scriptures That Will Forever Change Your Life
God's Promises to Bless You and Prosper You
Jesus Christ, Our Great Healer
God's Emergency Phone Numbers When You Find Yourself in Need
Prayers in Times of Trouble
The God of All Comfort Devotional
Prayer for Every Circumstance
God's Loving Kindness
The Power of Prayer to Change a Life
How to Be Sure You Are Saved
God's Promises for Your Every Concern
God's Promises to You in the Bible
Considerations for the God Seeker: Gems from Charles Spurgeon
Living Satisfied: Life Lessons from King Solomon and the Book of Ecclesiastes
7 Keys to a Victorious Life
How to Make Good Decisions–Practical Steps to Making God-Glorifying Choices
Secrets to Being a Happy Christian
Absolute Surrender–Surrender What You Can't Keep, To Gain What You Can Never Buy
The Greatest Prayer
How to Develop an Intimate Relationship with God
When God is Silent
How to Gain a Clear Conscience
The Unpardonable Sin – Is This Sin Really Unforgiveable?
A Woman of Powerful Prayer
Don't Be A Worry Wart – Accept God's Peace and Change Your Life
Breaking Free from Guilt and Shame
Getting Unstuck–Moving Beyond What's Holding You Back
The Christian Woman's Guide to Abundant Success
A Woman of Grace and Strength – Growing Strong in the Grace and Knowledge of our Lord
A Woman of Substance–Growing Spiritually Mature in an Immature World (Unabridged, 8 volumes in 1 book)
A Woman of Substance Series (8 individual volumes)

DEDICATION

I'd like to dedicate this book to:

My husband Rick

Our daughter Elisa

And our son Eric

As we continue to run our race, may we never forget God's wise counsel that makes us victorious.

CONTENTS

1	She Sets Goals and Plans for Success	9
2	Her Confidence is in the Lord	62
3	She is Saved by Grace—Discerning Real Conversion	115
4	She Understands Her Natural Sin Nature	150
5	She is Spiritually Mature	201
6	She Understands Truth	271
7	She Knows the Revealed Will of God for Her Life	321
8	She is Ever Watchful and Mindful of the Times	350

Prayer for Salvation	388
End Notes	395

THANKING YOU IN ADVANCE

I'd like to thank you for purchasing my book. If you find help and wisdom in it and believe it will help others too, please take a moment to leave a review on Amazon. Your feedback pushes the gospel "into all the world." Thank you, Lilliet

1

SHE SETS GOALS AND PLANS

FOR SUCCESS

*"Then the L*ORD *replied: 'Write down the revelation and make it plain on tablets so that a herald may run with it'" (Habakkuk 2:2).*

Successful people don't plan for failure. They make success a priority and do everything in their power and ability to plan for it. For them, planning is intentional and goes before execution.

People don't plan to fail—they simply fail to plan. If you find yourself with nothing of real value, perhaps it's because you've planned for nothing. No plans, no goals, and no aims typically lead to receiving nothing back in return.

Many fool themselves believing that living without goals equates to living spontaneously. But life has a way of carrying us along with the current, and with no intentionality the years quickly pass us by. Our negligence when it comes to purposeful living can have disastrous consequences for us. As God's Word puts it, "hasty shortcuts lead to poverty" (Proverbs 21:5).

We would be wise then to know not only what leads to success and resources, but also what leads to failure and deficiency.

God gave men and women a command. He told them to be fruitful and to multiply. God never gives people a command without giving them a blueprint for achieving that plan. God's Word holds all the wisdom keys we need for victory, increase, and achievement. It explains His methods of success and for multiplying everything we have. God wants us to triumph and if we'll study His methods—*we will!*

Goal setting is one method to realizing that success. God's Word makes clear to us the difference between worldly success, which can be lost, and God directed or sustained success, which is the *blessing* of God on our life.

By taking a serious look at what God planned for man—to take his rightful dominion and to overcome the evil one—we're able to achieve and maintain the success we were born for.

Characteristics of successful people.

1. Optimism
2. Aim, purpose, and vision
3. Willingness to work
4. Discipline
5. Integrated mind
6. Prolific reader
7. Risk taking
8. Realizing power of expectation
9. Mastery
10. Well-roundedness

Many laws that apply to the natural world have carryover value for us in the spiritual realm. It's God who gives us our temperament, personality, aptitudes, yearnings and dreams.

We can maximize our given potential by turning to God to make us into the perfect (complete) person He has in mind. By surrendering our puny plans and allowing Him to supersede them with His great and awesome plans, we work with Him to enhance our potential to become great.

When we surrender to Jesus, He makes the plan come about. With surrender comes a supernatural ability the Holy Spirit works in and through us. We can't circumvent the process, as this ability comes to us by no other person or means.

Since all of us have experienced some kind of failure, one of the most important life skills we can master is learning how to respond to it. Successful people know how to turn every failure into a learning experience to further their future success.

Setting goals is the first learning step toward turning around any failure. It may be necessary to write down what it is that brought about the failure. Then identify from God's Word the wisdom step needed to correct the problem. This is coupling intention with appropriate action.

Success requires diligence and planning for it requires that we know and understand God's methods for achieving that success.

> "In all your ways submit to him, and he will make your paths straight." (Proverbs 3:6)

> "Wise people think before they act; fools don't—and even brag about their foolishness." (Proverbs 13:16)

> "Good planning and hard work lead to prosperity, but hasty shortcuts lead to poverty." (Proverbs 21:5)

There are biblical laws or principles of success that successful people follow. By earnestly looking at what these laws entail and planning ahead for success, you can be assured of living a productive, contented, and victorious life.

Jesus lived with purpose, plans, and goals.

Jesus knew the Father and He purposed to do the Father's will. He knew beforehand what the Father had sent Him to accomplish. He understood that *His purpose was to glorify His Father* and to do *nothing* outside His will.

In Acts 16 we're told that Paul and the disciples followed plans. Although on more than one occasion those plans to present the gospel in a certain location were overridden by the Spirit of God. (See Acts 16:6-7).

Paul lived his life and ministry with balance: he planned yet remained sensitive to the Lord's directive.

There are two extremes in planning.

1. ***Not to plan at all.*** In Proverbs 6:6-11, the author rebukes the man who prepares for nothing, calling him a sluggard. He implores the sluggard to observe the ant, which "prepares her food in the summer, and gathers her provision in the harvest" (verse 8). According to Proverbs, the wise person in all things will establish objectives and prepare for the future.

2. ***To rely solely on our mind***—and to neglect our heart. When we're determined to run our life according to our own logic, we take God out of the equation. We neither ask Him for guidance nor believe that He knows better than we do how we should live.

It's true that God gives us our intellect for making decisions. And the most important decision we can make is to live according to His plans and purposes for us. The desire to do it God's way, by making use of His wisdom, will keep us from wasting our potential.

> Jesus replied: "'Love the Lord your God with all your heart and with all your soul and with all your mind.'" (Matthew 22:37)

When we live life as we see fit by clinging to our own reasoning, worry soon creeps in and takes over. When our plans go wrong, we become anxious about our future. The more we try to control our circumstances, the more fearful we become.

> "Therefore, do not worry about tomorrow, for tomorrow will worry about itself. Each day has enough trouble of its own." (Matthew 6:34)

Wise people recognize their limited, finite nature and subject their plans to the Lord. James speaks to those who plot out all their tomorrows without consulting God about the plans He has for them.

> "Now listen, you who say, 'Today or tomorrow we will go to this or that city, spend a year there, carry on business and make money.' Why, you do not even know what will happen tomorrow. What is your life? You are a mist that appears for a little while and then vanishes."(James 4:13-14)

James calls such presumption arrogance.

> "Instead, you ought to say, 'If it is the Lord's will, we will live and do this or that. As it is, you boast in your arrogant schemes. All such boasting is evil.'" (James 4:15-16)

In reality, James balances out these extremes. We're to use our minds and set goals, but we must do so in humility recognizing that God alone controls our destiny.

Setting goals is serious business. We ought not to be so anxious about life that we make rigid plans that are beyond our capacity to keep, nor should we fail to make any plans at all. Rather, with all humility, let us seek God's guidance and submit our plans to Him for His glory.

Only two choices.

We're given only two choices by God—to ***believe*** Him or to ***disbelieve*** Him! It's essential that we make the right choice.

God's abundant blessings are for those who love and obey Him. God is not miserly towards us, but rather full of grace, tenderness, and love. He does everything possible to draw us to Himself so we can obtain those blessings.

The book of Proverbs contains numerous wisdom keys for our victory. God's Word makes abundantly clear that God has both the plan and the methods for getting us to the good things He has for us. Those good things will come from making God's goals—our goals.

Vision comes with God-centered goals.

The book of Habakkuk tells us how goal setting will get us to those good things.

- "I will stand at my watch and station myself on the ramparts; I will look to see what he will say to me, and what answer I am to give to this complaint. Then the Lord replied: ***Write down the revelation and make it plain*** on tablets so that a herald may run *with it.* For the revelation awaits an appointed time; it speaks of the end and will not prove false. Though it linger, wait for it; it will certainly come and will not delay." "See, the enemy is puffed up; his desires are not upright—but the righteous person will live by his faithfulness." (Habakkuk 2:1-4)

Habakkuk 2:1–4 teaches us that we're to live by *vision* and establish God-centered goals for our lives. We can begin to discern the vision by first taking time to hear God's voice during prayer and from reading His Word. From that point on, as Habakkuk records, we should "***write down the revelation (the vision) and make it plain.***"

God's vision for each of us individually relates to His will for our lives. He asks us to write down on paper what we perceive His will and destiny for us to be. We can only do this accurately when we dig into His Word and learn what His will is for every person. Part of that will is for us to learn more about Him and accept Him personally.

According to the Jamieson, Fausset, and Brown Bible Commentary:

> "Write the vision—which I am about to reveal to you. Make it plain" (Deuteronomy 27:8): Is to write it in large legible characters upon tables—boxwood tables covered with wax, on which national affairs were engraved with an iron pen, and then hung up in public,

at the prophets' own houses, or at the temple, that those who passed might read them. Compare Luke 1:63, "writing table," that is, tablet. That he may run that reads it—commonly explained, "so intelligible as to be easily read by any one running past;" but then it would be, "that he that runs may read it." The true sense is, "so legible that whoever reads it, may run to tell all whom he can the good news of the foe's coming doom, and Judah's deliverance."

Run is not literal running, but "that he who reads it may run through it," that is, read it at once without difficulty.

Set your goals on heavenly gains.

Paul imparts the *secret of life* in Philippians 3:12–21. He tells us that God calls us to an improbable task. This task: *Pursuing intimacy with Jesus.* The fulfillment of this charge results in our gaining significance, purpose, and joy.

Paul urges each of us to set our goals on heavenly gains. He provides two ways to accomplish this task.

1. ***Pursue God's prize*** (Philippians 3:12–16). In these verses Paul likens the Christian life to running a race. The goal of this race is to win the prize. The race holds the image of our sanctification process. In other words, those who enter this race are believers who are called to *spiritual maturity—knowing Christ intimately and passionately.*

Paul was able to change the world through his focused life. Although he didn't consider that he had arrived at his goal, nevertheless, he continued to pursue the purpose of the Christian life. He kept his goal of continual sanctification in sight, to win the prize set before him.

- "Not that I have already obtained all this, or have already arrived at my goal, but I press on to take hold of that for which Christ Jesus took hold of me. Brothers and sisters, I do not consider myself yet to have taken hold of it. But one thing I do: Forgetting what is behind and straining toward what is ahead." (Philippians 3:12–13)

Paul had a humble dissatisfaction and a holy discontentment. He doesn't compare himself with other believers. He compares himself with Jesus. Consequently,

Paul says twice,

- "I press on toward the goal to win the prize for which God has called me heavenward in Christ Jesus." (Philippians 3:14)

2. ***To reach forward to what lies ahead.*** Paul is using an athletic metaphor of a runner who strains to wins the race—*to reach victory*. Paul is reaching forward and pressing on "toward the goal for the prize of the upward call of God in Christ Jesus." It's a heavenward call to Jesus Himself. Running to win this race

has eternal rewards with the message, "Well done, good and faithful servant!" (Matthew 25:21)

God's goals for all people.

God's goal isn't to make man good. God's goal is to reach down to man and show him the way back to relationship. It was love that motivated God not to give up on sin-prone man. Jesus is the bridge that God provides to make that way back possible.

God's desire is that we grow towards wholeness and maturity. When we see our inner weaknesses and deficiencies, we can bring them to God for healing. God wants us to rely on Him and see Him as a trusted friend, deliver, and counselor. As James said,

> "Therefore confess your sins [and faults] to each other and pray for each other so that you may be healed."

God's goal is to make us whole, for when we're whole we're free. Free to love our Lord entirely. God is the only One who can heal and restore us completely. He's the only One who can forgive our sin and satisfy our deepest longings to be unconditionally loved and accepted.

If your first goal is to turn to the Lord for the guidance He offers, God will make your path straight. Since God is light, it stands to reason that where God is—there is light. If you have God, then you have His light within you. There's no light whatsoever in Satan—nor any darkness in God!

God's goal to make you whole is achieved when you surrender your life to Him. He then sheds light into your darkened mind and heart. And with that light, your path is illuminated. By asking the Holy Spirit for His guidance and wisdom, we can stay within the light and avoid the darkness into which we'd stray were we to insist on going our own way.

> "There is a way that seems right to a man, but in the end it leads to death." (Proverbs 14:12)

Wholeness comes when we accept God's goals for us.

1. God's will (or desire) for every human being is ***salvation***, though He leaves the decision to accept His offer up to us.

2. His will for every Christian is ***sanctification***.

The basic meaning of *sanctification* is "to be set apart." Man is born with a problem. That problem is sin, for sin creates conflict within us. For the believer, there must be an ever-increasing sense that although sin remains, it isn't in control. It is one thing for sin to live *in* the believer, but it is quite another for the believer to live *in* sin.

The solution to man's problem is the Holy Spirit. He's the agent of sanctification who works within us to subdue sinful impulses and produce right actions.

The Greek word for sanctification is a form of the word "holy." To be sanctified is to be made holy. That is, to be set apart for God and changed into the moral and spiritual person God has purposed us to be. Sanctification doesn't happen through good intentions but through the inner working of the Holy Spirit (Romans 8:13; 2 Corinthians 3:17-18; Galatians 5:22).

- "For this is the *will of God*, your *sanctification*." (1 Thessalonians 4:3).

Our responsibility is to agree to cooperate with this process. Sanctification is the process of being practically changed into the person God intends, set apart and made holy.

Our ultimate goal is salvation and sanctification.

When we receive the salvation that's offered to us through Jesus, we obtain a peace we've never before experienced. It's His promised favor to those who accept Him. Those who come seeking Him with a humble, repentant heart are guaranteed to find Him.

Christian goal setting is a vital process toward reaching a greater degree of personal and spiritual maturity. Goal setting helps us achieve the success we desire in all areas of life, because when we get the *first* priority right all else follows.

> "But seek ***first*** his kingdom and his righteousness, and all these things will be given to you as well." (Matthew 6:33, bold italics added)

Spiritual goals are the most important objectives you'll ever set for yourself. Many neglect this vital area, choosing rather to focus on education, family, or career ambitions. But for the Christian, goal setting takes on a whole new meaning. There's power in setting spiritual goals. Without them Satan will quickly distract you from what's really important in life.

It starts with covenant relationship.

When marriage occurs there's a legal change of status. We go from being single to being married. In the same way our status changes once we accept Christ as our Savior. We move from being a lost sinner, to becoming a justified "saint" and start a lifelong process of change that will culminate in our own resurrection. The process starts when we respond to God in relationship, drawing near to Him in love and gratitude and offering our lives to Him in humble, lifelong service.

Your life as a married person starts with your marriage vows. Marriage is a covenant relationship, the bonding together of two quite different people. Eventually the two of you meld into "one" person, as God intended for individuals united in marriage. This process, painful as it may sometimes be, helps us mature as we learn to give and take, negotiate, love unconditionally, and become increasingly selfless.

Receiving salvation results in a covenant relationship with the Lord. The same process that occurs in marriage takes place within the born-again believer whose old sin nature is being transformed into Christ's likeness. We move from being self-indulgent individuals to submitting our will to Christ and living in partnership with Him. We co-labor with Him in a marriage relationship.

Afflictions and sanctification.

Our times of greatest difficulty often lead us to repent. The desire for change usually doesn't occur when we're operating in comfort or in accomplishment. Our self-pride at such times may keep us from seeing ourselves clearly. We may perceive ourselves to be quite acceptable and accomplished, while in reality we are tragically blind to the realities of who we are apart from Christ.

If we'll make ourselves willing recipients, God will do everything necessary to make us partakers of His holiness and useful in His service.

- "Pride leads to destruction and arrogance leads to downfall." (Proverbs 18:18)

Without sanctification there would be no change, no walking in the Spirit, no purpose, and no hope of living a life that's pleasing to God. The Holy Spirit helps us change our beliefs, attitudes, and actions so that we might reflect Christ's image.

Don't become discouraged if you feel this process is taking too long. Humility and a sincere desire to submit to God's goals for you can speed it up to a certain extent. But we must keep in mind that the task of looking daily to God to change us from within, is in itself an exciting adventure.

When we look back we can see that we have indeed made progress. When we continue on, we continue to progress. This steady, incremental growth spurs us on to greater works and revelation, while helping us avoid any desire to return to our former way of living.

> "Sometimes it takes a painful situation to make us change our ways." (Proverbs 20:30, GNB)

God wants us firmly dependent on Him every day.

God provided manna one day at a time for the Israelites in the desert. Those who refused to depend on God's daily provision, who tried to set aside a portion of one day's supply for the next, soon found the hoarded manna to be unfit for eating.

God wants you to rely on Him daily for your provision and spiritual growth. Don't be tempted to grow for a season and then expect that development to carry you through the rest of your life.

Consider God's revelation to Jeremiah.

> "For I know the thoughts that I think toward you, says the LORD, thoughts of peace and not of evil, to give you a future and a hope." (Jeremiah 29:11)

Pause for a moment to imagine God thinking about your future. He knows you're in need of hope: a confident expectation of blessing and provision. We may not be privy to all the details or know step by step how He'll do it, but we know His true nature. That's all we need to rest assured that He'll take care of us.

We weren't created to be omniscient, to know everything as God does. God reveals our future to us gradually as we grow in faith and knowledge of Him. God wisely reveals only what we're able at any given point in our spiritual maturity to perceive, understand, and apply. God is patient, and He waits for us to continue in our growth process so we can handle additional revelation from Him.

> "Behold, the former things have come to pass, and new things I declare; before they spring forth I tell you of them." (Isaiah 42:9)

> "Forget the former things; do not dwell on the past. See, I am doing a new thing! Now it springs up; do you not perceive it? I am making a way in the desert and streams in the wasteland." (Isaiah 43:18–19)

> "Remember the former things, those of long ago; I am God, and there is no other; I am God, and there is none like me. I make known the end from the beginning, from ancient times, what is still to come. I say, 'My purpose will stand and I will do all that I please.' From the east I summon a bird of prey; from a far-off land, a man to fulfill my purpose. What I have said, that I will bring about; what I have planned, that I will do. (Isaiah 46:9–11)

Careful study of these Scriptures shows us that God deliberately leads each of us to our specific destiny, with which He's already completely familiar.

There are three stages to the goal of sanctification.

Stage One: First, God's will is revealed with authority only in the Bible. We're to have a renewed mind, which results from a born-again spirit. Once we receive the Holy Spirit through salvation, we're able to understand what God's Word is saying to us. Without the renewed mind we'll invariably distort the Scriptures, seeking to avoid their radical commands for self-denial, love, purity, and ultimate satisfaction in Christ alone.

Paul says that the Scriptures are inspired and that they make the Christian "competent, equipped for every good work" (2 Timothy 3:16). Not just for some good works but for *every* good work. We become competent by getting to know the God of the work. This is done when we read the Bible, ask for wisdom and discernment, and seek God's face through prayer and worship.

Stage Two: The second stage of appropriating God's will for our lives is our application of biblical truth to new situations that may or may not be explicitly addressed in the Bible. The Bible doesn't tell us, for example, which person to marry (or whether to marry), what job to take, or where to live.

God desires for us a renewed mind that's shaped and governed by His Word and Spirit. The Bible contains His revealed will to us, and it's only with a renewed mind that we can discern what He's calling us to do. God's aim is to give us a new way of thinking and judging, not just new information. His goal is for us to be transformed, sanctified, and freed by the truth of his revealed Word (John 8:32; 17:17).

Stage Three: The third stage of adhering to God's will for us is to live and make decisions purposefully and intentionally based on our new spirit. Many of us tend to be spontaneous, not typically given to thinking before we act or speak. New decisions will now be premeditated, as our renewed mind becomes conformed to the image of Christ. Just as a new pair of shoes must conform to our feet, Christians must conform to the One they claim to follow. Christians are to be Christ-followers. Christ can't lead us unless we're willing to follow. A Christ-follower must take on the attributes of his or her leader—Christ. No longer does the flesh automatically act out and take over or the mouth speaks before considering the outcome. Our new spirit doesn't give in to the desires of the flesh or conform to the world.

- Jesus said, "Out of the abundance of the heart the mouth speaks. The good person out of his good treasure brings forth good, and the evil person out of his evil treasure brings forth evil. I tell you, on the day of judgment people will give account for every careless word they speak." (Matthew 12:34–36)

Why is this part of God's will for us? Because God commands us not to be prideful, greedy, jealous, envious, or angry, and lingering too long on these destructive emotions eventually produces actions that are both premeditated and calculated. These sensual emotions can flare up suddenly because our heart and mind aren't deliberately focused on what we're about to do.

Unregenerate man apart from Christ is naturally carnal. We're all guilty of having experienced these negative emotions because we're all natural. That is, until we're born-again. Only then can our natural tendencies be conformed to the image of Christ. Until our sin nature has been supernaturally transformed by the renewing of our mind, we find it utterly unnatural to be, or do good.

God's goal and will for you is: Transformation.

This renewal comes from learning God's ways for us. There is one grand task that characterizes the Christian life—*transformation of the mind*. All people are in desperate need of a new heart and a renewed mind.

Make the tree good and the fruit will be good, Jesus pointed out in Matthew 12:33. That remains the eminent challenge from God to us today. It's what God calls us to. We can't do this on our own. We're fundamentally in need of the Holy Spirit, whose working within us makes this possible. He alone makes us beautiful, pliable, and practical for His purposes.

We find our authentic selves when we give ourselves wholly, with abandon, to His process of molding. So immerse yourself in the written Word of God; saturate your mind with it. And pray that the Spirit of Christ will make you so new that the spillover will be good, acceptable, and perfect to your Creator—for this is the ***will of God.***

The will of God for us is that we become "holy," just as Christ is holy. This is clearly indicated by the other verse in which the phrase "this is the will of God" occurs.

> "...*give thanks in all circumstances;* for this is *God's will* for you in Christ Jesus." (1 Thessalonians 5:18)

God-centered goals come from God's will for us.

This affords us accountability and ensures eventual productivity. Christ-centered goals aren't all about what we want to do, but about what God can do through us! Christ-centered goals will make us more effective, as everything we do will be powered by the Holy Spirit. He enables us by grace to point ourselves toward the target of His perceived will for our life. With His will in mind we can make a measurable impact in His kingdom and significantly change our world by making goals we know agree with His.

Remember to make your goals S.M.A.R.T.

1. Specific

2. Measurable

3. Attainable

4. Realistic

5. Timely

What do you want from Jesus?

Jesus requires us to know what we want so we can ask for it by name. This is one of God's principles, the *principle of agreement*. A covenant agreement requires two or more people. What do you want Jesus to do for you? Are you seeking physical healing? Healing for your marriage? Restored relationships with children and/or other family members? Are you in need of emotional and mental healing? Are you seeking a business opportunity or a new job, to be debt free and financially stable? Are you seeking a church family or a new life by receiving salvation from the Giver of life?

No matter how large or small it may appear to be, if you have a need you must specify it to Jesus. You can't receive from Him if you neither know nor voice what you're in need of. God gave us a mouth to ask, so be sure you ask for the right things from Him.

> "Again, truly I tell you that if two of you on earth agree about anything they ask for, it will be done for them by my Father in heaven." (Matthew 18:19)

Jesus responds to people who know what they want. Remember, it's God who plants a dream within your heart and He desires to know whether you want the dream He has for you. Too many want only their dream, and God doesn't waste His dreams on those who don't aspire to them.

Until we've matured in our faith and learned to be steadfast and unwavering, we'll be tempted to doubt God's ability to come through for us.

We must guard against the temptation to grow impatient with God. God will not disappoint the believing expectations of those who wait to hear what He has to say to them. Though the promised favor may take some time to appear, be assured that *it will come!* God will richly compensate us for our patient waiting upon Him.

The Christian's life is not their own.

New Christians don't know how to navigate the Christian life yet. They don't understand what they possess or what's expected of them. They may not fully appreciate that they have been purchased by the blood of Christ and belong to Him.

We can avoid many pitfalls if we learn early that it's wise to consult God in everything we do. We often continue to pursue our own personal goals because we haven't learned that God has better goals for us. God's plans for us are always bigger and greater than ours, no matter how grandiose our own may seem. What we don't frequently recognize at this early stage is that God takes His time in perfecting us before we attain His goals. He wants us well equipped to hold on to what He gives us.

Many immature Christians turn back toward their own goals when they realize that God works much more slowly than we would like Him to. We want what we want, and we want it now! But Isaiah reminds us that those who wait upon the Lord will mount up as eagles (Isaiah 40:31). God has a special reward for those who are willing to wait upon Him.

Stepping out ahead of God means doing whatever we do "in the flesh" (Romans 8:1–17). And what we begin in the flesh can only be finished in the flesh. It's wiser and easier in the long run to refuse to take that bait from Satan, choosing instead to accomplish any task in the Spirit's strength and according to His timing. We're guaranteed success when we allow Him to go before us.

Five important areas of life for goal setting are:

1. Spiritual

2. Relational

3. Physical

4. Financial

5. Career

The call of God and the will of God on your life.

There are different names and purposes in Christian goal setting.

1. Our ***goal*** is to please Jesus and not ourselves.

2. Our ***pursuits*** are changed as a result.

3. Our ***desire*** is to get to know our God and Creator intimately.

> "***So we make it our goal to please him***, whether we are at home in the body or away from it. For we must all appear before the judgment seat of Christ, so that each of us may receive what is due us for the things done while in the body, whether good or bad" (2 Corinthians 5:9–10).

Knowing that God is leading and that He'll reveal His plan for us in His own time is invigorating. This assurance teaches us to trust Him and to wait patiently for His plan to unfold. Life is never boring when we decide to follow Jesus, for He always has more for us than we could imagine on our own.

You'll notice an increase in your energy level as you begin to live your life with anticipation. No longer do you believe that your life is haphazard, determined by fate only.

Your goal in life.

Our assignment from God, and indeed our reason for being, is to **glorify God and to enjoy Him forever**. You'll soon notice your mind becoming a magnet for attracting any information or opportunity that can help you achieve your spiritual goals.

Spending time immersed in the Word, with a goal of knowing your Creator better, will keep you from growing dull and dissatisfied with your Christian walk. Each time you let God know that He's your number one priority, He discloses a little more of Himself to you.

Retrain your mind to seek Him, not those accomplishments that will make you feel more significant. In God's eyes you're already of infinite value, so there's no point in trying to be "more" worthy. If you demonstrate your intent, God will give you the passion and drive to pursue Him. This one overriding spiritual goal—that of knowing your Savior more intimately—is God's will for your life.

Goals will help you reach the success God has in mind for you.

Your present circumstances won't determine your final destiny, they're just your starting point. The purpose of Christian goals is to focus your attention on the better future God has had in store for you since the beginning of time. When you pursue a goal, your power to accomplish it is enhanced. Your mind and heart aspire to achievement when they have clear objectives on which to focus. Goals afford you both a starting place and a destination. Without them we wander and waste the precious years God has given us.

It's God who plants dreams and desires within us. He gives them to us to move us in the direction He has planned. This is how we come into our destiny: by discerning what He wants us to do and then doing it.

Don't concern yourself with feelings of inadequacy.

God didn't give you your dream because He thought *you* could make it happen. He gave it to you because He wants the glory for making it happen *through* you. He's looking for the few faithful ones who will look to Him for their marching orders. He has His own purposes for giving you your particular dream.

Look to Him to fulfill your dream and be willing to wait for His perfect timing. Seek His face for clues as to the manner the dream will unfold. Be ever watchful for the people and opportunities He makes available to you.

Persistence is a significant key to getting what you want in life. It's a principle that's taught throughout the book of Proverbs. Persistence means never giving up! Appropriating your new life requires moving in a wholly different direction. Determine to remain focused on the dream God has given you, not the methods He'll use to get you there, or the dream "robbers" that Satan will send your way to steal it from you.

Always seek the Giver of the gift and not the gift itself. If you seek only gifts from God, your motivation is impure. God knows your heart; you can't keep this from Him anyway, so don't try to fool yourself. Ask God to reveal to you whether or not your heart is pure. If it isn't, give Him permission to make clear to you what you may not see in yourself.

Remember:

1. Keep your dream alive.

2. Visualize it daily.

3. Pray about it continually.

4. Seek wisdom for it.

5. Be cautious about your associations.

Godly friends will believe in the dream God has given you. They have dreams of their own from God and won't be inclined to disbelieve. Position yourself in the company of those who will remain in faith and agreement with you. Both you and your friends can rejoice when your dream comes to pass.

Be especially careful to whom you repeat your dream as unbelievers may scoff. Joseph told his brothers too much about his dream from God and they quickly became jealous and wanted to harm him.

Stay attuned to what God is doing in your life. Remain in the faith, especially when you're tempted to believe your goal won't come to pass or that God is taking too long. God's timing is always perfect. God is working on conforming you, and this takes time. Let Him do as He wills. Your life will eventually show the positive results of persistently waiting on Him.

Don't let your creativity become your enemy by focusing on too many desires at once. Go after one dream at a time. Harness it. You may be talented in many areas, but a God-given dream is different from a talent. God's dream deserves your undivided attention and it must become your unrivaled goal if you're to achieve it.

God wants you to discover your life's purpose.

Pursuing God's dream isn't a matter of pushing yourself harder, but of allowing God to pull you toward the life to which He has been calling you all along. The Bible contains our strategic life plan, a personal blueprint for our life. By faith and with intentionality we work out that plan.

No matter what position you find yourself in, determine your objective first. Until your thoughts are linked to a purpose there can be no accomplishment. After all, if you don't know where you're going, how can you expect to get there?

> "In their hearts humans plan their course, but the LORD establishes their steps." (Proverbs 16:9)

Categorize your goals—spiritual goals might look like this:

1. Spend time with the Lord daily by reading the Bible and by praying each morning.

2. Attend a Bible study at your church or in your community.

3. Join a small group for accountability to other believers.

4. Find a church home within six months or relocating to a new area.

5. Make a new Christian friend.

Find a new Scripture every day about God's love, mercy, forgiveness, or healing, whatever it is you need certainty about. Study and meditate on it, repeating it until your heart, not just your mind, knows it. Memorize and repeat this Scripture throughout the day. It will transform your outlook on life.

List the many ways in which the Lord cares for and blesses you and keep expanding it. Your gratitude will grow through the process. When you praise God for being good, your outcome will change. God loves to hear our praise because it acknowledges that He is indeed a good God.

Determine to find out what your spiritual gift(s) are so you can be a blessing within the body of Christ. You might want to take one of the free spiritual gifts assessments found on the internet. One site I particularly like is: *www.churchgrowth.org.*

Decide to become more comfortable with and natural at witnessing by simply giving your testimony of what God has done for you. A dying world is in desperate need of this "good news." Ask God to keep you from becoming self-conscious, keeping in mind that you are sharing something that will potentially change another person's path in life. Tell people you will pray for them, and then do it. Ask them whether you can pray for them in their presence. Many will agree.

Be a friend to someone who seems friendless. Give yourself away. This is one of the best ways to remain optimistic, as well as to dispel ingratitude and discouragement. Depression blows in when we isolate ourselves and fail to think of others' needs ahead of our own.

Let go of your past.

As was the case with many Bible characters, a God encounter is mandatory to the establishment of a new and better life. Merely wishing for a new future won't make it happen. Anything worth having requires something of you.

Ruth understood that her future success depended on her ability to let go of her past. She had to deliberately turn and depart from it, going with Naomi in disregard of her mother-in-law's selfless plea that she return to her own people. Ruth desired a new future, a good future. She most likely sensed that Naomi, for all the older woman's emptiness, had something that she didn't. Even in mourning Naomi was able to reveal to Ruth that God had done something in her life and Ruth wanted what Naomi had. When Ruth confronted Naomi with "your God shall be my God," she revealed her willingness to turn her back on her past to secure a better future. She understood that this would be found through her continuing relationship with Naomi.

What are you willing to see and go after?

Do you want a fresh start, a new future? This will require seeking and following a new direction—one that comes from God.

You'll never change your future until you change your destination. And you'll never change your destination, until you change the direction you're going.

The blind beggar in Luke 18 presents a good example. Seated by the wayside, begging, he asked those around him about an unusual commotion and was told that Jesus of Nazareth was walking through Jericho. Hearing this welcome news, the beggar cried out, "Jesus, son of David, have mercy on me." Even though those around him, embarrassed at what they perceived to be an unwelcome distraction, tried to silence him, he was persistent in his cries. His decision not to remain quiet resulted in receiving sight and a new future from Jesus.

Jesus commanded those present to bring the blind man to Him. Then he asked what at first strikes us as a surprising, perhaps even ridiculous, question: "What do you want me to do for you?" The blind man replied simply, "Lord, that I may receive my sight."

Jesus desires a new life for each one of us, but we must want it too—badly enough to pursue Him, to run Him down and ask for it no matter how obvious the request may sound. For only those who ask will receive.

> "When you ask, you do not receive, because you ask with wrong motives, that you may spend what you get on your pleasures." (James 4:3)

> "Ask and it will be given to you; seek and you will find; knock and the door will be opened to you." (Matthew 7:7)

"You desire but do not have, so you kill. You covet but you cannot get what you want, so you quarrel and fight. You do not have because you do not ask God." (James 4:2)

Some Bible characters who pursed the dream (goal) God gave them.

1. God gave Noah not only a vision, but a blueprint for the ark.

2. Abraham was told to look up at the stars; the analogy revealed God's plan to multiply his as yet unborn seed.

3. Abraham looked forward to the city with foundations, whose architect and builder is God. (Hebrews 11:10)

4. Moses was given the vision and plan for the tabernacle.

5. Ruth followed her mother-in-law Naomi, the first step in God's plan to give her a new future.

6. King David's desire "was to dwell in the house of the LORD all the days of my life, to gaze upon the beauty of the LORD and to seek him in his temple." (Psalm 27:4)

7. Solomon was given both abundant vision and the wisdom to construct God's temple.

8. Nehemiah's goal was to rebuild the wall of Jerusalem. The execution of this remarkable feat took only 52 days.

9. Esther, relying on God, was given the plan to save her people from destruction.

10. Mary chose "the better thing and it could not be taken from her" (Luke 10:42). The good thing, no. The best thing, choosing to sit at Jesus' feet and taking in the sustenance only He could give. Martha chose work, doing over being, and ended up stressed and frustrated due to her choice. The good is always the enemy of the better.

11. The hemorrhaging woman touched the hem of Jesus' garment, the initial step of faith that would activate God's plan for her new life of wholeness.

12. The blind man believed in Jesus, initiating God's plan to give him a future with sight.

13. The apostle Paul pressed on toward his goal: the prize of the upward call of God in Christ Jesus. (Philippians 3:14)

14. Paul was stopped on the Damascus road in a dramatic visitation from the Lord; this encounter was central to God's plan for proclamation of the new life in Christ based not on good works, but on faith.

Throughout history God has done miraculous things when His people participated with Him to fulfill their destiny.

Two questions every Christian should ask themselves.

1. *Who am I becoming?*

2. *Am I fulfilling God's calling and purpose for my life?*

We often assume that our everyday choices are negligibly minor. But in actuality, we're making major decisions when we decide whom to listen to, believe in, and trust. Following and trusting in the right person makes all the difference. If that person is someone other than the Lord Jesus Christ, pause to reconsider who alone holds all truth and loves you unconditionally. Perhaps a change is in order.

One simple practice of many an uncommon achiever is to write down seven objectives that can be accomplished every day. These practices will help you achieve your spiritual goals. Seven is the number of perfection, so don't be inclined to overdo it. Don't write down fifty. If you can't begin to achieve them all, or even to scratch the surface, you'll want to give up before you accomplish even one objective.

The list of biblical people who achieved God's dream for their lives and became successful as a result, should encourage you to notice how God may be working in your life. Reading biographies of godly giants of the faith will encourage you to seek the Lord for fulfillment of your own God-given dreams.

Every child of God needs wisdom to live a fulfilled life. Start by reading the book of Proverbs and writing down the lessons you learn from it. Proverbs teaches us the "way of wisdom." In other words, it tells us how to prosper, but also provides examples of what to avoid so failure won't be the end result.

Note what you learn from Proverbs. Notice general themes, principles, and real-life lessons. Keep a journal of your discoveries. Also, be sure to record what to avoid, as there's no wisdom in repeating costly mistakes.

Before we can mature in Christ, we must discern what to leave behind from our former life. After this, we can begin to build the positive character traits needed to go the distance.

Write down godly goals. Put them before your eyes every day and repeat them daily to yourself. This will keep the vision and goals fresh in your mind.

Do some study on writing down dreams, goal setting, and making plans. You'll start to see that "increase" is the natural outcome for every believer in Christ. You'll discover that those who regularly write things down are far more likely to see their dreams come to pass than those who don't take the time to discipline themselves in this way. Remember, it's how we finish that matters.

> "Suppose one of you wants to build a tower, will he not first sit down and estimate the cost to see if he has enough money to complete it? For if he lays the foundation and is not able to finish it, everyone who sees it will ridicule him, saying, the fellow began to build and was not able to finish." (Luke 14:28–30)

> "Do you see a man skilled in his work? He will serve before kings; He will not serve before obscure men." (Proverbs 22:29)

> "For this reason, since the day we heard about you, we have not stopped praying for you. We continually ask God to fill you with the knowledge of his will through all the wisdom and understanding that the Spirit gives, so that you may live a life worthy of the Lord and please him in every way: bearing fruit in every good work, growing in the knowledge of God, being strengthened with all power according to his glorious might so that you may have great endurance and patience." (Colossians 1:9–11)

> "Whatever you do, work at it with all your heart, as working for the Lord, not for human masters, since you know that you will receive an inheritance from the Lord as a reward. It is the Lord Christ you are serving." (Colossians 3:23–24)

Keep in mind as Paul reminds us, it's the Lord Jesus whom you are serving.

What are the secret desires of your heart?

What do you want God to do for you? What do you want to do for God? Has God put a desire in you that you now recognize originated with Him? Are you aware that you'll need Him to see it through to completion?

What personal goals do you have? What type of person do you want to be? If you're single and desire to marry, what kind of person do you envision as your spouse? Or if you're married, what kind of marriage partner do you wish to be? What kind of parent? What kind of employer or employee? What kind of inner spiritual life do you desire? Do you wish to be debt free and financially stable so you can bless others?

God is the giver of passion, giftedness, and calling.

1. Your *passion*—what you really get excited about.

2. Your *giftedness*—what you're really good at.

3. Your *calling*—God's unique purpose for your life.

What unlocks your passion? God made you distinct from others. What in particular can you identify that constitutes that difference? More often than not, it has to do with the direction in which God will take you. One way to know what you're called to do is to observe what you have a passion for. If you're not sure, ask yourself what you're good at or what others notice in you.

Seek to discover your spiritual gifts. The Holy Spirit has given every Christian at least one spiritual gift. Some receive several because of what God has called them to do in the kingdom. Your particular gift (strength) is your clue to what God has for you. He has equipped you for His purposes by giving you that gift(s).

God doesn't ask any of us to serve Him without first preparing us. Spiritual gifts equip us for ministering to the body of Christ. They aren't for our blessing alone. They're to be used for the edification of others in ministry. Yet even though your particular spiritual gift(s) aren't solely for your benefit, the fruit that come from using them will bless and edify you. These gifts and the resultant fruit are a blessing that encourages us in the work of the Lord.

Ask God for His guidance…then get moving.

1. ***Never lose sight of your goal.*** Take the time to review your goals every morning when you get up and every night before you go to bed. This will keep them fresh in your mind. If you think reviewing your goals twice a day is too much, maybe you should

reevaluate what it is you really want. Ask yourself, "How important is it to me that I attain my goals?"

2. ***Don't procrastinate.*** Understand that the only way to achieve your goals is to take action. Do something today that will help you to achieve your goals. There's no time like the present. Each step you take brings you one step closer to the life you envision.

3. ***Continuously evaluate your progress.*** Having an action plan isn't enough, for unforeseen obstacles often come up. We must make subtle changes that allow us to stay on course and not give up. In other words, notice what's working and what isn't. If an approach isn't proving to be effective, don't waste your time with it. Change your strategy instead. When one method no longer works, try another so you can stay on track.

Commitment precedes resources.

While resources are often required to reach a goal, commitment is invariably more important. God can get you the resources you need when He sees your commitment, especially if it's in obedience to something He has directed you to do. Until we commit, we'll always have some hesitancy.

The moment we dedicate ourselves to following through, God moves toward us, and a whole stream of events begins to flow. All manner of unforeseen incidents, "chance" meetings, influential persons, and material assistance begin to come our way when we determine to make a firm commitment.

Ruth made an initial commitment to her mother-in-law Naomi. That commitment led to opportunity and blessing.

Serving God has a great reward.

The decision to persevere in spite of difficulties, hardships, and times of testing will take you to your new future. If you decide the journey is too difficult and turn back, you will in effect be settling for your past. Living in the past won't take you to the abundant future God has for you.

God isn't looking for your perfection. He's looking for you to ***trust*** Him, for He's already made you perfect through His performance, not yours.

What should be the conclusion of a life lived well?

- "I have fought the good fight, I have finished the race, I have kept the faith." (2 Timothy 4:7)

What is our ultimate reward?

"Therefore, my brothers and sisters, make every effort to confirm your calling and election. For if you do these things, you will never stumble, and you will receive a rich welcome into the eternal kingdom of our Lord and Savior Jesus Christ." (2 Peter 1:10–11)

Beware the pitfall of believing that everything starts and ends with yourself.

Self-help books abound. Such books, no matter how convincing, repeat the message Satan wants to drill into our psyche—that **YOU** must make something good come out of your life. That **YOU** determine your future because **YOU** are the master of your life and destiny.

The danger in these books and their message is that everything emanates from **SELF**. **YOU** make it happen. **YOU** develop self-discipline, talent and ability. **YOU** determine your future and make it prosper.

Those who don't look to God for His direction rely upon themselves. This is the very self-sufficiency we must avoid if we hope to evade its pitfalls. Satan wants nothing more than for you to believe you're all-sufficient and that everything begins and ends with **YOU**. God desires that you rely upon and trust completely in **HIM** for **HIS** sufficiency and blessings.

A self-centered perspective doesn't bring lasting joy or fulfillment. Without a God-built foundation, self-sufficiency and prosperity all too quickly have a way of turning one's heart away from God. We have no doubt we can handle our wealth, but the unfortunate truth is that most often it ends up handling us.

Usually worldly success doesn't prove to be as fulfilling as we first anticipate, so we soon go looking for fulfillment in other things. These can be experiences, sexual conquest, trophies, prestige, recognition, power, winning an argument, or a thousand other rewards we may use to salve our egos and assure ourselves of our value. People want significance, but it is only God who can give it.

A wealthy man was once asked how much money a person needed to live. His telling response: Just a little more. Too many unwittingly live their lives according to this definition of success.

However worthwhile you may consider some of the secular material on success and prosperity know that financial or other success apart from the blessings of God, is often empty and vain. Yes, you may increase your wealth, but wealth without purpose is a poor substitute for abundant living. Wealth that isn't used to advance Christ's kingdom, is frequently spent on self. Its initial intoxication quickly fades, leaving no real or lasting satisfaction.

God has created eternal appetites in us.

Man is unique among all living species as God created him with the ability to contemplate a future. This capacity was given because

God wanted us to desire a relationship with Him. A future built with God, is indeed, a *very good* future. After all, God made us in His own image (Genesis 1:26).

Our original nature was tainted by sin. That sin flows over into our appetites and desires. Sin alienates us from God, from others, and even from our true selves. Rather than setting our desires, hopes, and ambitions on eternal things—things that won't wear out, give out, or die out—we make our self-driven notions our gods. These *gods* quickly become our lifelong goals.

"Claiming to be wise, they became fools…they exchanged the glory of the immortal God for images resembling a mortal human being or birds or four-footed animals or reptiles…they exchanged the truth about God for a lie and worshiped and served the creature rather than the Creator." (Romans 1:22–25)

Attaining worldly success is not the same as fulfilling your life's purpose, which is implanted in you by the Holy Spirit. Many individuals are able to reach their goals through worldly success principles, but this isn't the primary purpose of their being. You could be a resounding success in the eyes of the world, your family, and your friends, and still be a dismal failure by God's standards.

Jesus once told the story of a man who had achieved his self-defined goals in life.

> "The land of a rich man produced abundantly. And he thought to himself, 'What should I do, for I have no place to store my crops?' Then he said, 'I will do this: I will pull down my barns and build larger ones, and there I will store all my grain and my goods. And I will say to my soul, Soul, you have ample goods laid up for many years; relax, eat, drink, be merry.' But God said to him, 'You fool! This very night your life is being demanded of you. And the things you have prepared, whose will they be?' So it is with those who store up treasures for themselves but are not rich towards God." (Luke 12:16–21)

Is Jesus saying that we shouldn't have goals? That we shouldn't work hard or earn money? Not at all!

But the first question we must clarify in our mind is: What is the single, overriding purpose of my life? From what source do I derive my ultimate meaning, purpose, and fulfillment? The answers to these questions can only come from God. We must get to the point and ask God pointedly what it is He wants to do through us.

Keep in mind that His answer may take some time in coming. This may well be a test to see how we'll respond when we don't receive an answer instantly. At this critical juncture, many will turn from God and return to doing things their own way. If we're willing to stay with it, God will reveal in time, the full vision of what He has planned for us.

If some of us were enabled to see too far down the road we would become fearful, as our perceived inadequacy to do all that God is asking would overwhelm us. Prior to God's full disclosure, we're to continue to pursue godly things, assured that in His good time He'll reveal a clearer picture of His direction.

> "Now faith is the substance of things hoped for, the evidence of things not seen." (Hebrews 11:1)

> "But seek *first* the kingdom of God and His righteousness, and all these things shall be added to you." (Matthew 6:33)

Consequences of living without goals.

Children live their lives with abandon. But adulthood requires responsibility and making good choices. The adult who thinks of nothing but play, who wants no part of the responsibility of providing for self or others, is essentially still a child. When we take on adulthood, we're responsible for our own choices—choices that lead us to either prosper or fail.

If we fail to initiate a plan to be successful, we'll invariably fall victim to happenstance. Consider some people you know who didn't plan well. At the end of their lives many express regrets over lost years that produced nothing of lasting value. Even the secular world relies on success principles that coincide closely with biblical principles. Practicing what the Bible teaches, without necessarily even making the connection, has tremendous benefits. Goal setting develops self-discipline and an awareness of the bad habits that may impede our progress.

A woman of substance knows where to find her fulfillment. A fruitful, productive, peaceful life comes as the direct result of intimacy with her Savior. That uncanny ability to prosper in everything you lay your hands on comes only from God.

> "Delight yourself also in the LORD, and He shall give you the desires of your heart." (Psalm 37:4)

> "By humility and the fear of the LORD are riches and honor and life." (Proverbs 22:4)

> "A faithful man will abound with blessings, but he who hastens to be rich will not go unpunished." (Proverbs 28:20)

Success is your birthright.

Remember that God created you to be successful. He has

equipped and gifted you with everything you need for success to be your ever-present reality.

Everything God created is good and is intended to express His excellence. God is the Master Creator and nothing that was ever created was made without Him. He's immensely pleased with His handiwork.

Keep in mind that you're the only part of His creation into which He breathed His Spirit and made in His own image. He didn't make the animals after His image, nor did He impart His own Spirit into them.

We're His pride and joy. He loves to show us off, just as any proud father does. When we have successful relationships and are joyful and optimistic about our future, the world becomes curious. When we've gained the proper perspective regarding wealth, and long to be generous to others, people take notice. God has many reasons why He wants the world to recognize that *His children* are prosperous and well.

God desires for you to achieve outstanding success. There can be no pride in mediocrity. If you're born-again, success is your kingdom right. Jesus paid the price to give it to you, but you must seize it and claim it for yourself.

Our Lord stated that we're to be the salt and light of this world. What's more, He likened us to a city set upon a hill that can't be hidden. It's our duty to remain on that mountaintop where others can see our light, to refrain from spending our days in the valley of discontent and mediocrity.

We've been raised up to be an example for all, entrusted with the secrets of the kingdom to arouse the jealousy of the entire world. God's wisdom secrets are for all those who will accept His Son. God is the Giver of all good gifts. Jesus, salvation, wisdom, treasure, wealth, and success are only a few.

Success is both a gift and a choice. While it's the birthright of all saints, the individual's choice determines his portion. Your choice is the compass that points to your destination. God has destined you for success. Success in your walk with Him; in your marriage and relationships; with your children; your career, finances, health, and home…and the list goes on. God has equipped you to stand out wherever you are.

God has assured us that whatever endeavor we undertake will prosper. It takes secrets to succeed. And the Bible holds all the *secrets* God has for those who will diligently seek after Him.

> "Then the LORD your God will make you most prosperous in all the work of your hands and in the fruit of your womb, the

young of your livestock and the crops of your land. The LORD will again delight in you and make you prosperous, just as he delighted in your fathers." (Deuteronomy 30:9)

What's the goal of the Christian life?

Changed character is the evidence of a changed life, and spiritual growth involves the formation of character. With your consent, the Holy Spirit is working Christian character into your being. This character change, reflected in the transformation of your various attributes, will make you more like the Lord and less like the unbelieving world around you.

We become different from the inner core of our being outward. When our heart is changed, our person (our character and our very identity) is changed too.

A woman of authentic Christian character reflects the Christ who has called her. This is the goal of the Christian's life.

2

HER CONFIDENCE IS IN THE LORD

"Being confident of this, that he who began a good work in you will carry it on to completion until the day of Christ Jesus. (Philippians 1:6)

Does the Bible hold secrets related to our identity? Does it address such issues as confidence, strength, and fearlessness? And what about opposite emotions like fear, anxiety, and worry?

Confidence certainly has its advantages, as most of us want to follow those who appear confident and successful. But what exactly is confidence and how do we gain it if we feel we're lacking?

Confidence is often defined as: *self-assuredness*, or *self-assurance in one's personal judgment, ability,* or *power.*

If that's the kind of confidence we're after, how can we become more astute judges of ourselves and the world around us? How can we improve our aptitude and increase our influence with others? What traits define a confident person, and how can we walk the thin line between confidence and arrogance?

The Bible is our best resource for making this determination.

Traits of a confident person:

Helps others and builds them up.

Accepts responsibility for their choices.

Is balanced in attitude and outlook. Looks to God for their future.

Is flexible and loving toward people and situations they encounter.

Thinks and speaks towards self positively stating what God has already said about you in His Word.

Traits of an arrogant person.

Views self as superior.

Is incisive in transactions with others.

Never admits mistakes.

Revels in the blunders of others.

A healthy level of confidence may seem like an impossible quest for someone who feels worthless, but God's Word offers us the tools we need for gaining strong confidence.

Everyone trusts in something, but not all objects of trust are worthy or bring genuine confidence. Unfortunately, our choices are frequently misdirected. Real and lasting confidence comes when we put our trust in things that have eternal value, rather than temporal things like education, possessions, wealth or fame.

The correct kind of confidence.

Many believe that while they must focus on their self-esteem issues to gain a better view of themselves, they need to guard against going too far in that direction and risking arrogance. Even arrogant people will admit that they dislike those who perceive themselves as self-important. The problem is that people have difficulty differentiating the two and try to mask their low esteem issues with feigned arrogance.

Of course, the real question isn't one of high or low *self*-esteem, but of what correct or appropriate confidence looks like. The great English preacher Charles Spurgeon offered us this insight: "Self-confidence is acceptable only if it is rooted in God-confidence."

Correct confidence is a complex concept that includes:

1. Aspects of faith in God

2. Certainty

3. Assurance of one's relationship with God.

Intimacy with God brings confidence and boldness. Assurance comes from a conviction that our future is secure in God. Developing confidence in the Lord provides the basis for Christian assurance.

In the Old Testament the verb "*batah,*" conveys "putting one's trust in" something or someone, appears 118 times. A common term in the New Testament that expresses a similar idea, *"paressia,"* appears 31 times. This word can suggest plainness, openness, clarity of speech, confidence, courage, or boldness. A study of these terms can be helpful in a time like this, when many Christians are oppressed by fears or restrained by a spirit of timidity. It's helpful to consider the subject from both a negative and a positive vantage point.

If we put our ultimate trust and confidence in human ability, ours or that of others, we're investing them in false gods. It's foolish to attribute any real value to the world or its operating systems, as God's Word tells us that the world we know will one day pass away—that it was never meant to be eternal (Judges 9:26).

Self-esteem versus God-esteem.

Self-esteem asks *"What do I think of me?"* and is often influenced by a misguided view of self. If our confidence level is based on self-esteem, whether high or low, we're on shaky ground as our identity can quickly disintegrate if our talents, abilities, or achievements shift due to unforeseen circumstances. Many falsely tie their confidence to achievement and have no sense of identity beyond their own accomplishments.

But correct confidence, God-confidence, asks *"What does the Lord think about me?"* God's Word tells us that if we've accepted

Jesus as our Savior, we can reprogram our thinking by teaching ourselves to focus on the One who resides within us. When we turn from a narcissistic view of our self-importance we can develop a kingdom perspective. Our basic identity is now tied to Jesus and what He has achieved for us.

For the past several decades our society, schools, and even our parenting style have been built on teaching children to have confidence in themselves. Our children have been told that they can do and be anything. We've shifted from a society focused on doing good for society, to one concentrated on doing good for self. There are no failing grades as everyone is a winner. But this method has backfired. What we produced was a self-indulgent, entitlement-mentality generation exhibiting traits of narcissism and self-absorption. Many don't understand that developing esteem apart from God is empty and ultimately unsatisfying.

Where "stinking-thinking" comes from?

Low self-esteem is one of Satan's deadliest weapons against an unsuspecting society. All of the greatest weapons in his arsenal are psychological, with fear and doubt being two of the most common. Our society has seen an escalation of fear as times have become increasingly uncertain. Anger, hostility, worry, and pervasive guilt are hard to avoid. Even Christians suffer from these pessimistic emotions. Multitudes fail to understand where this thinking comes from or what it produces for us. They simply assume they have psychological problems and turn to doctors, who fail to understand the root cause of such torment.

Frequently with low self-esteem comes self-condemnation, Satan's most powerful psychological weapon of all. He especially loves to use it on Christians because he knows that Jesus came to set us free from condemnation.

Low self-esteem is a gut-level feeling of inferiority, inadequacy, and low self-worth. It isn't the same as humility, as some believe. Peter directed us to be sober minded, to understand our actual position through Christ. We're forgiven and redeemed from the curse of sin and condemnation. It isn't that we're to think more highly of ourselves, but that we're to think less often of our self, and more about appropriating the righteousness that comes from being one with Christ.

Studying God's Word and understanding that Jesus came to set you free provides not only confidence, but liberation from the bondage of depression, condemnation, fear, and torment. A low self-image actually results from spending too much time thinking of ourselves. God didn't intend for us to be self-occupied. He created us for fellowship with Himself and others.

Freedom comes with new thinking. When we turn to God and

ask for deliverance from fear, He fills us with His peace—a peace that far surpasses our ability to comprehend. This new focus comes from renewing our mind through His Word. Staying close to Him through prayer, submission and humility, fellowshipping with other believers, and praising and worshiping Him will keep our thinking victorious. If your lips are expressing gratitude rather than complaining, you're rewiring your brain. You won't get stuck on defeat and misery when praise is flowing forth from you.

- "And the peace of God, which transcends all understanding, will guard your hearts and your minds in Christ Jesus." (Philippians 4:7)

Confidence comes when we long to know our God.

All successful Bible characters had one thing in common: a fervent longing to be in God's presence. Moses valued God's presence even above His promises, and he refused to settle for less.

David had sinful weaknesses, but he longed for his God. His psalms are full of his desire to know Him more intimately.

Paul spoke about his confidence in carrying out the tasks God had given him to do in spite of crushing hardships.

- "Such is the *confidence* that we have through Christ toward God. Not that we are sufficient in ourselves to claim anything as coming from us, but our sufficiency is from God." (2 Corinthians 3:4-5, ESV)

- "Him we proclaim, warning everyone and teaching everyone with all wisdom, that we may present everyone mature in Christ. For this I toil, struggling with all his energy that he powerfully works within me." (Colossians 1:28-29, ESV)

It's clear that God expects us to trust Him completely. But it's also clear that we're to use the strength and gifts He gives us to serve Him. This is the balance of which Paul spoke.

Confidence comes when we identify our real "daddy."

Gaining an understanding that God is your "Abba," your daddy, will fill you with confidence. Frequently, people lack confidence because they don't know to whom they belong or who really loves them. Some have grown up in fatherless homes and have never experienced the love of a dad.

How many of us really know or understand love, or how to properly receive it when it's offered? Many believe they must work hard, and even compromise who they are, to receive what they so desperately want—to be accepted and cherished.

If you've grown up without a father or have grown up with one who is distant in his affection, or has been cruel and abusive, know that you can ask God to be the Father you've never really had. If you're unaccustomed to receiving love, it may be difficult at first for you to accept His love. If that's an issue for you, ask Him to show you how to accept love, and then relax and allow Him to father you. This will fill that empty place in your heart, and He'll be the best and most loving Father you could imagine. He adores you and wants you to know that above all else. He will never leave you, take from you, or offend you. He simply wants you to know deep in your heart that He has nothing but unconditional love for you. That means that He cherishes you, not just when you're cleaned up, presentable, and "perfect," but right now this very moment, just as you are!

Confident people know to whom they belong.

It's fundamental to develop an accurate sense of self-worth based not on your own attributes, intelligence, or performance, but on God's assessment of you. God loved and valued us, after all, to the point of sending His own Son to die on our behalf. Because you have such worth in His eyes, you have value—period!

Self-worth derived from God's love confers assurance, and assurance gives us the confidence that we're worthy purely because God considers us so. It's the only source of self-confidence that can't be taken from us. In fact, it has nothing directly to do with us but everything to do with Christ and His work. It's based not on what we, or others believe about our self, but on what Christ knows to be true about us. True and lasting confidence comes only from the Lord. He never changes, nor does His opinion about you.

Godly confidence radiates from within and comes with assurance of salvation. It's unique and the world is perplexed by it. This radiance comes from God's purposes and flows out of our intimacy with Him. It comes when we spend time in His presence. There is no substitute for time. It's required for building any quality relationship. God enjoys being with us so much that He gets jealous when we spend too much time with other things or people.

Too many seek spiritual activity, rather than spiritual substance. They're always *doing* rather than *being*. Develop a hunger for God. Be satisfied with nothing less than being in His presence. Your relationship with Him will grow when you share intimately with each other.

When you're in love, you can't wait to get back together and share the news of the day. Why should your relationship with God be any different? If we neglect the relationships that matter most, they shrivel. Give your relationship with God the attention it deserves, and you'll be pleasantly surprised to see it thrive.

- "'Let not the wise man boast of his wisdom or the strong man boast of his strength or the rich man boast of his riches, but let him who boasts boast about this: that he understands and knows me, that I am the LORD who exercises kindness, justice and righteousness on earth, for in these I delight,' declares the LORD."(Jeremiah 9:23–24)

How the world views confidence and self-esteem.

Perhaps no other self-help topic has spawned so much advice or so many conflicting theories. Since self-esteem is thought to be integral to happiness, fulfilling relationships, and achievement, a secular self-esteem test is designed to evaluate your general level of self-esteem and determine whether you need to work on your self-image. Most people never progress beyond this secular level of esteem, for psychology focuses on improving self without considering any other source of esteem.

If we want to achieve and maintain a healthy mental state, we must look beyond ourselves for fulfillment. If our knowledge isn't based on the sole source of truth, God's Word, it will be limited and faulty.

None of us can ever be everything to ourselves (self-sufficient); we were created with a "God void" for a reason. As God's Word reminds us:

- "For by the grace given me I say to every one of you: Do not think of yourself more highly than you ought, but rather think of yourself with sober judgment, in accordance with the faith God has distributed to each of you." (Romans 12:3)

- "The heart is deceitful above all things and beyond cure. Who can understand it?" (Jeremiah 17:9)

Seeking confidence in self brings us a curse.

There's no true wisdom apart from God—because **GOD IS WISDOM!** God is the author, originator, and only true source of wisdom. We have no understanding of spiritual things, let alone of the supernatural, apart from God. To make forward progress we must seek out the Holy Spirit, the Giver of enlightenment. As Solomon declared,

- "Trust in Jehovah with all your heart, and *lean not upon your own understanding.* In all your ways acknowledge him, and he will direct your paths." (Proverbs 3:5–6)

All too frequently we look to our own understanding because we aren't aware there's any other kind. When we get into God's Word, we discover for ourselves that He has sound counsel from which we can profit. This counsel doesn't come from the world or from psychology, which contains humanly perceived answers that are useless to God, and so to us. The Holy Spirit helps us understand that Word and offers the guidance we need to make right decisions based on it.

Pride elevates man, while Christian confidence elevates Christ. When we place our confidence in Jesus, He empowers us. Life on earth is meant to be a temporary state in which we learn and grow. We weren't created for this present world but for God's kingdom, which is our permanent domain.

God tests us and teaches us to wait upon Him. This waiting and testing brings forth patience and endurance, both of which are needed to overcome this world and Satan. Satan wants us to abandon God's plan for our lives. If we determine not to throw away our confidence or eternal inheritance, we **will** reign with Christ for all time—this is His promise to us.

Difficult situations become dire when we lack the confidence in Christ to endure. Weak faith will not allow us to deal with a crisis well. Soon we see our situation as hopeless and forget about the God who can change everything.

Frequently, God lets us deal with our difficulties for a season to develop our character. He's at work behind the scenes, nurturing us to the point that it becomes natural for us to trust Him *first* and *only* in any given situation.

Once we learn to stand firm in the face of opposition, we gain the confidence that leads to perseverance. Boldness rather than cowardice, God-confidence rather than fear, build in us a strong, unshakable, godly character.

If you let God work what He wills into your being, you'll attain the confidence you've been seeking. This will give you assurance and peace, and, more importantly, will bring Him glory.

The folly of earthly riches.

Confidence is not to be found ultimately in human strength as the prophet Jeremiah made clear. Those who place their confidence in their own resources will be cursed. Jeremiah goes on to say that such a person "will not see prosperity when it comes" (Jeremiah 17:5–6).

A hefty bank balance or retirement fund, investments, and assets can become a substitute for trusting God. God tells us that He notices even when a sparrow falls to the ground (Matthew 10:29). If God cares so much for the birds of the air, how much more will He care for us?

- "Those who trust in their riches will fall, but the righteous will thrive like a green leaf." (Proverbs 11:28)

When we believe God will provide for us, God takes our little and impressively multiplies it.

Confidence in our own abilities will lead us either to uncertainty, or to arrogance. Worry, fear, and anxiety are polar opposites of confidence. Chronic worry for the child of God must be questioned and dealt with head-on. This trait comes from the enemy and has no place in the life of an abiding Christian. When we seek our significance in God, the only One who will not change or fail us, we have a confidence built on solid ground.

- "So we say with confidence, 'The Lord is my helper; I will not be afraid. What can man do to me?'" (Hebrews 13:6)

- "Put your hope in the LORD both now and forevermore." (Psalm 131:1)

Satan wants God's children wallowing in doubt and fear. For when we're confident, we're mighty! The enemy employs strategies of fear to keep Christians impotent. When that doesn't work, he reverts to perceived self-sufficiency and arrogance. Arrogance is the bait of Satan. Pride brings us down quickly as Scripture reminds us.

- "When pride comes, then comes disgrace, but with humility comes wisdom." (Proverbs 11:2)

- "To fear the LORD is to hate evil; I hate pride and arrogance, evil behavior and perverse speech." (Proverbs 8:13)

- "Do not keep talking so proudly or let your mouth speak such arrogance, for the LORD is a God who knows, and by him deeds are weighed." (1 Samuel 2:3)

- "But blessed is the one who trusts in the LORD, whose confidence is in him. They will be like a tree planted by the water that sends out its roots by the stream. It does not fear when heat comes; its leaves are always green. It has no worries in a year of drought and never fails to bear fruit." (Jeremiah 17:7–8)

Our confidence grows as we deepen our relationship with God. When we see our true identity which is in Christ, we're able to look beyond ourselves. The Bible gives us both a direction and a person in which to place our confidence. It is the only resource for an accurate sense of self. This is the confidence we have in approaching God:

- "…that if we ask anything according to his will, he hears us. And if we know that he hears us—whatever we ask—we know that we have what we asked of him." (1 John 5:14–15)

Jesus desires for us to accept what He died to give us: His confidence, acceptance, and love. These gifts complete us so that we no longer need to look for love and acceptance elsewhere.

Jesus makes us what we need to be, by giving us what we need in Him. We build up our endurance when we operate in His confidence. This allows us to grasp the prize of our high calling. He renews us to run the race, to mount up on wings as eagles and soar forth strong and confident (Isaiah 40:31).

Learning more about our God-given purpose gives us confidence.

While still a young man, David killed the giant Goliath and kept the lions from killing his sheep. David became strong and confident through these experiences. Eventually God trusted David to be the king who would, under God's own guidance, lead his people. These experiences taught David that he could trust the Lord to help and protect him. With each reinforcing incident David's confidence in the Lord increased as he experienced God firsthand as his source of success.

Later in life King David experienced grave failures, yet God called him a man after His own heart. How could God say that about someone who had committed adultery and murder? For the very reason that when David failed, he turned to God rather than running from Him.

When we ask God to help us with our human frailties, He

empowers us to overcome our limitations. God's Spirit is our deliverer, our sustainer, and the One who gives us the power to overcome. If we aren't plugged in to His power, we have no power to draw on.

When we accept the experiences God allows in our lives, rather than running from them, we become confident as David was. It's especially valuable to learn to trust God while we're still young, as our future experiences will be positively affected.

God wants the world to witness how He makes His children strong, confident, and successful. He wants them to be jealous enough to seek those traits for themselves.

Understanding God's true character will give you confidence.

Jesus is the manifestation of the heart and character of God. His words and actions reveal seven characteristics that are crucial to our self-esteem. He is:

Our *Father*.

Our *pursuer*.

Our *lover*.

Our *Savior* and *Lord*.

Our *restorer* and *redeemer*.

Our *conqueror*, winning every battle for us.

And our *supplier*.

Unless we know that God loves and accepts us, we'll be tempted to look elsewhere for it. God's love precedes ours. It's only through this love that we can respond positively to Him. God is the definer, essence, and embodiment of love. He teaches us how to love by experiencing His love firsthand.

God's love for us never changes.

God isn't deterred by our disobedience, nor is His character dependent on our response or actions. He's completely consistent, and that includes His love. All His purposes are consistent with that love too. He was love (its embodiment and essence) before He created the world, and He'll be love through all eternity. Unlike fickle people, He isn't loving sometimes, and indifferent at others. "God is Love" is a simple phrase we've all heard. These three words occur together only twice in the Bible, both of them in 1 John

4:

> "Whoever is without love does not know God, for God is love." (1 John 4:8)

> "We have come to know and to believe in the love God has for us. God is love, and whoever remains in love remains in God and God in him." (1 John 4:16).

Examine God's character and the implications of His love for you.

1. He never gives up on you. (Luke 15:3–32)

2. He is patient with you and is interested in the intimate details of your life. (Mathew 6:25–34)

3. He sent His son to die on your behalf, even though you were undeserving. (Romans 5:8)

4. He stands with you. (Hebrews 13:5)

5. He died to take upon Himself your sickness, pain, and grief. (Isaiah 53:3–6)

6. He values you. (Luke 7:28)

7. He comforts you. (Luke 7:28)

8. He strengthens you through the Holy Spirit. (Ephesians 3:16)

9. He cleanses you. (Hebrews 10:17–22)

10. He broke death's stranglehold on you. (Luke 24:6–7)

11. He communes with you through prayer. (John 14:13–14)

12. He is aware of your needs. (Isaiah 65:24)

13. He has prepared a special place for you to spend eternity in relationship with Him. (John 3:16)

14. He provides a way of escape for you. (1 Corinthians 10:13)

15. He offers you a certain hope. (Romans 15:13)

16. He helps you in temptation. (Philippians 2:13)

17. He endured death on the cross so you could live in freedom. (Galatians 5:1)

Accepting the Savior frees you from constant burdens.

Guilt and shame put us under a terrible burden we were never intended to carry. Jesus was sent to free us from *all* our burdens. In fact, you won't experience true and lasting freedom until you agree to hand Him all your problems. When you do, you'll enter into abiding rest and experience lasting joy and victory. The Holy Spirit is waiting in the wings to manage our affairs for us—but He's waiting for our permission.

The greatest burden for us to carry is often *self*. Apart from God, that's the most difficult thing we have to manage. In our natural fallen state—with our fluctuating emotions, weaknesses, temptations, and inclination to listen to the enemy—we bring inward demons and battles to bear on our situation.

This worldly condition leaves us profoundly burdened. But when we grasp the enormity of our limitations and accept God's free gift of salvation, we give Him permission to "manage" us. What enormous freedom this brings!

Ask yourself: Do I truly believe in God?

This one question is the most important you'll ever ask. Just as *whom you choose to believe* is the most important decision you'll ever make.

Your future destination, as well as the quality of your present, rests solely on this momentous choice. No other decision compares.

Jesus didn't come into the world to condemn us, but to save and free us.

- "For God did not send his Son into the world to condemn the world, but to save the world through him." (John 3:17)

God sees you as infinitely worthy and significant. If you were the only person on earth, you are worthy of His sacrificial death. Understanding this truth fully, can't help but elicit a response from us. But sadly, though exposed to this reality, we can shortsightedly choose to resist, run, or close our heart to Him. Incredibly, even such a negative decision can't change how He feels about you.

Learning to see ourselves as God sees us comes when we respond to His wooing and recognize the extent of His love for us.

- "I am writing to you, dear children, because your sins have been forgiven on account of his name. I am writing to you, fathers, because you know him who is from the beginning. I am writing to you, young men, because you have overcome the evil one. I write to you, dear children, because you know the Father. I write to you, fathers, because you know him who is from the beginning. I write to you, young men, because you are strong, and the word of God lives in you, and you have overcome the evil one." (1 John 2:12–14)

Do you envision a good future based on God's love for you?

Too many burdens associated with day to day living keep our eyes fixated on the pavement. Dreams quickly fade when worry takes over. Many good people, and even many Christians, become bored and restless with life. Believers can become indifferent to the world around them because they lack a vision for the future. They don't discern who they are in Christ or embrace His purposes for them.

The Bible has no relevance to our everyday situations if we don't understand the role God wants to play in our lives. When we come to know His plans, His true character and nature, we start to connect the dots and life begins to make sense. We understand that God holds the big picture, of which we're seeing at any given point, only an isolated piece. Unless we can catch a glimpse of the whole, which is revealed to us in His Word, we'll be convinced that the Bible is too complicated to understand or doesn't apply to our lives today.

Understanding your value to God gives you confidence.

Jesus entered an impossibly sinful and arrogant world

environment. He came as a radically different rabbi who carried a radically different message. According to the historian Josephus, the women of Jesus' day faced rigid prejudice. Although Jewish men were taught through the Talmud that women were inferior, they were only too willing to use them for prostitution and sexual gratification in polygamous relationships.

But Jesus treated women in a drastically different way that must, ironically, have seemed scandalous to those around Him. He regularly taught women the Scriptures and spoke with them in public (a social taboo). In fact, He first revealed Himself as the Messiah to a woman (John 4).

With words and actions Jesus consistently affirmed women. He affirmed their intellectual capabilities by teaching them the Scriptures. He met their social needs by befriending them. And He acknowledged their emotional needs by refusing to condemn or talk down to them.

Our Lord used women in His everyday examples while teaching, spending time listening and ministering to them, and trusting them to be the first witnesses of His resurrection. He freely offered women everything He had come to earth to supply: salvation, healing, forgiveness of sins, and eternal life. To this day, Jesus is still a radical rabbi.

The greatest lie ever told!

In every nation that devalues women, the men unwittingly are left wanting. Women are natural nurturers endowed with that propensity by their Creator. Studies show that a married man enjoys better health, longer life, greater financial wealth, heightened morality, and decreased violence and selfishness in comparison to his unmarried counterparts.

With an increase in selfishness comes a decrease in love, empathy, devotion, commitment, affection, and tenderness. When the fruit of real love is absent, we're left to ourselves. In our natural, unchanged nature we're mean, selfish, demanding, lacking in love and tenderness. This is man's evil doing—not God's—and the situation can only be rectified by a God-intervention. This desire to intervene on our behalf is the very reason God sent His Son Jesus, who came in part to teach us how to love one another. Love is, in fact, the *mark* of the true Christian.

God esteems woman because she too is His creation, fashioned in His likeness. God purposed for her to complete man by adding to him tenderness, nurture, kindness, and gentleness. God made her different from man for a reason; her intended role is also different. God was deliberate and intentional in creating two complementary genders.

Through His gift of woman, God was providing for man by

giving him an altogether *good* and *perfect gift.*

Consider that Adam and Eve shared the same DNA.

God created Adam and later fashioned Eve from Adam's rib. Though separate from Adam, she was in effect his female form—resulting in both a male and a female Adam. Before God presented Eve to Adam, He informed Adam that it was not good for Him to be alone. Adam's work in the garden, which included naming the animals, allowed him to observe that the animals had mates and enjoyed companionship. It may have taken some time before Adam recognized his aloneness.

God didn't create Eve and place her in the Garden at the same moment He did Adam. Why? I believe God wanted Adam to understand that it was less than God's best for him to be alone. The *best* God had in mind for man included the complement of a companion, an equal partner. By putting Adam to sleep and allowing him to awaken to his beautiful counterpart, God ensured Adam's understanding that He had provided him a very good gift—a helpmate suitable for him in every way. It additionally brought longing into Adam's heart, since there had been no courtship between the two. Adam understood from the circumstances that he was in no way instrumental in the process. Eve was a ***good gift*** from God alone.

When women see from Scripture that God has planned for and

values them, they're liberated to value themselves. That value is based on the truth of God's Word. Eve was valuable not for what she could do for Adam, but based on God's desire for her to be an integral part of His creation.

Men are also called to value women when they see from God's Word that God's female creation is a very "good thing." Where would man be without God's perfect companion? Man lacks the ability to reproduce himself. That is a critical function of woman and man in cooperation. When Adam and Eve were expelled from the garden, God's command was that they be fruitful and multiply.

Accept your God-given significance.

1. ***You were created for God's good pleasure.***

Satan's favorite tactic is to take from, decrease, and detract from people. Consequently, he must convince man that woman is his problem—the direct opposite both of God's intention for women and the reality of the situation.

God ordained that women are to complete and help men and add to their lives. Each of us is an immense asset, not a liability as Satan wants men to believe. The Christian faith is intensely practical. God employs experience to teach and develop us. Yet He's much more interested in our interaction with Him than in the learning process itself. Everything God has created is at His disposal to use as a teaching tool for us. He's infinitely interested in our personal and spiritual development and desires us to be confident.

If the information on which we base our life is flawed, we end up with a faulty conclusion. The same is true of our self-image.

So how can we enjoy the uniqueness and special gifts God has given us? What does it mean for us to be God's beloved? How can we cultivate a godly view of ourselves and become truly confident?

> Revelation 4:11 tells us that all things were created by God for His pleasure.

Only human beings can give God the love, adoration, and worship He desires. He created each one of us to be distinctive, suited to functioning in a unique manner within the body of Christ. The confident woman learns that her time, love, adoration, submission, and devotion to her Creator bring Him great joy and pleasure.

2. ***You have been brought into an intimate relationship with God.***

We'll never be able to fulfill our intended purpose without an intimate relationship with the One who confers purpose. Simply knowing some things about God doesn't produce intimacy any more than knowing who our president is means that we know him personally. Neither does knowledge of biblical facts produce a relationship. The very word *intimacy* implies a relationship built on trust, love, and vulnerability. Giving of ourselves necessitates access to our innermost being, the part of us to which we allow no one else access.

God gives us in His Word, a model of the epitome of intimacy—the Trinity (one God in three persons: Father, Son, and Holy Spirit). Since we were made in the image of God, we're capable of intimacy and love by association.

Our closeness with God first began in the garden. Adam and Eve in the beginning of their relationship with God experienced an extraordinary intimacy with Him as they walked together in the cool of the day. When Adam and Eve chose to disobey God by eating the forbidden fruit, they chose to sever that intimacy.

Adam and Eve had no relationship with the serpent (Satan) before his appearing to them in the garden with his lies and half-truths. They had to this point shared an exclusive, intimate relationship with their Creator God.

What made them choose a superficial, cunning deceiver over a benevolent and wholly good God? The introduction of **PRIDE**! Pride is the desire to exalt self. Yet God wanted them to exalt Him. When the serpent promised that they "could be like God," the offer sounded too good to pass up and pride was ignited. But intimacy and pride can't cohabitate. And pride can't be present if we hope to share intimacy with God. Pride elevates man, while Christian confidence elevates Christ. Obedience and humility are crucial for enjoying a relationship with our devoted Father.

The possibility of intimacy is blocked when a willful, prideful heart, intent on getting what it wants, gets in the way. When pride is present, we forfeit any possibility of enjoying the benefits of intimacy with a Father who is all-knowing, all-wise, all-powerful, everywhere present, and wealthy beyond measure. He alone has the ability to reward, provide for, and bless those who choose Him over their pride.

Adam and Eve were overcome with shame and guilt immediately after their disobedience to God's command. Yielding to the temptation "to know good and evil" brought permanent, irreparable damage to their relationship with their Father. Disobedience brought long-term, dreadful consequences not only for themselves, but also to their future offspring.

Yet God doesn't leave man in his sin—as His nature is love. His love provides a way out. God understood when He gave man free will that some would obey and reciprocate His love, while others would go their own way. God accepts this freedom from His control and protection as a necessary part of total freedom and refuses to dictate our reaction to His love.

In response to the first couple's tragic choice, God had an immediate plan of provision and recovery: He covered Adam and Eve with animal skins. The shedding of blood required in the process symbolized the sacrifice Jesus would make on our behalf, rendering fellowship with God once again possible. It was through this restoration process that God kept humanity from forever being outcast.

As gracious and merciful as our loving Father is, though, He'll never demand that we accept His provision for our sins. God allows every person to freely choose…life or death. His provision for our redemption and restored intimacy with Him is there for our taking, no strings attached. If we desire to remain estranged from Him, He must allow us to go our own way. But before that final and irrevocable outcome, He'll do everything possible to bring us back to Himself.

> "God made him who had no sin to be sin for us, so that in him we might become the righteousness of God." (2 Corinthians 5:21)

> "He himself bore our sins' in his body on the cross, so that we might die to sins and live for righteousness; 'by his wounds you have been healed." (1 Peter 2:24)

"For there is one God and one mediator between God and mankind, the man Christ Jesus." (1 Timothy 2:5)

"God is faithful, who has called you into fellowship with his Son, Jesus Christ our Lord." (1 Corinthians 1:9)

Believers have the benefit of an intimate relationship with God, Jesus, and the Holy Spirit precisely because Jesus was obedient to His Father. His action made possible for us a restored relationship with our heavenly Father. *And this is the reason for our confidence!*

3. ***You've been given an exalted position.***

The book of Ephesians tells us that Christ has not only been given supreme honor in heaven but that He has lifted us up to share that exalted position with Him. We're adequate in Christ for everything life may demand of us. The better we learn who Christ is and who we are in Him, the more we're able to transform into His likeness and take on His attributes, of which confidence is just one.

The book of Esther provides an account of a young Jewish girl, Esther, who was chosen to be the bride of the Persian king. Because of her relationship with God, rather than focusing on this new love relationship, Esther recognized her purpose—to attain freedom for her people. By seeking favor with the king, she gained the ultimate favor she was seeking, the blessing and salvation of her people.

The result of honoring and obeying our Heavenly King brings us His favor. It additionally brings us beautification, adornment, increased influence, and wealth. The stories in the Bible were written not to entertain us, but to show us the way to God's rich kingdom.

To participate in kingdom endeavors we must understand how the Father and His kingdom operate. God never intended for you to receive anything from this world. You only inhabit it as your temporary dwelling place. Your real place is with the Father sharing in all the blessings of His kingdom.

When we seek to submit, honor, and adore our King, as Esther did, the kingdom will unfold for us too. Esther learned to look beyond her own interests and press on toward increased godliness. This is what Christian confidence looks like. When we move beyond our selfish position toward godliness, we too can impact our world.

Humility is the essence of intimacy with God.

Jesus is the solution for our sin problem, as sin is always a barrier to intimacy with the Father. Jesus' death bought for us the privilege of direct access to God. When we truly grasp the magnitude of what He did for us, our obedience and adoration become the all-encompassing passion of our life.

Pride will not permit us to love others unconditionally. It certainly won't let us love God with abandon, which is the very heart of intimacy with Him. Sin hinders our fellowship with the Father, but humility opens wide the door to the One who loves us beyond measure.

> "The LORD appeared to us in the past, saying: 'I have loved you with an everlasting love; I have drawn you with unfailing kindness.'" (Jeremiah 31:3)

Legitimate objects of our confidence.

There's only one legitimate object of our confidence—our Savior and Lord! He alone loves us unconditionally. No one else treats us with such compassion, unconditional acceptance, and love. No one else has mercy and goodness to follow us all of our days. No one else grants such wonderful things for us to enjoy. This is genuine love. The world offers us a cheap imitation and then unabashedly asks for something in return.

The kingdom of this world belongs to Satan. This is his domain. If you don't belong to Christ, you belong to the world! Belonging to the world, results in our death. If you want life, you must choose to *accept* Jesus and His deity—and *reject* all others. In choosing Him, we *actively* choose life. With that new life we receive a new image. He imprints upon our heart His image, and our self-awareness is changed as we begin to see ourselves as He sees us. We start to care about pleasing Him rather than others or ourselves.

"But blessed is the one who trusts in the LORD, whose *confidence* is in him. They will be like a tree planted by the water that sends out its roots by the stream. It does not fear when heat comes; its leaves are always green. It has no worries in a year of drought and never fails to bear fruit." (Jeremiah 17:7–8)

"But Christ is faithful as the Son over God's house. And we are his house, if indeed we hold firmly to our *confidence* and the hope in which we glory." (Hebrews 3:6)

"Let us then approach God's throne of grace with *confidence*, so that we may receive mercy and find grace to help us in our time of need." (Hebrew 4:16)

All of us, at some time or another, find ourselves in need. God longs to meet those needs with His grace, mercy, and overwhelming love. If we will remain faithful to Him and recognize and acknowledge the countless ways in which He provides for us, we'll come to understand this truth about Him.

Illegitimate objects of our confidence.

1. **Human wisdom:** There's no true wisdom apart from God…because **GOD IS WISDOM**. We must tap into His wisdom if we want His accompanying power. It comes only to those who ask for it by name.

- "Trust in Jehovah with all your heart, and lean not upon your own understanding. In all your ways acknowledge him, and he will direct your paths." (Proverbs 3:5–6).

"This is what the LORD says: Cursed is the one who trusts in man, who draws strength from mere flesh and whose heart turns away from the LORD. That person will be like a bush in the wastelands; they will not see prosperity when it comes. They will dwell in the parched places of the desert, in a salt land where no one lives." (Jeremiah 17:5–6)

2. ***Earthly riches and systems:*** God takes our little and multiplies it. When we look to Him *first* to supply all our needs, He comes through for us.

"Have no fear of sudden disaster or of the ruin that overtakes the wicked, for the LORD will be at your side and will keep your foot from being snared." (Proverbs 3:25–26)

"I can do all this through him who gives me strength." (Philippians 4:13)

"Let us then approach God's throne of grace with confidence, so that we may receive mercy and find grace to help us in our time of need." (Hebrews 4:16)

We're tempted, just as others throughout the Bible, to put our faith in something other than God.

Adam and Eve believed the lies of the serpent. Abraham, fearful in the presence of those who had no regard for God, not only lied so his life might be spared, but had difficulty believing that God could rescue him. King Saul, in the absence of certainty, engaged a medium for advice, a choice he would later regret.

We, likewise, are inclined to invest our faith in the world's systems and values. We entrust our money to secular companies that don't hold to ethical practices. We distrust God to come through for us during lean times and accept any job offer that may come our way settling for second best. We marry anyone who shows us the attention and affection we crave, not considering that God may have a better mate for us. We're afraid to answer honestly and boldly when put on the spot, resorting to a "white lie" because we don't believe God will reward us for honest character. And like the fearful Peter, we too easily deny the very Christ we profess to love.

When we allow fear to rule us, we misplace our confidence. Looking to the world or to non-Christians for solutions that only God grants is like building on a wobbly, crumbling foundation. Money has become the all-encompassing god of this world. As Jesus Himself cautions,

> "Do not store up for yourselves treasures on earth, where moth and rust destroy, and where thieves break in and steal." (Matthew 6:19)

3. ***Accomplishments and abilities:*** Scores of people place their confidence in their own abilities and accomplishments. In contrast, our trust as believers is never based on our wealth, career, influence, perceived power, or any other worldly criterion. Our earthly pursuits are finite. Scripture reminds us that they will rust and be taken from us by thieves. God places no value on what unregenerate man sees as important or worthwhile. Unimpressed by earthly status, celebrity, or fame, God focuses on people's character—on their heart, not their appearance.

When people are consumed by their own good fortune, physical beauty and status, they simply don't have room in their hearts to love God liberally. Acquiring and maintaining "all these things" requires their undivided devotion. They find themselves in continuous maintenance mode, desperate to hold on to what they fear losing.

Jesus instructed the rich young man to give up his possessions to follow Him. Why? He didn't tell everyone this. Because He knew that this man's heart was *set* on his wealth. Unable in his own power to do so, the man walked away full of sorrow (Matthew 19:21).

Christians often fail to comprehend that they're choosing the temporal over the eternal treasure. Many opt for fleeting happiness over permanent joy, the distinguishing mark that separates us from the rest of the world. In so doing we "gain" for ourselves unnecessary worry and unbelief. Our confidence and esteem must be grounded in Christian character.

> "Whoever fears the LORD has a secure fortress, and for their children it will be a refuge. The fear of the LORD is a fountain of life, turning a person from the snares of death." (Proverbs 14:26–27)

Confidence is every believer's calling.

God is preparing you for your future. A future beyond anything you can imagine. Fully embrace every season of that preparation. God has His own way of preparing you. It's your responsibility to cooperate with Him in this process. Being intentional about the time you spend with Him and listening carefully to His voice will aid you in this process.

Get excited about what the Lord has for you and where He wants to take you. That enthusiasm will help you say no to the enticements the enemy throws your way to distract you from your high calling. The more time and energy you devote to your transformation process, the stronger and more confident you'll become. One day you'll look back, no longer able to recognize the person you once were.

Scripture teaches us to be confident in our prayers.

Through prayer we accept Jesus as our Savior, asking Him to come into our heart and change us into a new creation. In the Old Testament the law reigned, and blessings came as a result of obedience. Jesus ushered in the new covenant (the New Testament), and with it a new way for God to relate to His children.

When we accept Christ, we intentionally turn our backs on our former lives of sin. We gain many benefits when we accept personally what Jesus died to give us. The privilege of prayer is just one of those benefits. What a profound comfort to be able to pour out our hearts to a God who is deeply concerned about every aspect of our lives.

God isn't mad at you. He doesn't focus on your sin. He sees you and longs for you, so there's no need to fear Him. He wants you to be confident *in* Him. He's never too busy, too preoccupied, or too impatient to hear from you. He's always waiting, longing for you to turn to Him. If you ask Him for direction and counsel, you can do so in the assurance that He'll provide it. He offers solutions to your every problem and need. He won't withhold one good thing from those who ask.

We optimize our success when we ask for right things. Our first priority is asking Christ to come into our lives. From that connection point on, we can be assured that He's always with us.

When we're young in Christ, we've yet to learn that God doesn't always answer our requests immediately. We fail to discern that much of what we ask for could be damaging for us. Nor do we comprehend that we may need added maturity to handle what we're requesting. God knows not only what we need, but at what point we're ready to receive it.

The fact that God desires to converse with us is astounding. Often, we're not at a point of appreciating all that God offers. We take it for granted. But, if we'll pause and think about it, what an amazing privilege it is to have a Creator who's deeply and personally devoted to us.

If you're born again, the Holy Spirit is permanently residing in you. He's always willing and ready to communicate with your spirit. What a blessing! Have you thanked your Lord for giving you the Holy Spirit?

> "Jesus replied, 'Anyone who loves me will obey my teaching. My Father will love them, and we will come to them and make our home with them.'" (John 14:23)

> "Here I am! I stand at the door and knock. If anyone hears my voice and opens the door, I will come in and eat with that person, and they with me." (Revelation 3:20)

> "Examine yourselves to see whether you are in the faith; test yourselves. Do you not realize that Christ Jesus is in you—unless, of course, you fail the test?" (2 Corinthians 13:5)

The Spirit ignites within us a desire to talk with God, to listen to Him, and to experience more of His tremendous power. That's what prayer is.

We express our thanks, faith, love, devotion, and hope to God in prayer. And we receive from Him answers, assurance, guidance, peace, strength, power, and revelation of who He is and what He wants to do in us.

- "Ask in faith, nothing doubting: for he who doubts is like the surge of the sea driven by the wind and tossed. For let not that man think that he shall receive anything of the Lord; a double-minded man, unstable in all his ways." (James 1:6-8)

> "And this is the confidence that we have toward him, that, if we ask anything according to his will, he hears us." (1 John 5:14)

We can be confident in the providential (beneficial, advantageous) operation of God. God operates in an orderly fashion and He's completely truthful in everything He says. God's system operates differently from the world's and comes with a guarantee too good to ignore. The world offers no warranty or protection—its buyer beware! But with God there's always protection and reward.

We can have the character of confidence.

By taking a careful look at the "fruit of confidence" in God's Word, we can push forward in the direction He's calling us, understanding that He has equipped us to succeed. He isn't looking for our failure, but our triumph. Confidence comes when we understand that although we're responsible for obeying, we don't control the outcome.

Doubt, uncertainty, unbelief, and distrust are all opposites of trust. If we allow these negative feelings to take hold of us, we'll be limited in our thinking and ability. We'll end up placing our trust in others or in ourselves. But apart from the power that comes from the Holy Spirit, our feeble and temporary abilities won't see us through. Our attempts at self-importance lead us to pride, and pride detracts from our power source.

We lose our confidence when we fixate on our problems rather than on the One who came to free us from those problems.

> "He replied, 'You of little faith, why are you so afraid?' Then he got up and rebuked the winds and the waves, and it was completely calm." (Matthew 8:26)

Christians are called to one purpose.

It's impossible to find true fulfillment apart from discovering why we were created. We've been called to co-labor with Christ, to unite with Him in one Spirit and for one purpose. This alone gives meaning to our lives. It's virtually impossible to serve God without keeping His purposes in mind. If we don't know what those purposes are, how will we fulfill them? For that we need to go back to the Word.

> "This is the message we have heard from him and declare to you: God is light; in him there is no darkness at all. *If* we claim to have fellowship with him and yet walk in the darkness, we lie and do not live out the truth. But *if* we walk in the light, as he is in the light, we have fellowship with one another, and the blood of Jesus, his Son, purifies us from all sin. *If* we claim to be without sin, we deceive ourselves and the truth is not in us. *If* we confess our sins, he is faithful and just and will forgive us our sins and purify us from all unrighteousness. *If* we claim we have not sinned, we make him out to be a liar and his word is not in us." (1 John 1:5–10, bold italics added)

That lowly conjunction "if" is integral to this passage. It's the prescription for our high calling. We must ask ourselves whether these evidences of faith can be found in us. An affirmative answer is confirmation that we belong to Him.

When we don't know what to do or where to turn, we can look beyond ourselves to God. With the Spirit's power in us, we become a powerhouse. By first accepting Him and then surrendering our will to His infinitely greater will, we discover our confidence. Only then do we begin to know what to do and where to turn.

Ask Jesus to mold and fashion you into His likeness. Yield yourself as pliable, workable clay to be used in the potter's hand to fashion as He wills. When He's finished, He'll turn you into something beautiful, valuable, and good, equipped to accomplish every good work he has purposed for you.

As you begin to see evidence of your transformation, you'll be assured that you can trust Christ implicitly. He's fully engaged in making something beautiful and useful from the hard lump of clay you've offered Him. And you and I can possess peace and confidence in knowing that what He started He'll see through to completion.

1. A confident woman understands that salvation brings knowledge of the Savior.

2. A confident woman knows God, first personally and then intimately.

3. A confident woman understands the sanctification process.

4. A confident woman longs for her Savior's presence; as David did, she thirsts for Him, her lover.

5. A confident woman understands repentance and the forgiveness of sins.

6. A confident woman understands that she is redeemed.

7. A confident woman understands that the "fear of the Lord" is the beginning of wisdom.

8. A confident woman has a healthy self-concept, and her esteem comes from God—her true lover.

9. A confident woman understands her spiritual inheritance.

10. A confident woman recognizes her role and calling in God's overall plan.

11. A confident woman understands herself to be a divine original, a priceless treasure to God!

12. A confident woman seeks her substance in Christ and not in herself.

A confident woman understands God's absolute goodness.

Absolute goodness resides in God alone and He shares His goodness with those who seek fellowship with Him. This personal bond sheds light on truth, and truth reveals more truth. The more we let God change us, the more we're freed up to love ourselves and others.

We must seek and chase down all available spiritual truth. Ask God to give you the capacity to understand, and then be willing to put that truth into practice as opportunities present themselves. Without truth there can be no understanding of goodness.

> "The wicked, through the pride of his countenance, will not seek after God: God is not in all his thoughts." (Psalm 10:4)

> "Even him [the Antichrist], whose coming is after the working of Satan with all power and signs and lying wonders [falsehoods], and with all deceivableness of unrighteousness in them [the unsaved] that perish; because they received not the love of the truth, that they might be saved." (2 Thessalonians 2:10).

Salvation in Christ leads us to truth, and truth gives us confidence.

There are so many false prophets today that it's difficult to discern real truth, yet we're commanded to seek it. But how can we be sure we're going after the right thing when we're surrounded by deception? There are foundational doctrines of the Christian faith that if denied, leave us without truth. Without truth, we're vulnerable to deception. Ask yourself whether these foundational Christian truths are being taught in your church:

The godhead (Father, Son, and Holy Spirit).

The deity of Jesus Christ.

The sinfulness of man.

The virgin birth.

The sinless life of Jesus Christ.

The literal blood sacrifice of Jesus Christ.

The bodily resurrection of Jesus Christ.

The existence of a literal hell.

> "Then you will know the truth, and the truth will set you free." (John 8:32)

> "So if the Son sets you free, you will be free indeed." (John 8:36)

We're told in 2 Timothy 3:5, that in the last days there will be false prophets. Religious people who will have a form of godliness, but deny its **POWER**.

Be aware that those who deny the power that comes through receiving Jesus Christ as Savior are promoting a different gospel.

Many cults profess to follow Jesus. But if you investigate carefully, you'll discover that they're speaking of a "different" Jesus and that they follow their own scriptures, which they place above the Bible. There are many imitators, but only one original.

When something isn't right in the believer's life, the Holy Spirit provides a "warning" through our conscience. Be sure to heed His warning for it's meant to protect you. This is one of the ways He speaks to us. Those who are taught not to question, to believe "every wind of doctrine" without searching the Scriptures for themselves, will be left wanting. God has given us the Holy Spirit to help us navigate through a world of Satan's falsehood. Ask for discernment to avoid being deceived. Ask for the wisdom and assurance to know you're following the one true God.

The end times will be marked by numerous impersonators, but there is only one author and originator of truth. Remember that the Bible, in sharp contrast to cults and false religions, teaches that salvation is a supernatural miracle—a gift from God—in response to one's faith in Jesus Christ, the Son of God, for the forgiveness of sins.

> "Everyone who calls on the name of the Lord will be saved."
> (Romans 10:13)

If you're part of a religious group that tells you you're not good enough, or that you must rely upon your works to get you into heaven, you're buying into a lie. Satan is behind all such messages. They're meant to keep you from coming to Jesus and receiving your full inheritance in the kingdom of God.

> Jesus answered, "Very truly I tell you, no one can enter the kingdom of God unless they are born of water and the Spirit." (John 3:5)

> "Yet to all who did receive him, to those who believed in his name, he gave the right to become children of God." (John 1:12)

> "For you know that it was not with perishable things such as silver or gold that you were redeemed from the empty way of life handed down to you from your ancestors, but with the precious blood of Christ, a lamb without blemish or defect." (1 Peter 1:18–19)

We come to Jesus as sinners seeking a Savior. Nothing else is required. You don't have to clean yourself up first, as salvation doesn't come from anything you can do. It comes from what Jesus accomplished and nothing else. He gave up everything, so you could be redeemed. This Jesus did because He loves you. Accepting Jesus' finished work on the cross will give you the confidence that you are loved and saved.

- "Having confidence of this very thing, that he who has begun in you a good work will complete it unto Jesus Christ's day" (Philippians 1:6).

3

SHE IS SAVED BY GRACE —

DISCERNING REAL CONVERSION

"That being justified by His grace we might be made heirs according to the hope of eternal life" (Titus 3:7)

Perhaps you've known identical twins who looked so much alike that without a distinguishing mark, like a birthmark, you couldn't tell them apart.

True believers have distinguishing marks too that set them apart from all others. Their "birthmark" is Jesus. Since He marks us as Christians and changes our identity, we no longer resemble our former selves.

Possibly you've heard the words "saved," "born again," and "conversion" and have wondered what they really mean. These terms are basically synonymous. Spiritually speaking, *conversion* refers to "a change." But first we must answer the questions "What is a person changed from?" and "What are they changed to?"

Being converted or born-again is a miraculous, life-transforming event and is impossible without the active participation of the Holy Spirit. He initiates our conversion by inviting us to participate with Him. Until this awareness of our need for a Savior, and indeed asking Him to come into our life to save us occurs, it's impossible for us to fully understand Scripture or Jesus and His works.[1]

Do you know your eternal destination?

Some people believe it's impossible to know for sure whether or not they're saved. This one question brings so many to a state of anguish because they have no assurance that they'll go to heaven after they die. If you've asked this very question, take heart: The Bible tells us we can know for certain we're saved.

Since God is no *respecter of persons* (meaning that He plays no favorites) He makes eternal salvation available to all who will choose Him and come to Him. That we can gain absolute assurance of our eternal destination is made clear in the book of 1 John. The word "know" is used 39 times in this short book. John is saying that there are some things—our salvation in particular—we can know for sure. Paul agrees:

> "The Spirit himself testifies with our spirit that we are God's children." (Romans 8:16)

Since God gave us His Word on so grave an issue, no one need struggle any longer regarding their eternal destination.

Earthly life is a gift. And when its brief span is gone there's eternity to face. If we don't get this one central question firmly answered, there's no turning back to get it correct.

Understanding our human nature.

We were born into sin and sin makes us selfish. We have no ability on our own to change our nature. Change occurs only when we see things for what they really are and make a decision to do an about-face. But the question for so many isn't what to turn "*from*," but what to turn "*to*."

1. ***Our fleshly, selfish desires get us into trouble.***

The Bible tells us that Satan is a master manipulator. Our sinful nature comes with inborn weaknesses. And those weaknesses combined with the devil's influence, leads the whole world into sin (Revelation 12:9). Because of Satan's deceptions and our sinful tendencies, the Bible says that "all have sinned and fall short of the glory of God." (Romans 3:23)

The devil can't make us sin, but our lack of awareness of his tactics allows him to influence us through our own fleshly weaknesses.

Galatians 5:19-21 tells us these weaknesses are sexual immorality, impurity and debauchery, idolatry, witchcraft, hatred, discord, jealousy, fits of rage, selfish ambition, etc. (see Romans 1:24-32). These human weaknesses make us especially vulnerable to Satan's deception and manipulations.

2. *We're naturally devious.*

Some synonyms for the word *devious* are: deceitful, scheming, underhanded, conniving, sneaky, cunning, crafty, or sly. Think about it, who possesses these traits? Satan does!

Because we're born into sin, we're naturally like Satan until our nature is transformed. We can't be transformed without Christ. To accept and embrace Christ means we're making a decision to turn from this sinful state to become more like Jesus.

Prior to conversion, justifying is a natural part of our innate thinking process. We naturally look for ways to justify, or rationalize our conduct, lusts, and sinful desires. When we accept Jesus, we see that we've been justifying our sinful behavior. We ask Him to come in and change our inclinations.

> "The heart is deceitful above all things and beyond cure. Who can understand it? "I the Lord search the heart and examine the mind, to reward a man according to his conduct, according to what his deeds deserve." (Jeremiah 17:9–10)

3. *We resent having to restrain our fleshly desires.*

In Romans 8:5–8, Paul puts it this way:

> "Those who live according to the sinful nature have their minds set on what that nature desires; but those who live in accordance with the Spirit have their minds set on what the Spirit desires. The mind of sinful man is death, but the mind controlled by the Spirit is life and peace; the sinful mind is hostile to God. It does not submit to God's law, nor can it do so. Those controlled by the sinful nature cannot please God."

These weaknesses and the propensity to act on them belong to our human nature, which Paul calls the "flesh." Satan uses them as entry points into our heart and mind. He appeals to our selfishness, greed, and immaturity by persuading us to rely upon ourselves for fulfillment of our self-centered desires. This is natural to us because we want what we want. Without the positive influence of God's Spirit in us, we simply aren't inclined in the direction of God's plan.

> Paul warns, "For if you live according to the sinful nature, you will die; but if by the Spirit you put to death the misdeeds of the body, you will live, because those who are led by the Spirit of God are sons of God." (Romans 8:13–14)

The Word of God makes it plain that repentance includes changing our thoughts. Mark 7:20–21 tells us that what defiles us starts from within.

> "What comes out of a man is what makes him 'unclean.' For from within, out of men's hearts, come evil thoughts, sexual immorality, theft, murder, adultery, greed, malice, deceit, lewdness, envy, slander, arrogance and folly. All these evils come from inside and make a man 'unclean.'"

> "Let the wicked forsake his way and the evil man his thoughts. Let him turn to the LORD, and he will have mercy on him, and to our God, for he will freely pardon." (Isaiah 55:7)

Isaiah makes clear that God pardons us when we forsake our sinful thoughts and ways. Since sin is intrinsic to all of us, we must all deal with it. What one person struggles with may not be the same as what someone else does. But in some form or another we all suffer from self-centeredness.

Being pardoned means we examine ourselves and recognize our own particular weaknesses in both thought and deed. If you're not aware of what those weaknesses are, ask God to reveal them to you. With the Holy Spirit's help, you'll see what He sees. When you see those shortfalls clearly, ask Him to give you the strength to change them. This is a life-long process for most of us. Some weaknesses God will take from us immediately. Others He may allow us to struggle with for a time, to teach us to lean on Him for complete deliverance.

- We are told to "grow in the grace and knowledge of our Lord and Savior Jesus Christ." (2 Peter 3:18)

What is repentance?

Repent isn't a word we hear widely in our day, so few understand its full meaning. In both Greek and Hebrew repentance refers to a *change of heart*, a significant shift in our thinking, a transformation of purpose, with emphasis on modifying one's conduct.

> Peter urges us, "Repent, then, and turn to God, so that your sins may be wiped out, that times of refreshing may come from the Lord." (Acts 3:19)

> And Paul explained that the "reward" of sin is death. (Romans 6:23)

The term *convert* means "turn." When we repent, we not only turn from our sin, but surrender our will to God. Repenting of our sin means acknowledging that we're a sinner in need of a Savior.

When a crime is pardoned by a judge, the judge, on the basis of that pardon or act of grace, expects the person to turn from their life of crime. He doesn't pardon the individual so they may continue on in their lifestyle of lawbreaking. In the same way we're to change, to turn from our sinful deeds and thoughts.

God commands our repentance.

Throughout Scripture we're told of our need to repent. The response to that message varies. Some openly rebuke it and dismiss the thought of needing to change. Others may at first be interested but realize with time that they don't want to give up what they perceive as pleasure.

But some consider the *Good News* the best news they're ever heard. They understand that repentance is the only way to a new and better life. They embrace it wholeheartedly, never to return to their old life of sin and depravity. To them the gospel message is a pearl of great price—news like no other. They're completely captivated, immediately and irreversibly changed.

Man was not originally created to die. Death was the result of sin (Romans 3:23; 5:12; 6:23). Like Adam, we're responsible for our own actions and attitudes toward God. As the Scriptures point out, this present world is spiritually blinded by Satan (see Revelation 12:9; 1 John 5:19). But God is calling, and a few will respond.

> "Each one is tempted when he is drawn away by his own desires and enticed." (James 1:14–16)

> "Jesus said, 'Out of the heart proceed evil thoughts, murders, fornications . . .'" (Matthew 15:19)

Men and women must acknowledge that they're sinners. By believing the gospel, repenting of sin, and accepting Jesus as Savior and Lord, we can be freed from our sinful nature.

> "Jesus said, 'He who believes and is baptized will be saved.'" (Mark 16:16)

Repenting has two components—believing and receiving.

Acts 16 records Paul and Silas's imprisonment in Philippi before an earthquake loosed their chains and opened the doors to their cells. The jailer, recognizing a miracle from God, asked Paul and Silas what he must do to be saved. Their answer:

> "Believe on the Lord Jesus Christ, and you will be saved, you and your household" (Acts 16:31, bold italics added).

Merely having a *belief* that Jesus is the Savior won't make you a true believer. True believers believe in His message, His promises, and His instructions. It goes beyond belief to *accepting truth* and *receiving it* into our being.

God calls us to "genuine" repentance.

True repentance goes deeper than self-reproach; it involves a sense of grief over having denied God. Even very young children have a sense of right and wrong and know when they're doing something for which they may receive punishment. The boy caught by his mother standing on the kitchen counter, one arm still in the cookie jar and chewing as fast as he can, turns to her and simply says "I'm sorry." He's sorry he got caught and was unable to finish the cookies in the jar, not that he was doing something he was told not to do.

We have the same attitude about confessing our wrongdoing—we're sorry we got caught, but not sorry for what we did. Genuine repentance is so much more than feeling sorry and a world away from feeling sorry for ourselves.

Genuine repentance comes when we see ourselves clearly rather than pretending, we aren't as bad as others. We're skilled in our self-deception. With enough practice we become masters at it. Only when the Holy Spirit convicts us of our sinful condition apart from God, do we see ourselves honestly. The Holy Spirit doesn't reveal our sins to shame us, but to draw us to the One who has made provision for them. Suddenly we see that we have grieved our Lord with our perverse heart, with our wrong attitudes and words, disbelief, and total disregard for and rebellion against Him.

Remorse over having spent our lives in denial of Him sends us to Him to receive the healing we're so eager for. True repentance brings salvation, and salvation brings forgiveness of sins. We can move away from shame and guilt because we've been made whole through Jesus.

Shame and guilt come from Satan, not God. They're the devil's number one tactic to keep people from the very One they need. When true repentance occurs within our heart, the Holy Spirit pours His power and strength into us. This makes possible our ability to remain strong against Satan.

The Holy Spirit sheds light on how much Christ loves you.

In his letter to the Ephesians, Paul writes these powerful words:

> "I pray that out of his glorious riches he [God] may strengthen you with power through his Spirit in your inner being, so that Christ may dwell in your hearts through faith. And I pray that you, being rooted and established in love, may have power, together with all the saints, to grasp how wide and long and high and deep is the love of Christ, and to know this love that

surpasses knowledge—that you may be filled to the measure of all the fullness of God. Now to him who is able to do immeasurably more than all we ask or imagine, according to his power that is at work within us, to him be glory in the church and in Christ Jesus throughout all generations, for ever and ever! Amen." (Ephesians 3:16–22)

Without question one of the most remarkable Christian doctrines is that Jesus will dwell in any human heart that welcomes Him. Until we accept Jesus as Savior and understand His messages to us, it just isn't possible to live a holy, transformed life. This inclination and ability come only through repentance. Jesus is God's provision for you. God is the giver of all good things, and His Son is above all other good things.

- "He went on to say, 'This is why I told you that *no one can come to me unless the Father has enabled them*.'" (John 6:65)

What is the mark of a true believer?

Spiritual conversion: A true believer is a person who believes, first, that Jesus is the Christ. But this is not just a mental acknowledgment of the fact, as it requires acceptance of that truth in our *heart*. Many may believe "*about*" Jesus, and many more will take the step of believing "*in*" Him. The truth is, though, that the true

Christian trusts Jesus Christ as Lord and Savior; the converted person "***believes***" Him.

When we repent our eyes are opened and we're able to see that our previous thinking and behaviors were not only wrong, but hurtful to Christ, ourselves, and others. Repentance brings us to salvation, and salvation turns us from our wrong ways.

> "He replied, 'Because the knowledge of the secrets of the kingdom of Heaven has been given to you, but not to them.'" (Matthew 13:11)

This is a major distinction between someone who identifies them self as a Christian and someone who is a true Christian. Genuine belief comes by way of saving faith. It's coming to the place where one trusts in nothing else and no one else but Jesus Christ for salvation.

What God promises to do He'll do! Consequently, if you've trusted Jesus as your Savior, according to the plan laid out in His Word to you, you are saved.

- "When they heard this, they had no further objections and praised God, saying, 'So then, even to Gentiles God has granted repentance that leads to life.'" (Acts 11:18)

God will lead us to repent when we respond in faith to His messages to us. Spiritual blindness is a curse from Satan. But spiritual vision is life itself.

Obedience: Salvation makes it possible for us come into agreement with God's ways. Genuine repentance is more than an emotion of the moment. Our lives must change, for God's light saves us from our spiritual blindness and enables us to understand Scripture.

As we mature spiritually and continue to gain wisdom from the reading and hearing of God's Word, we recognize that faith, confession, and obedience are all necessary for maintaining our intimacy with the Lord. When we ask Jesus for forgiveness, we need to believe that we're forgiven.

> Earlier Jesus had asked, "But why do you call me 'Lord, Lord' and not do the things which I say?" (Luke 6:46)

Disobedience will keep us from receiving the good things God has for us, all of which come to us by grace through faith. When we trust God's Word and believe that He forgives us, we gain confidence to continue to confess, understanding that confession brings us back into intimacy with Him. A pure heart comes by way of confession and keeps us free and undefiled. The true Christian is obedient to Christ's message. [1]

What does such belief require?

Faith believes that Christ delivers—that He offers salvation and forgiveness of sins and will fully meet our needs. Confession through prayer gives the Holy Spirit the power and authority to go to work on our behalf, continually interceding for us before the Father. Jesus does the same for us.

When God shines light into our heart, we're able to see that receiving this new knowledge is going to require a decision from us: whether we're for Christ or against Him. If we're for Him, we must *accept* Him. We can't have it both ways. God doesn't tolerate a lukewarm response to the truth He gives.

> "I know your deeds, that you are neither cold nor hot. I wish you were either one or the other! So, because you are lukewarm—neither hot nor cold—I am about to spit you out of my mouth." (Revelation 3:15–16)

Those are strong words, but they give us a picture of how God views our being wishy-washy. The Bible also tells us,

> "Simply let your 'Yes' be 'Yes,' and your 'No,' 'No'; anything beyond this comes from the evil one." (Matthew 5:37)

If you're having difficulty letting others know you're a Christian, consider more carefully what the verse above is saying: that this "comes from the evil one."

God has and will always exist.

God has no beginning or end. His kingdom will last forever as the book of Psalms assures us.

> "Before the mountains were born, or you brought forth the whole world, from everlasting to everlasting you are God." (Psalm 90:2)

People are born and live for a short time in their physical bodies. Our time is calculated and measured out by God and our bodies eventually die. Upon death, we return to the dust from which we were taken.

But because we're made in God's image (Genesis 1:26), and since His Spirit resides in us, we're eternal beings and our spirit never ceases to exist.

Eternal life is more than an existence that never ends. It's a life that's lived infinitely, and it'll be lived forever either in joy or in torment. It will not be neutral; it will be one or the other. If we belong to Christ and His kingdom, we'll experience joy for all eternity. But if we reject God's free gift of salvation, offered through His Son Jesus, we'll receive torment for all eternity.

The Apostle Paul warns us against rejecting God's grace.

Eternity is forever. Although some don't want to think about it, the Bible tells us that to fail to consider our eternal destination is foolish.

Paul begins a discussion of the wrath of God against wicked men who suppress the truth in unrighteousness.

- But God shows his anger from heaven against all sinful, wicked people who suppress the truth by their wickedness (Romans 1:18, NLT).

The apostle teaches that all men have knowledge of the true God and because of this knowledge should glorify God. That is, they ought to render to God the honor He deserves because of who He is. Beyond this, all people owe Him thanks for all His benefits, even our very existence. We have a moral obligation to worship and serve the true and living God who gives us life.

But what do people do? They reject God. They turn away from Him and create idols: false worldviews, erroneous philosophies, and satanic religions.

What is involved in this rejection of God? Paul teaches us that idolatry and all other sin begins in the human heart or mind. It involves a darkening of the heart of man. Paul used different terms in Romans 1 to describe the corruption of the human mind:

"Their foolish hearts were darkened" (verse 21),

"They became fools" (verse 22),

"They became futile in their thoughts" (verse 21), and

"God gave them over to a debased mind" (verse 28).

Until we receive Jesus as our Savior, even if we have knowledge of Him, we can't know Him *personally*. Just as you may know of someone famous coming to your town, unless you know that person personally, they won't be spending one-on-one time with you.

The Bible tells us that in our natural state we're spiritually dead and that our nature is opposed to God. We won't be able to comprehend who God is apart from spiritual rebirth.

- "As for you, you were dead in your transgressions and sins." (Ephesians 2:1)

"The person without the Spirit does not accept the things that come from the Spirit of God but considers them foolishness, and cannot understand them because they are discerned only through the Spirit." (1 Corinthians. 2:14)

"For God so loved the world that he gave his one and only Son, that whoever believes in him shall not perish but have eternal life." (John 3:16)

But the person who chooses God over wickedness will experience a joyous eternal life. This is the essence of the Christian faith, and Jesus spoke of it several times. Eternal life is not a destination but an everlasting relationship with the triune God. This relationship starts here on earth and continues in heaven

Who can receive eternal life?

Everyone who trusts in Jesus by faith as Savior receives life everlasting. This is God's single method whereby we can enter into a relationship with Him.

"Jesus answered, 'I am the way and the truth and the life. No one comes to the Father except through me.'" (John 14:6)

"For my Father's will is that everyone who looks to the Son and believes in him shall have eternal life, and I will raise him up at the last day." (John 6:40)

Jesus fulfilled His Father's plan—and modeled humility, obedience, self-sacrifice, and total dependence on the Father. Jesus is our example of how to respond to the Father.

Repentance involves living under Jesus' lordship and authority.

God the Father gave His Son the name that's above all other names: that of the Lord Jesus Christ. Jesus was given complete authority over heaven and earth by His Father. Although most reject His authority, this in no way negates the reality that *His lordship will never end.*

As a result of man declining to accept Christ's lordship, sin runs rampant and shipwrecks many lives. The gospel is called the Good News because God has a good plan that won't be stopped by any created being. One day every person will acknowledge the authority of Jesus. Just as God has said, all created beings in heaven, on earth, and under the earth will kneel before Him—including those who have rejected Him as the Son of God. What a triumphant and glorious time that will be.[2]

> "...that at the name of Jesus every knee should bow, in Heaven and on earth and under the earth." (Philippians 2:10).

Christians will be forever changed!

The world is a fearful place in which we all experience pain and suffering. As a result, when something dreadful happens to us we may feel that our lives will never again be the same. But in a powerful sense, just as evil harms and steals from us, being born again renews and gives life back to us. It gives us back the life we were meant to live. We have authority even now to take back what the enemy has stolen from us. When this takes place, we actually become stronger and better for it.

From the moment we accept Jesus as our personal Savior and Lord, our lives are forever changed. This change involves more than assurance of eternal life with God. The rebirth experience means that we're now "followers" of Christ. Belonging to and following Him bring us a completely new and invigorated life.

There are several immediate benefits to salvation.

1. Our sins are forgiven (past, present, and future.) (2 Corinthians 5:21)

2. We are a "new creation" in Christ. (2 Corinthians 5:17)

3. We walk in newness of life. (Romans 6:4)

4. We put on the "new man." (Ephesians 4:24; Colossians 3:10)

Jesus came to reconcile the world to the Father through His death on the cross (2 Corinthians 5:18–19). As a result, those who accept and follow Him are transformed to reflect His will.

Transformation begins a process that involves . . .

- Your mind being renewed by the Word of God. (Romans 12:2)

- Walking in accordance with the leading of the Holy Spirit. (Galatians 5:19–25)

- Functioning in the wisdom of God rather than by human reasoning. (James 3:13–18)

- Living according to the teachings of Jesus. (Colossians 2:6)

- Desiring to do His work, not from guilt but in joy. Turning from our old habits to working in His way, with His methods, and in His likeness. (2 Corinthians 5:20)

- Having Christ in us, the hope of glory. (Colossians 1:27)

- Pressing on to the goal of eternity with Jesus. (Philippians 3:8–14)

Transformed people walk in the light received.

John illustrated for us that those who are saved have a desire to "walk in the light." Jesus is that light.

- "There was a man sent from God whose name was John. He came as a witness to testify concerning that light, so that through him all might believe." (John 1:6–7)

- "When Jesus spoke again to the people, he said, 'I am the light of the world. Whoever follows me will never walk in darkness, but will have the light of life.'" (John 8:12)

Light completely changes the atmosphere of a dark room. Where once there was no vision because of the darkness, light reveals what was there all along. Salvation sheds light on our formerly darkened heart. With that new light come new desires. The desire to fellowship with Christ is a theme that runs throughout the book of 1 John.

A truly saved person will gravitate toward the things of God. Desires change as one begins reading the Bible, finding and attending a church, praying, and enjoying fellowship with other believers.

- "And without faith it is impossible to please God, because *anyone who comes to him must believe that he exists* and *that he rewards those who earnestly seek him*." (Hebrews 11:6)

Blessings unspeakable come to those who earnestly seek the giver of light. With prayer and study, a true believer begins to know what God wants. She seeks God's commands and develops a desire to obey them. In doing so, she starts to see her purpose in the Kingdom. Genuine salvation is proven by a desire to obey God.

> "If you know that he is righteous, you know that everyone who does what is right has been born of him." (1 John 2:29)

Transformed people are unable to continue in their sin.

The true believer can't continue to live a life of sin. When John tells us that those who are saved don't sin, he isn't teaching sinless perfection. Sinning is a part of our human condition from which we can't escape during this lifetime. But when we come to Christ, we have a new dynamic force working in our heart—the power of the Holy Spirit. We sin, but we find it impossible to continue living in sin habitually.

When the genuinely converted person sins, there's an immediate sense of wrong. They sense that they've damaged their intimate relationship with the Lord. That discomfort will drive them to confess, to restore that cherished relationship built on fellowship, trust, and unconditional love,

> "'…because the Lord disciplines the one he loves, and he chastens everyone he accepts as his son.' Endure hardship as discipline;

God is treating you as his children. For what children are not disciplined by their father? If you are not disciplined—and everyone undergoes discipline—then you are not legitimate, not true sons and daughters at all. Moreover, we have all had human fathers who disciplined us and we respected them for it. How much more should we submit to the Father of spirits and live! They disciplined us for a little while as they thought best; but God disciplines us for our good, in order that we may share in his holiness. No discipline seems pleasant at the time, but painful. Later on, however, it produces a harvest of righteousness and peace for those who have been trained by it." (Hebrews 12:6–11)

Once the light of Christ enters our heart, we can no longer enjoy sinning for long. There will come a time, if blatant sin is present, that we'll feel the sting of lost intimacy with the Lord. The Holy Spirit is present in us to convict us, not to condemn us. That conviction draws us back.

God has directed us to "work out our salvation." This means that it's our responsibility to go to God's Word to see what it is He's already given us.

His Word holds the key to overthrowing the strongholds of sin in our life. He expects us to do what we need to do, because we derive strength from taking responsibility for our spiritual growth and overcoming the enemy.

Yes, we're human, and human beings' sin, but we've given the power of the Holy Spirit to overcome sin. If we refuse to stay away from "forbidden fruit," we'll end up in bondage. Freedom is deciding that bondage is not our inheritance and we'll no longer accept it.

"Turning from," means taking action to destroy the strongholds that have overtaken us. When we expose and confess our sin to God and our loved ones, we bring it out of the dark and into the light. That exposure holds us accountable. Turning from sin enables us to walk in the light that's already been given.

So many refuse to take responsibility for the negative things they allow into their lives. They prefer to make someone else the scapegoat for their problems. When we operate under a handout mentality, we're always expecting someone else to make our situation better for us. But God refuses to be an enabler.

It's up to us to grow into maturity. We must take responsibility for where we are in our life's journey. God has made provision for everything we need. That provision comes through the shed blood of Jesus. That precious blood is our power source and God expects us to claim it for ourselves and live in the freedom it provides.

If God disciplines you to bring you back into fellowship with Himself, willingly accept His discipline. Only fathers who love their children and want good things for them bother to chastise them.

Fathers who don't really care, ignore their offspring. God longs for you and His discipline is designed to bring you back to Himself.

> "Those whom I love I rebuke and discipline. So be earnest and ***repent***." (Revelation 3:19)

Transformed people receive the Word of God with gladness.

Another mark of genuine conversion is that a saved person *receives* the Word of God when they hear it. They don't respond with doubt or unbelief, nor do they try to dispute or debate it. The saved person will hear God's voice through His Word and respond to it affirmatively. Jesus said this would be a characteristic of His sheep.

> "My sheep listen to my voice; I know them, and they follow me." (John 10:27)

The desire to hear, understand, and do what God says in His Word is an indicator of a spiritually converted life. When Jesus saves a life, He literally changes that person from the inside out. They are a brand-new creation.

> "Therefore, if anyone is in Christ, the new creation has come: The old has gone, the new is here! (2 Corinthians 5:17)

> "The person without the Spirit does not accept the things that come from the Spirit of God but considers them foolishness, and cannot understand them because they are discerned only through the Spirit." (1 Corinthians 2:14)

Transformed people have love towards others.

Jesus said that we would be known for (identified by) our love for others. This is not a love that can be easily explained. Although a believer will, like Jesus, love all people. A Christian may at times experience a greater love for those within the family of God than for members of their own family who may be outside of God.

> "Anyone who claims to be in the light but hates a brother or sister is still in the darkness. Anyone who loves their brother and sister lives in the light, and there is nothing in them to make them stumble. But anyone who hates a brother or sister is in the darkness and walks around in the darkness. They do not know where they are going, because the darkness has blinded them." (1 John 2:9–11)

> "We know that we have passed from death to life, because we love each other. Anyone who does not love remains in death. Anyone who hates a brother or sister is a murderer, and you know that no murderer has eternal life residing in him." (1 John 3:14–15)

Transformed people have the power of the Holy Spirit.

The Holy Spirit resides in every saved person. He's our individual power source for overcoming the evil one and the things of the flesh. The Holy Spirit is also a witness to others of what has occurred in the heart of the believer. His job is to seal us, lead us, and assure us of our salvation. The presence of the Holy Spirit changes our being from mortal to immortal and is proof that we belong to the Lord!

> "The Spirit himself testifies with our spirit that we are God's children." (Romans 8:16)

> "And do not grieve the Holy Spirit of God, with whom you were sealed for the day of redemption." (Ephesians 4:30)

> "And you also were included in Christ when you heard the message of truth, the gospel of your salvation. When you believed, you were marked in him with a seal, the promised Holy Spirit, who is a deposit guaranteeing our inheritance until the redemption of those who are God's possession—to the praise of his glory." (Ephesians 1:13–14)

> "But when he, the Spirit of truth, comes, he will guide you into all the truth. He will not speak on his own; he will speak only what he hears, and he will tell you what is yet to come." (John 16:13)

These are mysterious concepts for an unbeliever. But for the believer these truths are the essentials of the faith. When the Holy

Spirit invades a person's life, He not only speaks to their heart, but guides, directs, and protects them too. He'll warn us when needed, give abundant wisdom when we ask for it, guide us with knowledge in areas where we're lacking, and lead us to learn more of Jesus. He offers us comfort in times of suffering, teaches us all truth so we won't be deceived, and assures us beyond doubt that we belong to the family of God.

> "And hope does not put us to shame, because God's love has been poured out into our hearts through the Holy Spirit, who has been given to us." (Romans 5:5)

The Holy Spirit is the Spirit of God who resides within the heart of every believer. That continuous presence brings us immense peace as we start to understand who we are and to whom we belong. Having the Holy Spirit residing in our being changes our very nature and desires. We begin to develop an appetite for the person, work, and worship of God.

If there's no peace, then there can be no assurance. Unrest may be a sign that you've not really received the gift of new life the Lord desires to give you. When salvation is genuine, there's communion between the Spirit of God and your spirit. If it isn't there, it may be that He isn't there.

This condition can also be caused by unconfessed sin in the life of the believer. It's when we're walking in the light that the Holy

Spirit bears witness within us that we most assuredly belong to God's family.

> "…who will transform our lowly body that it may be conformed to His glorious body, according to the working by which He is able even to subdue all things to Himself." (Philippians 3:21)

> "Behold what manner of love the Father has bestowed on us, that we should be called children of God! Therefore the world does not know us, because it did not know Him. Beloved, now we are children of God; and it has not yet been revealed what we shall be, but we know that when He is revealed, we shall be like Him, for we shall see Him as He is. And everyone who has this hope in Him purifies himself, just as He is pure." (1 John 3:1–3, NKJV)

When John says, "it has not yet been revealed what we shall be," he means that we don't know some of the specifics about what our nature will be like. No other creature has been given God's Spirit. That Spirit came from God and was breathed into Adam at the beginning. Angels were not given God's Spirit and animals certainly don't possess it. This makes possible our transformation into His likeness. Our spirit, connected to His Spirit, is the means to being conformed to Him.

Transformed people live decisively.

A woman of substance knows how to live decisively with purpose. Purpose comes when we understand that God has a plan for us and that He will direct us to that plan.

- Joshua heard God's directive: "March around the city once with all the armed men. Do this for six days." (Joshua 6:3)

Joshua was able to obey, because he *heard* God speaking to him. We too must be quiet enough that we learn to listen. Once we hear from God, we must obey.

God is Holy, and if we're to bear His likeness we must pursue holiness as a way of life. This isn't natural to us, but God provides the Holy Spirit to make it possible. Prayer is the avenue for asking for what we need. And what we need most is holiness—it's what keeps us close enough to hear God when He speaks, even in a whisper.

For days Joshua led his men on a march around the enemy city of Jericho. Finally, at his command, the army shouted. Then the walls of the city crumbled, and the residents were at the mercy of the Israelites. We can become so accustomed to hearing these stories that we lapse into the belief that they're just Bible stories of old, holding no real value to us today.

However, these stories were written down as examples for us, to enable us to live in the same faith. As it's *faith* and *obedience* that take us to a better life—a life filled with miracles, healing, and possibilities. Notice that Joshua obeyed.

> "And he ordered the army, 'Advance! March around the city, with an armed guard going ahead of the ark of the LORD." (Joshua 6:7)

Joshua faced three potential stumbling blocks.

1. ***He could have questioned God's orders.*** Marching around the city didn't sound like an effective plan for overtaking powerful people.

2. ***He could have felt obligated to explain this strange plan to his men.*** Because this directive didn't correspond with the usual military method, Joshua could have felt the need to justify his leadership ability or rationalize for the army this unusual strategy. Perhaps he worried that the men might lose respect for him and his leadership, wondering how in the world he had come up with such a strange strategy. Many in this situation would look for approval and agreement.

3. ***He could have feared failure.*** Joshua's example to us reveals that, in fact, he did none of these. Upon hearing God's voice he simply obeyed without hesitation, not thinking first about himself and his reputation. As a result

God honored his obedience: "The wall fell down . . . and they took the city" (Joshua 6:20).

Joshua's example shows us that:

1. He knew instinctively that when God gives an order *it cannot fail.*

2. He was *willing* to do what God said.

3. He was willing to be *obedient* regardless of what the command sounded like or how he felt about it.

4. He had complete *confidence* and *trust* in the Lord his God.

5. He had learned to *trust* God more than himself.

6. He *knew* God's *voice* when he heard it, and he followed through immediately, without wavering.

Shouldn't we emulate this kind of faithfulness to receive as Joshua did?

The importance God puts on overcoming this world.

Repentance that brings true conversion is the only way to defeat the enemy. Since the enemy rules this earth, we must possess the

Holy Spirit by receiving Christ as Savior. Turning from Satan's endless lies and accepting Jesus' power, gives you His authority to overcome in this evil world.

Willpower is not sufficient. The enemy is too crafty and has been doing what he does—lie, steal, and kill—for far too long for you to outsmart him. Most people are unprepared for the battle he wages against them.

Receiving salvation and the Holy Spirit is the secret power behind defeating Satan and your natural sin nature.

Salvation ensures that you can end up winning…not only in this present life, but also in the life to come.

4

SHE UNDERSTANDS HER NATURAL SIN NATURE

*"Watch and pray so that you will not fall into temptation. The spirit is willing,
but the body is weak." (Matthew 26:41)*

Y ou may not know it—but you're at war! We all are! We're at war against our own sin nature.

The good life competes for our attention and devotion as much as our desire to stray. When a seduction or temptation to sin appears, it comes because people are prone to sinning. The outward forms usually come from three sources:

1. From our own *flesh*.

2. From the *world*.

3. From *Satan*.

According to the apostle John, the world "is under the power of the evil one" and falling in love with it is *enmity* (meaning hostility or hatred) against God.

Our environment and the people around us seduce us. More than ever before, we're surrounded by willful, conscious seducers and corrupters of our youth.

> "Jesus said, 'Whoever causes one of these little ones to stumble and sin, it were better for that man that a millstone be tied around his neck and he be cast into the sea.'" (Matthew 18:6)

Sin is a spiritual cancer that damages all three aspects of a person—mind, heart, and will, or body, soul, and spirit. People aren't always aware of the gravity the decision to rebel against God brings. The consequences of sin are so grave that it takes a Savior to redeem us.

Sin brought with it a whole host of evils that fall under the category of death. Death isn't a simple matter. It isn't merely about the human heart ceasing to beat. Sin brought the death of our innocence and *automatic* fellowship and intimacy with our Creator. It brought death of a our perfect, protected environment, one without thorns, thistles, and endless hard work. But more significantly, it brought about our spiritual and physical death.

Understanding the nature of sin and how it first originated.

The decision by Adam and Eve to rebel against God brought sin into the world. Ever since, man has experienced conflict. Adam and Eve's own children were skilled in strife and jealousy which led to murder. Cain's hardened heart caused him to lie to God when God asked him about his brother Abel's whereabouts. Instead of confessing to God, Cain asked God in a haughty tone, "Am I my brother's keeper?"

Sin deceives us. When we're deceived, we believe we can successfully deceive others and even God. The hardened heart doesn't perceive its own wickedness.

The outcome of sin.

Man's fall into sin brought several immediate results.

1. ***The knowledge of good and evil.*** Immediately after the fall Adam and Eve lost their innocence, recognizing the difference between good and evil and realizing that they were naked, they experienced fear and shame for the first

time. They would now have to rely on human knowledge, rather than the wisdom of God. (Genesis 3:7)

2. ***Self-righteousness.*** Adam and Eve tried to make clothing from fig leaves, an outward example of what people try to do spiritually. Realizing that we're sinners and thinking that self-improvement will correct our sin problem (Genesis 3:7) we try to "better" ourselves. But our self-righteousness is as inadequate to cover our sins, as the fig leaves were to cover Adam and Eve. Scripture tells us that all our self-righteousness is no better than filthy rags. (Isaiah 64:6)

3. ***Fear and shame.*** On that day, when God arrived to fellowship with Adam and Eve in the garden, as was His custom, rather than meeting God in joy and anticipation, they hid themselves in shame and fear, turning from His presence (see Genesis 3:10). Shame and guilt make us want to turn away, too, from the very God who desires to save and restore us. Shame over the past and fear of the future, are the basic causes that generate all other negative emotional responses.

4. ***Separation from God.*** God didn't remove Himself from man's presence, rather Adam and Eve removed themselves from God. They had become self-conscious rather than God-conscious as they had been before they sinned. Their act of

rebellion—their choice to disobey God's explicit instruction—brought about their immediate spiritual death, which was separation from God.

- "Then the man and his wife heard the sound of the LORD God as he was walking in the garden in the cool of the day, and they hid from the LORD God among the trees of the garden. But the LORD God called to the man, *'Where are you?'* He answered, 'I heard you in the garden, and I was afraid because I was naked; so I hid.'" (Genesis 3:8–10)

What was different?

Since God is all-knowing, He didn't ask His question to find out their physical location in the garden. God was really asking "Where are you spiritually, Adam?" Their answer immediately reveals their altered spiritual status. Adam answered that he had heard God's voice and was afraid because he was naked, so he had hidden himself from God's presence. Adam, of course, had always been naked; he was created that way. In his sinless state he had no need of clothing. Both Adam and Eve were clothed in God's glory, so the issue of nakedness had never before affected their relationship with God.

God confronts sinful people with the same question today. We must address this question to recognize our true spiritual condition apart from Christ. We must see and acknowledge that we stand naked without Him. Christ clothes us in His own righteousness, and we're made righteous *in Him*. He alone is our covering.

God's next response was also a question:

> *"Who told you that you were naked?* Have you eaten from the tree that I commanded you not to eat from?" (Genesis 3:11)

God already knew, of course, that Adam had eaten of the tree. His purpose in questioning was to get Adam to see what his rebellion had done to their relationship, and to see if Adam would confess his sin to restore the severed union.

> "If we confess our sin, He is faithful and just to forgive us our sin and cleanse us from all unrighteousness." (1 John 1:9)

Adam's answer demonstrated his inability to accept blame. In blaming Eve, he also blamed God.

> "The woman you gave me, she gave me of the tree, and I did eat." (Genesis 3:12)

Then God asked the woman, "What is this that you have done?" Following the pattern set by her husband, Eve also refused to accept any responsibility. She blamed the serpent for her sin.

God had given the first sinners an opportunity to be honest with Him. Honesty would have restored the severed relationship. But their sin had made them prideful and they refused to do so.

When we refuse to repent and ask for forgiveness, God has no other alternative than to pronounce the penalty for our sin—we are, after all, guilty! Adam and Eve were under the old covenant; the new covenant, under Jesus, hadn't yet been established.

The penalty for Adam and Eve's sin.

Disobedience to God defines sin. Our continual desire to be free from God, to go our own way, sets us on the path to our own destruction. God desires to turn us *from* our ways so that we won't self-destruct. On the surface we see the immediate results of sin, but we need to dig deeper to observe that there are additional penalties as God pronounces judgment on the serpent, the man, and the woman.

Many don't realize that sin has lasting consequences. The story of the rebellion in the garden is recorded as a rebuke for us to learn from. Jesus is the provision that keeps us alive and free. He makes possible a restored relationship with the Father.

The penalty placed on the serpent.

1. ***A changed physical form.*** The serpent originally walked upright, but once cursed by God, it has slithered on its belly through the dust.

2. ***There would be enmity between Satan and man.*** This was the beginning of "spiritual warfare," with Satan struggling for the soul of man. A warfare that continues to this day.

3. ***Christ would ultimately crush Satan's head.*** The third penalty on the serpent is actually a promise to sinful man. Although Satan would spiritually "bruise the heel" of man through sin, the seed (descendant) that would come from woman (Jesus) would crush Satan's head.

> "And I will put enmity between you and the woman, and between your offspring and hers; he will crush your head, and you will strike his heel." (Genesis 3:15)

This was the first promise of a Savior from man's sin. Although Satan would adversely affect all of man's descendants through sin, a Savior would be sent by God through a woman, and the power of sin would be crushed. The tragedy of sin came through the fall of one woman, but redemption would also come through a woman—the one who would birth the Lord Jesus Christ.

Adam's penalty for sinning against God.

1. ***He would toil all his days.*** Adam would now experience labor by the sweat of his brow and weariness. Prior to sinning, Adam had tended the ground in ease and contentment, but now he would have to labor to get it to produce. Earth's environment had changed; the ground that was once fertile and without pests or weeds became subject to decay and covered with thorns and thistles.

2. ***He would experience death.*** The penalty of natural death was imposed on Adam. God made it clear that the man's body would return to the ground.

> "By the sweat of your brow you will eat your food until you return to the ground, since from it you were taken; for dust you are and to dust you will return." (Genesis 3:19)

Spiritual death was also a penalty of sin. Without forgiveness, man would die the spiritual death of eternal separation from God.

> "God said, 'The one who sins is the one who will die. The child will not share the guilt of the parent, nor will the parent share the guilt of the child. The righteousness of the righteous will be credited to them." (Ezekiel 18:20).

Eve's penalty for disobeying God's command.

1. ***She would have sorrow in childbirth.*** The curse of pain and sorrow was placed upon childbearing. Eve would now bear her offspring in pain as a remembrance of the innocence she had lost.

2. ***She would experience subjection.*** Eve would become subject to her husband. She had acted independently; now that independence would be frustrated by subjection to another.

Penalties on both Adam and Eve.

God removed Adam and Eve from the beautiful environment of the garden, to a world filled with sorrow, pain, thorns, hard labor, and death.

The promise of Christ.

The only bright spot in the entire chapter of Genesis 3 is the promise of the coming Redeemer who would crush the power of Satan (verse 15). The answer for our hard work and sorrow would come when Jesus entered our sin-damaged environment to travail on our behalf. When we accept Jesus, we're pardoned from our harsh sentence.

"After he has suffered, he will see the light of life and be satisfied; by his knowledge my righteous servant will justify many, and he will bear their iniquities." (Isaiah 53:11)

Jesus takes what we deserve.

Subjection: He was made subject to the law that He might redeem us from the law. (Galatians 4:4)

Thorns: He was crowned with thorns on our behalf. (Matthew 27:29)

Sweat: Jesus sweat great drops of blood for us. (Luke 22:44)

Sorrow: Surely He bore our sorrows. (Isaiah 53:4–5)

Death: He replaced death's penalty by bringing eternal life. (John 3:16)

Jesus bore every penalty for our sin. Through His life, death, and resurrection, the head (power) of Satan was crushed. This was not a single occurrence, for by accepting Christ we are changed, exonerated from forever bearing this curse. [1]

God's original intent for people.

Let's rewind back to the beginning, back to God's original intent for mankind. God Himself said that man was **very good**! This was an expression of delight as God was pleased with every facet of man's creation. Every part of man was good and pure—his nature, his temperament, his will, his intellect, his physical being, and his heart. After all, *man was made in God's own image*, and that image was very good indeed. Man at this point was inclined to love God, knowing that God had loved him first.

> "God saw all that he had made, and it was ***very good***. And there was evening, and there was morning—the sixth day." (Genesis 1:31)

After the fall, man's original nature and goodness was radically changed. Disobedience to God's command now made him hostile to God.

- "The mind governed by the flesh is hostile to God; it does not submit to God's law, nor can it do so." (Romans 8:7)

Disobedient, rebellious human nature develops as we communicate with spirits other than God's Spirit. Satan and his demons have some authority on this earth. When people listen and submit to his evil plans, they're agreeing and communicating with the demonic principalities of the spirit realm. These spirits are influences and strongholds that take hold of us as we relinquish our God-given authority to them.

> "These are the things God has revealed to us by his Spirit. The Spirit searches all things, even the deep things of God. For who knows a person's thoughts except their own spirit within them? In the same way no one knows the thoughts of God except the Spirit of God. What we have received is not the spirit of the world, but the ***Spirit who is from God***, so that we may understand what God has freely given us." (1 Corinthians 2:10–12)

If man's creation was "very good," why has human history been steeped in violence, war, murder, suffering, and anguish? Why do we continually experience anger, hatred, greed, jealousy, pride, and lust against each other?

Nowhere in God's Word are these called good or acceptable, as they're opposed to the very nature of God. God didn't create anything less than perfect, so we must be careful never to accuse Him of evil.

> Paul said, "I know that nothing good lives in me, that is, in my sinful nature. For I have the desire to do what is good, but I cannot carry it out." (Romans 7:18)

If these aren't godly traits, where do they come from? God is loving, kind, generous, good, and merciful. But after the fall, man was the very opposite of these positive traits.

Pondering this human condition, we're compelled to ask ourselves, "Would something God pronounced 'very good' produce what we see in this world?" No, these traits came from the "spirit of this world" Satan.

What does the Bible say about sin and its nature?

To sin means to transgress, "to step across" or "go beyond a set boundary or limit." Adam and Eve were given limits by God. They were told of which trees they were to eat and which tree they were to avoid. God made His intent abundantly clear: to keep them from harm and to protect them, not to permit them to be "like God," as Satan had claimed.

Children derive comfort and protection from playgrounds with fences. This clear definition of limits brings children reassurance. They understand that they aren't to go beyond the boundary, nor can anything from the outside come in and hurt them.

God's limits are for our protection. They protect us from the evil that lurks all around us. When we question God's limits, we begin to question whether God really has our good in mind. Once the seed of doubt about God's goodness is planted in our mind, we give in, as

Eve did, and follow through with a willful act of disobedience. Eve didn't stop first to see where this thought had come from. She didn't tell the serpent she would ask God first about the matter. She **acted** on *false* information because she didn't inquire of God before proceeding.

Similarly, in our deception, we believe we know best what's good for us. We don't readily see that we're rebellious, prideful, and disobedient. Yet we have limited perspective about what is good. When we decide to cross over the boundaries God has set up, we've made the choice to be our own god. We determine for ourselves what's good and right. This sets us up for immense sorrow and eventual tragedy, because we're naïve about the evil that's in this world.

We may have good intentions. We may want to do what we perceive to be good. But apart from God, we don't understand the concept of good or evil. We miss the mark by straying off course. Satan comes to trip us up, and before we know it, we're on his path.

God has something in mind for each of His children to do in the kingdom of God. But once we stray we no longer seek after that purpose, or even after God. We're first *distracted* and then *deceived*. We no longer conform to God's standard because Satan convinces us that we can determine our own. To sin, then, is to transgress the boundaries God has set for us, to miss the target altogether.

What setting our own standard causes?

Man, apart from God is dying. Death produces for people a darkened mind and an inclination toward rebellion and error. Our thinking, our being, our actions, and our daily living are all affected by our darkened mind. Light must enter in if we can hope to escape everlasting darkness.

Sin not only darkens our mind but ravages our heart. It binds and entangles us to the point that we no longer have the ability to escape on our own. It inclines us toward seeking our own pleasures and earthly attachments and producing selfishness rather than good. What is harmed most, however, is the capability of our will to affect our intentions. Man's willpower has no strength, especially when it comes to doing God's will. The apostle Paul speaks of this weakness of will when he says,

> "For I fail to practice the good deeds I desire to do, but the evil deeds which I do not desire to do are what I am always doing." (Romans 7:19)

Jesus said of humanity, "Whoever practices sin is the slave of sin" (John 8:34). In this sinful state, unregenerate man perceives sinning to be freedom, while in reality, struggling to escape its net, it's actually slavery.

The topic of sin is seldom preached today.

Sin isn't a popular topic and many churches have moved away from preaching on it for fear of offending members. Some churches have gone so far as to deny that man even has a sin problem. When they do preach on the topic, many pastors and theologians have a tendency to refer to sin as a transgression of law, rather than evidence of a lack of love for God.

Sin isn't merely an act; it's the evil condition of the unregenerate heart of man. It's man's true nature apart from God. People left in their original condition are already condemned. When we choose not to turn from that condition, we've sealed our own fate. Christ won't force us to accept the hope He offers, but He makes it available to all who will hear.

- This is what Jesus meant when He told Nicodemus that "unless one is born of water and the Spirit, he cannot enter the kingdom of God." (John 3:5; Titus 3:5)

Is the human heart really deceitful and corrupt?

Only Scripture tells us the truth.

> The prophet Jeremiah stated that "the heart is deceitful above all things, and desperately corrupt; who can understand it?" (Jeremiah 17:9)

> When Isaiah received a vision of the Holy One of Israel, he cried "Woe is me! For I am lost; for I am a man of unclean lips, and I dwell in the midst of a people of unclean lips; for my eyes have seen the King, the LORD of hosts!" (Isaiah 6:5)

> The reaction of Peter to Jesus when He displayed His deity was similar: "Depart from me, for I am a sinful man, O Lord." (Luke 5:8)

> The letter to the Hebrews warns against anyone who has "an evil, unbelieving heart." (Hebrews 3:12)

> And Jesus declared that "what comes out of the mouth proceeds from the heart, and this defiles a man. For out of the heart come evil thoughts, murder, adultery, fornication, theft, false witness, slander. These are what defile a man." (Matthew 15:18–20)

Understanding Satan's many schemes against you.

Knowing Satan's numerous schemes against you is vital to your victory. God has equipped you to fight the battle, but you must take up the armor and learn to fight. Understanding spiritual warfare is a must for every believer.

The Bible teaches us that Satan's primary strategy is the power of deception. Paul warned that Satan has strategies for destroying our lives and causing us to live in constant confusion. Satan's plan is to deceive and deprive you of your spiritual inheritance. To rob you of the countless blessings God has prepared for you. The devil wants to attack you where you're most vulnerable—to fill your mind and heart with dread, by sowing seeds of fear, doubt, distrust, hopelessness, and despair. He causes us our greatest confusion because we don't fully understand his methods of warfare, or our inclination to fall for his varied schemes.

The first truth we must cling to is that Jesus has already defeated our enemy, Satan! Jesus is coming back (the second coming of Christ) to redeem His own and will rule in victory during the Millennium. Satan will once and for all be silenced. He will be consigned to "the pit" for all eternity. *Understand that Satan is already defeated.* Jesus' death bought for us victory.

The Holy Spirit is the power source for victory in *every* area of life. When we cease walking our own way, and walk obediently in His ways, we're walking in the Spirit. The Holy Spirit protects us against Satan's numerous attacks and deceptions.

Many women aren't interested in studying the concept of war. However, there are aspects of armed conflict that intrigue me as a military spouse. From a leadership point of view, I'm interested in how Generals think and strategize. I see the connection between freedom for our country and freedom for the Christian.

Those who study the history of war notice that effective results are achieved by knowing the tactics of the enemy. They know where the enemy is strong and where they're weak. Victories are won by armies that disguise their true intentions, surprise their opponents, and catch them ill-prepared.

Many Christians, especially those new to the faith, are surprised by the battles they face. Trusting in their own skills and resources, they fail to see that Satan's strategy is to disguise his true intentions. He's effective because he catches us by surprise and because we're ill-prepared.

Satan attacks our emotions, health, finances, relationships, and thinking. He affects whole families and even the family of God, the Church. One of his key tactics is to try to snatch away the "Word" once it's been heard. He tells us lies so we'll replace our faith with doubt.

Be alert and stay on guard! A strong prayer life and a mind filled with God's Word and promises are the best armor against his attacks. Without spiritual weapons, many Christians are defeated soon after a battle begins. They are ill equipped and even ignorant that a battle is going on around them. Most aren't warned in advance that soon after becoming a Christian, the battle will heat up. Since few are skilled at warfare and their church neither prepares nor teaches them the tactical defense strategies they'll need for victory, many suffer and are critically wounded. Suddenly they find themselves on a battlefield with no shield or weapons to defend themselves. They're weak, vulnerable, and untrained to fight. Nor do they comprehend that their enemy, Satan, is shrewd and deceptive. He won't announce his attack plan. He confuses people with mixed messages and preys on their weaknesses and ignorance.

The nature of sin.

Through His Word, God gives us methods for living in peace with Himself and others. When we sin, we choose to violate those methods. God sets limits for our protection because He loves us. Most people think that sin is solely about committing acts that are contrary to God's law. But God doesn't just look at our actions. He looks deep into our heart, at the *attitudes* and *motives* behind our actions. The sins of the heart go beyond physical deeds.

Why do we sin?

Paul expressed the frustration all Christians experience with regard to sin.

> "For I do not understand what I do. For what I want to do I do not do, but what I hate I do." (Romans 7:15)

We, like Paul, have limited natural ability to conform to God's values. Jesus explained that we may be willing to do what's right yet fail because our flesh is weak and susceptible to temptation, leading us into sin.

> "Watch and pray so that you will not fall into temptation. The spirit is willing, but the body is weak." (Matthew 26:41)

Know the cycle of sin.

Walking in places of temptation: going where you shouldn't.

Enticing others to sin: influencing others to sin with you.

Hearing Satan's voice: listening too long and giving consideration to his messages to you.

Partaking: entering into the sin.

Seeing the forbidden sin: considering it for too long and even admiring it.

Accepting the temptation to sin: committing the sin and staying in its grip.

Satan's tactics of war are:

The world. Our society operates under an anti-Christ and anti-God system. Abraham was a friend of God, but his nephew Lot was a friend of the world. If we're not aware, we become involved in the world gradually. Our friendships can lead us to love the world, and this makes it easy for us to conform. The believer "is married to Christ" and our relationship with Him requires faithfulness to preserve the intimacy. As in earthly marriage, adultery breaks down trust and shatters fidelity. When we're unfaithful to Christ, we're guilty of spiritual adultery. We treat God with disrespect and cast Him aside to go after spiritual prostitutes and idols. If you're a friend of the world, you can't be a friend to God. God will have no part of the world.

The flesh. Our old nature is inherited from the first Adam and is prone to sin. The flesh is not synonymous with the body, which in itself is neutral, not sinful. The body may glorify God from the influence of the Holy Spirit. Or the flesh may influence the body to serve sin and the devil. When a sinner yields to Christ she receives a new nature, but the old nature desires to reign. The old nature is neither removed nor reformed. For this reason we battle against it continually.

> "For the sinful nature desires what is contrary to the Spirit, and the Spirit what is contrary to the sinful nature. They are in conflict with each other so that you do not do what you want." (Galatians 5:17)

When we live for the flesh, we grieve the Holy Spirit. He jealously guards our relationship to God and is grieved when we sin against His love for us. Living to please the flesh is synonymous to declaring war on God.

> "The sinful mind is hostile to God. It does not submit to God's law, nor can it do so." (Romans 8:7)

When we permit our flesh to control us, we lose the desire for intimacy with God because our spirit is at war. We must decide which spirit will control us—our fleshly, carnal spirit, or the Spirit of God.

Abraham had a conformed, spiritual mind and he walked with God. The result: *he enjoyed peace*. In contrast, Lot had a carnal mind and didn't walk with God. The result: *he experienced turmoil*.

> "The mind of sinful man is death, but the mind controlled by the Spirit is life and peace." (Romans 8:6)

Our pride. The devil opposes the Son of God. Pride is one of Satan's chief weapons in his warfare against Christians. God desires for us to be humble. Satan wants us to be puffed-up with pride. God wants us to depend on His grace. The devil wants us to depend on ourselves. Satan is the author of all "do-it-yourself" spiritual endeavors. He's the originator of "religion," which is man's attempt to fill up his own spiritual void. Religion has manmade rules and works attached to it. It's all about man attempting to reach God. But it has at its heart

rebellion, because unregenerate people refuse to receive and accept God's free grace and the gift of Jesus.

Satan derives pleasure when man's ego is inflated and attempts to work independently of God. Even when God warns us, we fall prey to Satan's deceptions. Peter fell into Satan's snare by acting impulsively, pulling out his sword to defend Jesus, believing that was what He wanted.

The devil's primary objective in the life of a believer is discouragement.

Satan wants all believers to give up—especially on God. He tempts us to sin so we'll live in disobedience and defeat. When we continue to sin and refuse to repent, we're telling the Holy Spirit to stay out of our life. Yet, His presence keeps us from harm as He gently guides us and speaks to us about all things.

When we refuse the Spirit's protection, we're susceptible to all the lies, doubt, discouragement, and depression Satan throws at us. Fully deceived, we soon accept defeat easily.

> "Have I not commanded you? Be strong and courageous. Do not be terrified; do not be discouraged, for the LORD your God will be with you wherever you go." (Joshua 1:9)

We never have a valid reason to become fearful when we understand that God loves us with an everlasting love and continually keeps watch over us. Yes, we need to be *aware* of Satan's many schemes and disguises, but we don't need to live in dread of him. Paul warned us to guards our heart and minds. To be successful in our warfare, we need only to wear God's armor and be alert in prayer.

> "And pray in the Spirit on all occasions with all kinds of prayers and requests. With this in mind, be alert and always keep on praying for all the saints." (Ephesians 6:18)

Can the endless cycle of sin be broken?

Yes! The cycle of sin has already been broken through the power of Jesus' finished work on the cross. The moment we accept Jesus as Savior we're given the Holy Spirit. He is our power source to resist sin. Only by *staying in Him* are we kept from the full force of temptation and the compulsion to give in to it.

There are two paths to take in this life. One is the path of salvation. We receive it when we hear, understand, and accept the gospel message. Receiving the gospel gives us deliverance, salvation, and life.

The other is the path of sin. Satan's pathway leads to death, damnation and torment. Satan has no life to give.

We must be on guard at all times against the attacks of our spiritual adversary.

> "Be alert and of sober mind. Your enemy the devil prowls around like a roaring lion looking for someone to devour." (1 Peter 5:8)

The natural, carnal mind.

The word carnal refers to anything pertaining to our *natural* body (e.g., the sensual, pertaining to our five senses: hearing, sight, smell, touch, and taste, our natural, physical needs; and our appetites, including the sensuous or sexual). We typically don't operate much beyond the level of our senses.

> As Paul wrote, "For those who live according to the flesh set their minds on the things of the flesh, but those who live according to the Spirit, the things of the Spirit. For to be carnally minded is death, but to be spiritually minded is life and peace. Because the carnal mind is enmity against God; for it is not subject to the law of God, nor indeed can be." (Romans 8:5–7)

Living in the flesh will keep you from coming into spiritual maturity. Only the Holy Spirit can produce godly fruit in you.

> Second Peter 1:3–11 says it well: "His divine power has given us everything we need for life and godliness through our knowledge of him who called us by his own glory and

goodness. Through these he has given us his very great and precious promises, so that through them you may participate in the divine nature and escape the corruption in the world caused by evil desires. For this very reason, make every effort to add to your faith goodness; and to goodness, knowledge; and to knowledge, self-control; and to self-control, perseverance; and to perseverance, godliness; and to godliness, brotherly kindness; and to brotherly kindness, love. For if you possess these qualities in increasing measure, they will keep you from being ineffective and unproductive in your knowledge of our Lord Jesus Christ. But if anyone does not have them, he is nearsighted and blind, and has forgotten that he has been cleansed from his past sins. Therefore, my brothers, be all the more eager to make your calling and election sure. For if you do these things, you will never fall, and you will receive a rich welcome into the eternal kingdom of our Lord and Savior Jesus Christ."

Out with the old nature.

Our "old nature" is our natural, unregenerate human nature, our nature before receiving salvation. In Paul's terminology, it's our "flesh," which is carnal, selfish, and hostile to God (Romans 8:7).

God can work miracles. He can free us from destructive habits that imprison us. With God's sanctifying help we are changing little by little, day by day, being renewed. (Romans 6:16). By faithfully studying God's Word, we become sensitive to facets of our lives that are in need of transformation.

- "For the word of God is alive and active. Sharper than any double-edged sword, it penetrates even to dividing soul and spirit, joints and marrow; it judges the thoughts and attitudes of the heart." (Hebrews 4:12)

The transformation process can't take place in the flesh. It requires a God intervention. The Word and the Holy Spirit help in this process. With our testimony we can offer others the hope of being transformed too.

In with the new.

If "*we*" strive to change ourselves, the process of overcoming will be deficient. God must build into our character the positive traits that overcome sin.

Staying in our pre-conversion environment after we've been born-again may hinder our ability to become mature and self-controlled. When we hold on to our previous thought patterns, behaviors, habits, and often friends, we thwart our forward progress.

As He did with Abraham, God may be calling you to a new way, asking you to leave the old life, with its old associates behind. If you're willing to obey, your growth will come sooner, and you'll be able to rejoice in your new life.

What we need.

Our need is for a *new* nature, one that is inclined toward loving and honoring God and not ourselves. People attempt through religion and spirituality to remake the old nature, but God gives us a *brand new nature*—not a remake. Our unregenerate nature is contrary to God's nature, which is holy and without sin. We're born into sin and stay in our sinful condition until we recognize it and ask God to come into our heart to change it.

God is Spirit and we're called to worship Him in spirit and in truth. But with our old nature at work, continually at odds with God's Spirit, we aren't fully capable of worshiping Him as He desires. [2]

Paul warned us to carry around with us our shield of faith.

> "Finally, be strong in the Lord and in his mighty power. Put on the full armor of God so that you can take your stand against the devil's schemes. For our struggle is not against flesh and blood, but against the rulers, against the authorities, against the powers of this dark world and against the spiritual forces of evil in the heavenly realms. Therefore put on the full armor of God, so that when the day of evil comes, you may be able

to stand your ground, and after you have done everything, to stand. Stand firm then, with the belt of truth buckled around your waist, with the breastplate of righteousness in place, and with your feet fitted with the readiness that comes from the gospel of peace. In addition to all this, take up the shield of faith, with which you can extinguish all the flaming arrows of the evil one. Take the helmet of salvation and the sword of the Spirit, which is the word of God. And pray in the Spirit on all occasions with all kinds of prayers and requests. With this in mind, be alert and always keep on praying for all the saints." (Ephesians 6:10–18)

Our armor.

A strong defense is mandatory! We become superior when we're equipped for offensive warfare. Wearing the full armor of God for protection keeps us victorious. We must eliminate any areas of unbelief and disobedience that would give the devil a foothold in our life. Only a life fully submitted to Jesus can resist the devil.

> "Submit yourselves, then, to God. Resist the devil, and he will flee from you." (James 4:7)

Living a life of truth and putting on the breastplate of righteousness; being armed with the sword of the Spirit, which is the Word of God; filling our life with prayer and seeking always to please the Father—is the armor that keeps us safe and secure. This is how we *gain ground* and make Satan flee!

The Holy Spirit is eager to help you.

Before Jesus left this earth, he told his disciples that He would send them a "helper," the Holy Spirit. God has also assured us that He will never leave nor forsake us. True to His promise, He gave us the Holy Spirit, who is always with and within us.

When God's Spirit dwells in us we're able to walk in His ways and walk away from the sin that entangles us. The Holy Spirit is essential for us to win the battle set before us. He's the One who's tirelessly working on our behalf.

The problems the enemy brings into our lives can't be resolved through other people, possessions, addictions, or flight. Sin and the devastation it brings must be tackled straight out with God's power.

If sin has you firmly in its grip, respond by doing something different. Call on the Holy Spirit today. Ask Him to give you the strength, power, and assurance of knowing you can walk away from your sin. The battle may take some time, but the Holy Spirit will empower you to walk in the newness of life that Christ alone provides.

Jesus was born and made possible the forgiveness of your sins. His power allows you to conquer Satan's strongholds. Both Jesus and Satan have a vested interest in your choice. Jesus wants you to win. Satan wants you to lose. Position yourself on the winning side by asking the Holy Spirit to equip you for every good work.

Be self-controlled.

Self-control is a fruit of the Spirit that allows you to properly manage your desires. God expects you to ask Him to help and direct those desires for His greater purpose.

We have not because we ask not. It's our job to ask for this help. God knows we can't master these evil desires on our own. Failing to ask for this help leaves us with unmanageable desires that will soon overtake us. The Holy Spirit helps us conform to God's standards and keeps our desires from overwhelming us and breaking our resolve.

Do not quench the Spirit but stir it up.

Paul admonished believers, "Do not quench the Spirit" (1 Thessalonians 5:19). He urged the young evangelist Timothy,

> "For this reason I remind you to fan into flame the gift of God, which is in you through the laying on of my hands. For God did not give us a spirit of timidity, but a spirit of power, of love and of self-discipline." (2 Timothy 1:6–7)

Paul likened God's Spirit to a live ember in a dying fire. He encouraged Timothy to stir up that coal, to fan it into flame. It's our responsibility to fan the flames in our own lives and make them once again produce a raging fire within us. We must guard against neglecting that small, isolated ember. We're not to neglect the gift of God's Spirit and grow cold toward it.

Satan is always on the sidelines waiting for an opportunity based on whatever weakness he may detect. Having a raging fire of passion and love for the God within us, and a fervent desire to please Him, keeps Satan at a distance. Paul advises us to stand fast in the truth we have learned, concentrating on righteous living, regardless of our circumstances.

> "Instead, by taking up the whole armor of God that you may be able to withstand in the evil day." (Ephesians 6:13)

We're to co-labor with Christ. He doesn't expect you to be passive and leave everything up to Him. If you want good fruit in your life, you must go to work to produce it. God's Word is the sword that cuts through all deception that may be keeping you from it

Which spirit will you seek?

> Paul contrasts God's Spirit with that of "bitterness and wrath": "Get rid of all bitterness, rage and anger, brawling and slander,

along with every form of malice. Be kind and compassionate to one another, forgiving each other, just as in Christ God forgave you." (Ephesians 4:31–32)

We quench God's Spirit when we refuse His leading and indulge in corruption. Satan thrives in an environment where deception is present. By seeking God's Spirit and leading, we can live a godly life by putting on the spirit of the "new man."

This doesn't mean we'll never sin again, but neither do we need to become discouraged in the face of our sins. We have reason to be confident because with the Holy Spirit residing in us, we don't need to live in dread of fulfilling those evil desires of the flesh.

> When we "submit to God" and "resist the devil," he will flee from us. (James 4:7)

> Paul explained, "Walk in the spirit, and you will not fulfill the lust of the flesh." (Galatians 5:16)

There's no need to lose hope. Scripture gives us every reason to be encouraged in our daily struggle against sin. Remember that Jesus Himself was tempted in the desert and throughout His earthly life. Yet, He provided us an example of how to deal with temptation.

> "For we do not have a high priest who is unable to empathize with our weaknesses, but we have one who has been tempted in

every way, just as we are—yet he did not sin. Let us then approach God's throne of grace with confidence, so that we may receive mercy and find grace to help us in our time of need." (Hebrews 4:15–16)

How do we get this help?

"Ask and it will be given to you; seek and you will find; knock and the door will be opened to you. For everyone who asks receives; the one who seeks finds; and to the one who knocks, the door will be opened. (Matthew 7:7–8)

Jesus didn't leave the disciples alone and He doesn't leave us abandoned and powerless either. When God's Spirit dwells in us, we're able to walk in His ways and away from sin. To maintain the victory we receive through the deliverance the Holy Spirit provides, we must be aware of the influences working to snatch that victory from us. Still these influences are no more than a nuisance to the Christian who is *strong in the Spirit* and *aware*.

Ignorance of how the enemy works to defeat you will only serve his purposes. God's Word makes clear to you how he works. Jesus died so you might be victorious in *all* things.

How do we bridge the gap that keeps us from intimacy with the Father?

There can be no victory until there's an awareness of the full impact of our sinful condition. Our sin doesn't need to make us feel guilty; we're all born into it and stand in need of redemption. When we submit to Jesus and desire to know Him, we bridge the gap that has kept us from Him.

God has a remedy for every problem we face. When we press into Him rather than fleeing from His presence, we become free. We may be in bondage at the moment, but through Christ there's always a way out.

HOW TO ONCE AGAIN ENJOY FELLOWSHIP WITH GOD

AFTER WILLFULLY SINNING.

Draw near to God. We do so by confessing our sins in true repentance. God graciously draws near to us when we deal with the sin that has been keeping Him at a distance. He won't share us. He insists on having us for Himself. Scripture tells us that a double-minded Christian—one who wants to have it both ways—is unstable in all his ways. Abraham and Lot, who were tugging in opposite directions, eventually had to part ways. Lawlessness and obedience can't travel in unison. Based on their own choices, Abraham received the blessings of God, while Lot did not. God will bless us too, but we must choose Him to receive those blessings.

Humble yourself before God. Since God knows our heart at all times, it's impossible to pretend we're submitted to Him when such is not the case. Since we're so easily deceived, we may be able to fool ourselves, but not God. Outward submission isn't the same as inward submission, which is always characterized by humility. God hates the sin of pride, which is conceit, self-importance, and arrogance. He will discipline any of His children who operate in it. We tend to treat sin too lightly, sometimes going so far as to laugh about it. But sin is serious business to God. When we grow into spiritually maturity, we see how serious sin actually is. The mark of true humility is facing the gravity of sin and dealing with our disobedience.

> "'Has not my hand made all these things, and so they came into being?' declares the LORD. 'This is the one I esteem: he who is humble and contrite in spirit, and trembles at my word.'" (Isaiah 66:2)

> "The sacrifices of God are a broken spirit; a broken and contrite heart, O God, you will not despise." (Psalm 51:17)

This is how we draw near to God and how He draws near to us. Our warfare with Him ceases the moment we ask for forgiveness and cleansing. We'll no longer be at war with ourselves either. We'll experience peace the moment we humble ourselves before God.

> "The fruit of righteousness will be peace; the effect of righteousness will be quietness and confidence forever." (Isaiah 32:17)

Submit to God. Unconditional surrender is the pathway to complete victory. Surrender is a military term that means submitting to another. We're insubordinate when we desire to override God's authority and will. If we accept and submit to His authority we receive one of His benefits—safety. Soldiers who act alone in battle find themselves in heightened danger.

We're to obey our Commander's orders. They're meant to prolong our life. God's commands are designed to keep us safe and secure. Not as Satan wants us to believe, to keep us from enjoying life.

This is the reason uncommitted Christians are unable to experience total freedom and victory. They have broken rank and gone AWOL. There's no protection from the enemy for those who wish to go it alone.

Satan devises cunning schemes to get a person to pull away from others and to commit sin in perceived isolation. To get at us, Satan needs a foothold into our lives. Paul cautions us in Ephesians 4:27

not to "give place to the devil," yet we readily do give him that foothold when we fail to submit to God.

David paid a high price for this warfare. When he finally sought restoration of his relationship with God, he experienced peace and joy once again. Like defiance, submission is an act of will. We must agree to say to God, "Not my will but yours be done."

The will of God comes from the heart of God.

James presents four arguments that reveal the foolishness of ignoring the will of God (James 4:13–14, 16).

1. ***The complexity of life.*** Think of the many things you have to do in any one day, about the people, places, duties, responsibilities, deadlines, activities, and goals you must deal with and address. Each day is characterized by a myriad of decisions. Apart from the will of God, life remains a mystery and it doesn't begin to make sense until we know Jesus as Savior. Without Him, the world is a baffling and threatening environment. In knowing Christ, we come to know peace and purpose. Even the physical world around us takes on new meaning. Suddenly we see purpose as we go about our day.

2. ***The uncertainty of life.*** Many people try to plan their whole lives when they don't even know for certain what tomorrow may bring.

- "Do not boast about tomorrow, for you do not know what a day may bring forth." (Psalm 27:1)

- "Whoever drinks the water I give him will never thirst. Indeed, the water I give him will become in him a spring of water welling up to eternal life." (John 4:14)

- "Now listen, you who say, 'Today or tomorrow we will go to this or that city, spend a year there, carry on business and make money.' Why, you do not even know what will happen tomorrow. What is your life? You are a mist that appears for a little while and then vanishes." (James 4:13)

In the parable of the farmer, found in Luke 12:16–21, Jesus reminds us of the foolishness of this type of thinking.

- "The ground of a certain rich man produced a good crop. He thought to himself, 'What shall I do? I have no place to store my crops?' Then he said, 'This is what I'll do. I will tear down my barns and build bigger ones, and there I will store all my grain and my goods. And I'll say to myself, "You have plenty of good things laid up for many years. Take life easy; eat, drink and be merry."'" (Luke 12:16–19)

What was God's response to this boasting?

- "But God said to him, 'You fool! This very night your life will be demanded from you. Then who will get what you have prepared for yourself?' This is how it will be with anyone who stores up things for himself but is not rich toward God." (Luke 12: 20–21)

Life is uncertain to us, but never to God. Only when we stay within His will can we be confident of tomorrow.

3. ***The brevity of life.*** This is a theme repeated often in Scripture. Life seems long to us. We measure it in years because we lack God's perspective on time. The Lord counsels us to number our days (Psalm 90:12) since He measures time in comparison to eternity. Our earthly life from His perspective is momentary and fleeting.

- "Man born of woman is of few days and full of trouble. He springs up like a flower and withers away; like a fleeting shadow, he does not endure." (Job 14:1–2)

Since life is brief, we can't afford either to spend or waste our lives. We're called instead to *invest* them in things that are eternal. God reveals His will to us in His Word to enable us to live lives full of purpose and fulfillment. But if people decline to read the Word, they won't learn the precepts, principles, and promises intended to guide them in every area. *Knowing* and *obeying*, comprise the surest recipe for success.

4. ***The frailty of life.*** Human beings boast to camouflage their weaknesses. They try to control their futures, not identifying that they have neither the wisdom nor the power to do so. Pride keeps people bragging, convinced that they are the masters of their fate, the captains of their souls. Because God has instilled people with intelligence and creativity, they may come to believe they can do anything. Unregenerate man is ignorant of the nature of God's will, convinced that he's at liberty to accept or reject it.

In reality, knowing the will of God isn't an option; it's an obligation. We can't "take it or leave it" because He's the Creator and we're the created. And since we'll never be the Creator, we're obliged to obey Him. As Christians our perspective on the matter takes on a much more positive spin. He's our Savior and Lord—and we're His children.

Misunderstanding this principle leads many to see God's will as a formula for misery. But God chastens us in love, not loathing. Just as loving parents correct their wayward children, God's correction affords us needed guidance. It's actually a comfort to a rebellious child to know that his parents love him enough ***not*** to let him go his own way, the way of folly. Rebellion, on the other hand, is the way of Satan. It brings great heartbreak, brokenness, and often irretrievable loss.

- As Solomon put it, "The lot is cast into the lap, but its every decision is from the LORD." (Proverbs 16:33)

God gives us but one life to live. A brief one at that! It's crucial that we neither boast nor waste it. The desire to be within God's will ensures that our life is lived well and productively.

Facing our sin.

What a blessing to read the accounts of men used by God though terribly flawed by sin. The Holy Spirit inspired these writings in God's Word for our reproof, that we too may be inspired to follow God despite our flaws and failings.

King David had an opportunity to get to know God in the midst of appalling sin and human weakness. Usually we know when we've committed sin in a particular area. But until someone else draws attention to it (as the prophet Nathan did for David) we somehow believe the situation isn't all that serious. Our hardness of heart leads us to believe we can cover up our sin with no one being the wiser. It's often only when we're confronted, that we see the enormity of what we've done.

David was suddenly awakened from his complacency toward his sin. The gravity of the situation overwhelmed him when he heard Nathan's convicting declaration, "You are that man!" His unconfessed sin had caused continued intimacy with God to elude him. When David at last saw, acknowledged, grieved over, and asked forgiveness for his sin, this bond of fellowship was restored.

> "Have mercy on me, O God, according to your unfailing love; according to your great compassion blot out my transgressions. Wash away all my iniquity and cleanse me from my sin. For I know my transgressions, and my sin is always before me. Against you, you only, have I sinned and done what is evil in your sight, so that you are proved right when you speak and justified when you judge. Surely I was sinful at birth, sinful from the time my mother conceived me. Surely you desire truth in the inner parts; you teach me wisdom in the inmost place." (Psalm 51:1–6)

Like David, who admitted and confessed his iniquity, we must verbalize our sin to God in prayer. It's vital that we call it what it is—*sin*—not making light of it by declaring it a mistake.

- "If we confess our sins, he is faithful and just and will forgive us our sins and purify us from all unrighteousness." (1 John 1:9)

We restore fellowship with our Lord when we take this first step toward humility. When we confess to God, we take responsibility for our sin—as well as for our *desire to sin*.

Receive God's forgiveness.

You may grieve over your sin but be careful not to fall into Satan's snare by staying in grief for too long. While God wants our godly sorrow, He knows Satan's desire to use our very grief to condemn us and keep us in guilt.

God's remedy for sin is confession. After which He "remembers" the sin no more. After repenting, be sure to move on with God by keeping your eyes on Him, not yourself and your sin.

In 2 Samuel we see how David reacted after the news that the child conceived with Bathsheba had died.

- "Then David exclaimed to Nathan, "I have sinned against the Lord!" Nathan replied to David, "Yes, and the Lord has forgiven your sin. You are not going to die. Nonetheless, because you have treated the Lord with such contempt in this matter, the son who has been born to you will certainly die. David got up from the ground, bathed, put on oil, and changed his clothes. *He went to the house of the Lord and worshiped.* Then, when he entered his palace, he requested that food be brought to him, and he ate. " (2 Samuel 12:13-19)

David was well aware that the penalty for adultery and murder was death. But he also knew that God had forgiven him. David knew God deeply and intimately as a loving, caring Father who was more pleased with his acting in faith than He had been displeased with his sin.

As with David, the Lord knows all about our weaknesses. Nevertheless, He is still passionately devoted to us, as He was with His friend and servant David. God's love for him far exceeded any evil he could commit.

We have an even greater opportunity for such sweet fellowship and intimacy with our Lord than David did. Jesus has come to set us free from condemnation and guilt.

The cross and the empty tomb opened up for us immediate access to God's presence and grace. Jesus' sacrifice covers all our sin—past, present, and even future. We're no longer condemned because of our sin. The only source of condemnation for us as new covenant people is our refusal to accept what Jesus died to give us. When we decline His offer, we take the matter out of God's hands—and He won't over-ride our will.

God has made every provision for us to run to Him when we sin. Doing so keeps us in victory and out of defeat. His kindness, grace, and compassion are available to all repentant sinners.

God's Word produces good fruit in our life when we…

Meditate on it. (Psalm 1:1–3)

Speak it. (Luke 6:43–45)

Allow the Holy Spirit to work on our behalf. (Psalm 104:16)

What it is God wants for us?

God wants us to focus on Him, not on our sin. He told the woman at the well to go and sin no more. He wants us to be devoted to Him and look to Him for our fresh start.

Don't get drawn into the mindless chatter of the world. Stop seeking the approval of others. Don't listen to the lies that others spew out against our great and mighty God. Listening to godless people will only tempt you in their direction. That isn't the inheritance God has for you.

God's approval isn't based on your performance or on what others believe about you. His love for each of us is unconditional. It brings Him great joy when we surrender our lives to Him. He'll teach us how to live each day in the light of His goodness and blessings. Choose today to believe what He says about you, not what others say.

- "The righteous will flourish like a palm tree, they will grow like a cedar of Lebanon." (Psalm 92:12)

GOD REQUIRES SOME THINGS FROM YOU

BEFORE YOU CAN ENTER THE PROMISED LAND.

1. ***He requires your obedience to His instructions.*** We find what God desires from us in His Word to us. God's love is unconditional. But many of His blessings aren't. We must know what those blessings and promises are if we're to possess them for ourselves. He reserves them for the obedient. Over and over again He pledges, "If you'll do this . . . then I'll do that."

2. ***He requires clean hands and a pure heart (Psalm 24:4).*** Sin is a barrier to receiving God's promises. God who won't tolerate sin, made provision for it by sending His Son. Jesus' once-for-all sacrifice satisfied God's just wrath against sin, and confession brings us back into His presence. Jesus always responds to our humble confession with forgiveness.

3. ***He requires action.*** Faith is a fact, but it's also an ***act***. Faith without works, says James, is dead (James 2:26). We become conquerors through the power of the Holy Spirit to go in and possess the Promised Land.[3]

But first you must defeat your staunch opponent. Satan won't concede and give up any territory and gaining ground requires destroying his fortresses. The fight builds your spiritual fortitude. It makes you strong, confident, courageous, and fierce. Winning requires singleness of mind and heart. You must know who you are in Christ and that He's the power source behind your every victory.

This is how we overcome our natural sin nature to become women of faith and substance.

5

SHE IS SPIRITUALLY MATURE

"That you may stand firm in all the will of God, mature and fully assured" (Colossians 4:12).

What does it mean to grow up? Are there components to maturity that let us know whether or not we've succeeded? Is time or age a factor?

In the physical world most people understand the concept of growth. We expect babies to grow and develop, and if they don't, we suspect a problem.

Just as physical maturity and social development has a set of markers to measure growth, so too does spiritual growth.

We know what maturity looks like to society. It looks at characteristics like: Sincerity, personal integrity, humility, courtesy, wisdom, and charity (love). And most of us can discern whether or not a person is mature.

But a more important question is: "What does maturity look like to God?" "What particular traits is He looking for in me?"

Christian maturity has everything to do with **who we are in Christ**—it's our *spiritual character.* It's essential to grow in our faith because Godly character leads us to fulfilling the call God has placed on our life.

I read a quote recently that seems to be true for so many: "The tragedy of life isn't that it ends too soon—it's that we wait too long to begin it."

Perhaps you've found yourself feeling just that way. If so, be assured that with God you can always start over. He'll build into you the maturity and character you may lack. Remember that God can make happen in a day what we may strive to attain in a whole lifetime, for God's ways are not our ways—and His methods are certainly not ours.

All of us wish deep down that we could do everything right and avoid the pain and suffering that come from a lack of knowledge and wisdom. But we're born into sin and doing right is just not possible until our nature is changed by a God encounter. We were created dependent because God created us for Himself. This dependency requires us to seek Him out. Our neediness requires that we rely on Him to meet all our needs: physical, material, and emotional. We're like babies in need of constant care, protection, and knowledge. We know so little and there's so much to grasp and understand.

We can't learn it all on our own, so we need God to show us what we don't know and how to live rightly. In the end, we can consider our life a failure only if we've never reached the place of knowing that our human knowledge and wisdom are limited, and that it's God who reveals all things to us.

While we can't go back in time, we can start fresh now with God. Most of us want to reach some level of maturity, but we're often unsure how to go about it.

Spiritual growth may be defined as *maturity* or, to use a biblical term, *perfection*. Initially, when someone accepts Christ as Savior there're spiritually immature. With study and time, their old nature is gradually transformed into a new creation. Eventually a new Christian should develop the qualities that characterize the mature.

Many Scriptures describe the need to grow and mature spiritually, among them:

> "Be no longer children, but grow up in Christ." (Ephesians 4:14–15)

> "But grow in the grace and knowledge of our Lord and Savior Jesus Christ." (2 Peter 3:18)

> The Thessalonians "grew exceedingly in faith." (2 Thessalonians 1:3)

> Paul prayed "for their love to abound more and more." (Philippians 1:9)

The mark of a mature believer.

Maturity is a process that comes as we pursue spiritual understanding of ***who God is*** and what His ***attributes*** are.

> "If any of you lacks wisdom, you should ask God, who gives generously to all without finding fault, and it will be given to you." (James 1:5)

Becoming mature not only involves cultivating intimate communication and relationship with the Spirit of God ***in our heart***, but ensuring that our heart is ***captivated*** by that communication. Spiritual maturity involves integrating God's Word into our character to such a degree that it affects virtually every aspect of our lives.

One definition of maturity includes "*being perfect, complete, or ready.*" The word "perfect" is often misunderstood. We tend to think it means without flaw or error, but it also means *complete, mature, or healthy* (see Leviticus 22:21). Paul understood perfection was not God's intent for believers to fulfill His will.

> "Not that I have already obtained all this, or have already been made perfect, but I press on to take hold of that for which Christ Jesus took hold of me. Brothers, I do not consider myself yet to have taken hold of it. But one thing I do: Forgetting what is behind and straining toward what is ahead, I press on toward the goal to win the prize for which God has called me heavenward in Christ Jesus." (Philippians 3:12–14)

Paul knew the secret to reaching maturity.

- "We proclaim him, admonishing and teaching everyone with all wisdom, so that we may present everyone **perfect [mature]** in Christ." (Colossians 1:28, bold italics added).

"Until we all reach unity in the faith and in the knowledge of the Son of God and become ***mature, attaining to the whole measure of the fullness of Christ***." (Ephesians 4:13)

God has clearly defined objectives for each of His children.

1. That they might be "conformed to the image of his son." (Romans 8:29)

2. That they "leave the elementary teachings about Christ and go on to full maturity." (Hebrews 6:1)

The first step toward reaching spiritual maturity: A desire to grow.

Just as children want to grow and become just like Mommy and Daddy, we must desire to resemble our *Abba*, our heavenly "Daddy." We must become and remain excited about growing and learning more and more about our faith and about the Savior in whom that faith rests.

We relate differently to our heavenly Father as we attain maturity milestones. Maturity allows us to see Him as the relational God that He is. That advanced perception helps us *value* our relationship with Him to the point that we can't bear the thought of willfully hurting Him. With spiritual growth, we recognize that the world holds nothing of value for us, that Christ is indeed our only true treasure.

In the beginning of our Christian walk, God…

1. *Calls us*—"Come, follow Me,"

2. *Conforms us*—"And I will make you . . . ."

3. ***Commissions us***—"Go ye."

Before we attain some measure of spiritual maturity, we often mistake God's *calling* and *conforming,* for His *commissioning*. In our initial excitement at hearing from God what He may want to do with us, we assume He's asking us to go forth immediately.

For instance, Moses knew the *calling* of God, but it took another forty years for God to *conform* this future leader. Only then was Moses ready for God's *commissioning*.

Joseph's vision from God (his *calling*) came when he was just seventeen years old. But it wasn't until he was thirty that he stood before Pharaoh. The intervening years had constituted Joseph's *conforming* process. During that time God *conformed* Joseph from a boy inclined to tactlessly reveal too much to jealous brothers, to one who possessed incredible wisdom, maturity, and leadership ability. God had greater purposes for Joseph. This was his *commissioning*. And Joseph cooperated with God's vision for him.

Jesus knew His *calling* was to be about His Father's business. As a developing boy He grew in wisdom, in stature, and in favor with God and man. This was His *conforming* process. At age thirty Jesus was *commissioned* by the Father, and the Spirit of God (the Holy Spirit) was sent to rest on Him. Even Jesus was in need of the filling (baptizing) of the Holy Spirit before being sent out to minister—His *commissioning*.

Godly character involves conforming to Christ's image.

The pattern of *conforming* to Christ and increasing in spiritual maturity (and experience) must be operating in a believer's life before he or she is fully equipped to step into ministry.

Moses, Joshua, Abraham, and David are all examples of this principle. After a firm foundation and preparation for ministry requirements are in place, there's a final component to maturity: *the absolute willingness to obey God when He gives us our marching orders.* We too can be used in mighty ways. We need only to ask God what He has for us and then submit ourselves to His conforming process. In Paul's words, we won't be ready…

- ". . . until we all reach unity in the faith and in the knowledge of the Son of God and become **mature, attaining to the whole measure of the fullness of Christ**. Then we will **no longer be infants**, tossed back and forth by the waves, and blown here and there by every wind of teaching and by the cunning and craftiness of men in their deceitful scheming. Instead, speaking the truth in love, we will in all things ***grow up*** into him who is the Head, that is, Christ. From him the whole body, joined and held together by every supporting ligament, grows and builds itself up in love, as each part does its work." (Ephesians 4:13–16, bold italics added)

There are three stages (calling, conforming, and commissioning) in the life of the believer (1 John 2:12–14).

Conversion isn't the goal; it's only the gateway. We're to progress from strength to strength, and from glory to glory, because God didn't save us to stagnate.

Do you desire God to use you? Do you have a vision for what you could be? Then seek to spend your time well in building up your faith, which in turn builds your spiritual character. Spiritual growth often takes the same path as physical growth. We must learn to stand strong and certain at each stage before we can move on to the next level of maturity.

1. ***Children, represent salvation/conversion.*** A spiritual child, like an infant, has many deficiencies. He or she lacks strength, wisdom, insight, and purpose. A young child's world revolves around needs. Those around them must spend vast amounts of time and energy meeting those needs for attention, care, and protection. At this tender stage of life they have little to give, yet their demands are limitless. Paul told the Corinthians that they derived satisfaction in childish things, since children don't yet desire adult things. And if we, though physically adults, remain spiritually immature, we have the same kinds of deficits. Too many of us are content to live as babes, demanding constant care and attention, with little regard for the needs of others. The

minds of such people are tuned to themselves, not to the purposes God has at heart for them.

2. ***Young men and women, represent maturation.*** This group has left behind their childishness. They hunger for the Word of God. As the maturation process continues, they become increasingly strong, committed, and steadfast. Maturity is measured not by the absence of problems in our lives, but by how we engage with and handle those problems. At this stage believers become aware of the conflicts in which the enemy wants to embroil them. Young children are usually spared from discord, but the maturing process requires the fortitude to avoid being continuously swayed by conflict and changing circumstances.

3. ***Fathers and mothers represent consummation/reproduction.*** This stage represents those who are willing to go deeper to know God in intimacy and insight. Young men and women know God, but the fathers and mothers have the capacity to know Him more fully. Seeing things from God's perspective requires knowing His mind and purposes. Parents in the faith have experienced not only salvation but also maturation. They understand the mind of God well enough to discern His purposes for their own lives and for His Church. God sees the whole, not just the parts. And it's only when we see God in His fullness, from His beginning, that we can begin to understand

the need to avoid the perils of remaining immature, including susceptibility to errors and false teaching.[1]

At this stage we're fit to be *commissioned*. We need to place ourselves under an accountability structure, to learn under someone who has been engaged in ministry for some time and can mentor us properly. If we're to be effective in His service, we must learn from our fathers and mothers of the faith so that we're not devoured by the enemy before we've gotten started

We live in a day of situation ethics, decaying morals, and an almost complete vacuum of absolutes. The Church finds itself in desperate need of spiritual fathers and mothers. Spiritual maturity takes time and requires adaptability so we can readily adjust and respond to change.

Realize that God knows our natural bent for sameness and comfort. But He wants for us maturity—not comfort, conformity, or complacence. God already gave us our childhood to play and to be protected. As the perfect Father that He is, He won't permit us to remain immature.

> Brothers, do not be children in your thinking. Be infants in evil, but in your thinking ***be mature***." (1Corinthians 14:20, ESV)

Maturity takes time and effort. Many of us don't reach full maturity because we don't bother to pursue it. It isn't one of our goals. We must want it badly enough to work for it.

- ". . . until we come to such unity in our faith and knowledge of God's Son that we will be ***mature*** and ***full grown in the Lord***, measuring up to the full stature of Christ." (Ephesians 4:13, NLT)

According to this verse we can define spiritual maturity in one phrase: *being like Christ.*

Renew your mind.

The world has a pattern and most people seek to conform to it believing that it holds what they're looking for. But Paul instructs us to conform to a different pattern. How do we do that? *By the renewing of our minds!* The word *renewing* comes from the Greek word for "renovation." God starts a remodeling project on us beginning with our structural center, our mind and heart. When we accept Him as our Savior, He goes immediately to work on our character. Eventually we see a change in our thought patterns. And when we think differently, we start behaving differently too. Soon, with the reconstruction of our "house"—our personhood—our new home no longer resembles the former. This process of reconstruction starts with the heart. As we take in more of what God offers—the forgiveness of our sins, a new heart and spirit, and the hearing and reading of His Word—our faith grows. As we take in more of His wisdom and precepts and incorporate them into our lives, they *transform* us. The process happens so gradually that we may not even be aware it's taking place.

The result of this new conforming process.

Greater discernment and spiritual development! We can't reach maturity if we don't know and understand what God's Word has to say on the subject. If we don't know He loves us and has so much more planned for our lives, we'll try to live to the best of our inferior ability. We need to know the basics to make forward progress. The more we're immersed in the Word, the better we're able to "test and approve" God's will for us.

Desiring to know God's will is a natural concern for most new (and seasoned) Christians. But where many get confused is the idea of *discerning* God's will. How do we know what God wants us to be or do?

Paul specifies three qualities of God's will—***good, pleasing***, and ***perfect***. Good means just that—*good*. It's valuable! What God wants for you is good for you, even though it may not feel that way at the moment. Pleasing at its most basic means "*acceptable*." Something that's pleasing makes sense, and you come to accept and invest in it more and more as you come to know   God. God is maturing you, transforming you into His image. And that transformation leads us in a certain direction. Eventually we can see in retrospect the irony that our hard times have brought about our perfection and maturity. It's at that point that we exercise that very discernment by becoming grateful for those trials.

Growing into maturity requires seven practices.

There are seven basic practices every Christian needs for spiritual growth to occur. We grow by…

1. *Eating*—The Bible and Jesus are our bread of life.

2. *Breathing*—Prayer restores our spirit and makes us one with Jesus.

3. *Practicing good hygiene*—Confessing our sins keeps us clean.

4. *Investing in a caring family*—Fellowship with other believers keeps us accountable.

5. *Regular exercise*—Service to others exercises our spiritual gifts.

6. *Acknowledging our need of protection*—Taking our spiritual authority (understanding what Jesus purchased for us) tramples the enemy.

7. ***Practicing generosity***—Our joyful willingness to give financially reveals that money has no hold on us.

> "You have been Christians a long time now, and you ought to be teaching others. Instead, you need someone to teach you again the basic things a beginner must learn about the Scriptures. You are like babies who drink only milk and cannot eat solid food. And a person who is living on milk isn't very far along in the Christian life and doesn't know much about doing what is right." (Hebrews 5:12–13, NLT)

Spiritual maturity isn't automatic, immediate, or a prize that is won without discipline. It isn't even instinctive, as the process runs counter to our human nature. That's because being "born again" refers to a spiritual rebirth, a regeneration of the human soul or spirit.

- "Very truly I tell you, no one can see the kingdom of God without being born again." (John 3:3)

"Continue to grow in the grace and knowledge of our savior, Jesus Christ." (2 Peter 3:18, GN)

"Discipline yourself for the purpose of godliness." (1Timothy 4:7, NASB)

This discipline is a process and it takes steady effort. We need to monitor our intake of life's junk food—the garbage the world offers, its entertainment and morality. Taking such fare into our eyes and ears, the gates to our soul, contaminate us. We'll never reach a level of maturity unless we're *purposeful* in doing so. If this isn't the sole intent of our being, we'll gradually lose ground.

Four tests of spiritual maturity.

God's will is for every believer to experience growth and maturity. Far from being based on age, appearance, achievements, academics, or any other worldly criteria, this kind of maturity is determined by *truth* and *attitude*.

Our attitude determines our character. Without a commitment to spiritual maturity in relationships, for example, we can't truly fulfill Christ's command to love our neighbor as ourselves.

1. ***A mature person is positive under pressure.*** *How do you handle problems? How do you respond when you don't get your way?*

    "Consider it pure joy whenever you face trials of many kinds, because the testing of your faith develops perseverance. Perseverance must finish its works so that you may be mature and complete, not lacking anything." (James 1:1–2)

    "Blessed is the man who perseveres under trial, because when he has stood the test, he will receive the crown of life." (James 1:12)

2. ***A mature person is sensitive to others.*** *How do you treat others?*

   "If you keep the royal law found in scripture, 'Love your neighbor as yourself,' you are doing right." (James 2:8)

3. ***A mature person has mastered his/her mouth.*** *Have you learned to control your speech?*

   "If anyone is never at fault in what he says, he is a perfect man, able to keep his whole body in check." (James 3:2)

   "Do not let any negative talk come out of your mouth, but only what is helpful for building up others according to their needs." (Ephesians 4:29)

   "If anyone considers himself religious and yet does not keep a tight rein on his tongue, he deceives himself and his religion is worthless." (James 1:26)

4. ***A mature person is a peacemaker.*** *Have you learned to positively affect others? Are you able to bring people together in peace?*

   "What causes fights and quarrels among you? Don't they come from your desires that battle within you?" (James 4:1)

James specified that spiritual maturity involved five components.

1. *Patience* in testing (chapter 1).

2. Practice of the *truth* (chapter 2).

3. Control of the *tongue* (chapter 3).

4. Interest in *peacemaking*, not making trouble (chapter 4).

5. *Prayerful* attitude in times of adversity (chapter 5)

The mature believer understands the purpose of the cross.

If we're intent on living a God-honoring life that produces good fruit, we'll need a focus. Spiritual maturity is the primary focus for every believer.

Imagine being able to meet a first-century believer. What do you think this person would think of the state of today's Church? Lack of spiritual discernment keeps people in dead churches. Unless we understand Christ's intent and purpose for His people, we'll go through life bewildered by our existence and confused as to our life's purpose.

A foundation that's firmly built, is built upon the cross. We need:

1. ***Instruction*** for growing in God.

2. ***Understanding*** to enable us to serve God's purposes.

3. An ever-increasing ***desire*** for God.

4. Continuous ***training*** and reinforcement in the ***fear of the Lord***.

5. Lessons in ***conformity*** to Christ's character.

Paul writes in Colossians 1:16,

- "For by him all things were created: things in heaven and on earth, visible and invisible, whether thrones or powers or rulers or authorities; ***all things were created by him*** and ***for him.***"

Most of us don't grasp the reality that we were created ***for Him*** (Revelation 4:11). Truth is that we were created solely for *His purposes* and for *His good pleasure.* And since we neither conceived of nor fashioned ourselves, it follows that we don't belong to ourselves either.

To understand the purpose of the cross, it's vital that we're clear on God's original intent for man.

The account of man in Genesis.

1. Man's ***submission***: "The Lord God took the man [and]"

2. Man's ***location***: "put him into the garden"

3. Man's ***vocation***: "to cultivate it and keep it."

God chose not only man's *location* but also his *vocation*. God did, nevertheless, give man the prerogative to decide his own course. It was only after the fall of Adam and Eve that God gave man the freedom to be independent of Him.

- "We all, like sheep, have gone astray, each of us has turned to his own way; and the LORD has laid on him the iniquity of us all." (Isaiah 53:6)

God's original intent for humanity.

God originally intended for men and women to live with Him for all time (as in forever) in perfection.

Adam and Eve had a purposeful life. They were protected, loved immeasurably, and free from stress and hardship. But these partners opted to live life by their own terms, in consequence, invalidating God's original intent. Once they choose their own way, God would not stop the consequences that choice brought forth. He allowed them to reap what they had chosen. Self-government also brought self-interest. In tragic irony, this independence would now make life extraordinarily challenging and problematic.

The cross is God's answer to our need. In the fullness of time God would send Jesus to die on the cross and rise again as victor over sin and death. This act made intimacy and fellowship once again possible with the Father.

God would not give up on man. A restored relationship was always foremost in His heart. But His justice demanded that it would now come about in another way. Now, intimacy with Him would have to be *chosen* by each of us individually. God would fellowship only with those willing to choose Him over Satan—with those who would freely choose the more difficult path of obedience to Him.

God had a two-fold objective: To benefit Himself and to redeem and restore a remnant of humanity.

> "For none of us lives to himself alone and none of us dies to himself alone. If we live, we live to the Lord; and if we die, we die to the Lord. So, whether we live or die, we belong to the Lord. For this very reason, Christ died and returned to life so that he might be the Lord of both the dead and the living." (Romans 14:7–9)

We see here that Christ died for our sin but once again establishes His lordship over our lives. We receive cleansing and He receives us back as His own possession. God is interested in getting us back, not just in washing away our sins.

> "…who gave himself for us to redeem us from all wickedness and to purify for himself *a people that are his very own*, eager to do what is good." (Titus 2:14)

We don't hear enough today of how much God desires to "have" us. So many people, including many Christians, are joyless and troubled. They lack the basic understanding of their reason for being. They don't understand that it is God who wants them and loves them beyond measure. If we would accept and *receive* that fact, we would live as rightful daughters of the King. We would rejoice and cherish the knowledge that we belong to Him—the God of the universe!

The mature Christian woman understands that giving herself unreservedly, in total surrender to Christ, means attaining what she could receive in no other way. God desires for us to be rich and knowledgeable in all spiritual matters. He wants us to grow in love, grace, and mercy toward others.

Three issues in developing maturity: Ourselves, change, and God.

Just as there are stages to our sanctification, there are critical issues in the process of maturing. Not dealing with these issues will most likely delay our moving into spiritual adulthood. The issues have to do with our views of: ourselves, change, and God.

Let's look to Abraham once again as our example. Abraham's *attitude* toward himself can be symbolized by something he did continually. He built altars (see Genesis 12:7–8; 13:4, 18; 22:9). At the altar, the Old Testament believer met with God.

The lack of an altar pointed to those who knew little of pleasing God. For example, King Saul, whose life represented disobedience, instability, and eventual tragedy, was 42 years old before he built his first altar. He didn't see the value either of the altar or of glorifying God.

Abraham by contrast, is known for his faith in God. The altar was the place where he laid down his life before the Lord. He inquired of God there and expected His presence, practices he considered to be vital for life. From a lifetime spent surrendering and dedicating himself to God's purposes, he came to trust implicitly in God's character and nature.

Obedience brings understanding of who God is.

When we begin the process, as Abraham did, of laying our lives down at the altar, we begin to understand God. Our surrender brings revelation from God, and revelation produces consecration and obedience. To Abraham the altar represented both submission and self-sacrifice. These outcomes were for his benefit, not his destruction. Abraham came to such an understanding of and trust in God that he wasn't afraid to obey Him. Even when God commanded Abraham to sacrifice his only son, Isaac, on the altar, Abraham knew he could trust God to raise him back to life. The patriarch knew that God's testing wasn't unreasonable, even if what He was requesting sounded that way. When we come to understand God's true motives, we don't need to be afraid He'll ask something of us that would destroy us.

> "Abraham trusted God always had good in store for him, and not harm. By knowing God's true nature, he understood it was meant for his testing." (Genesis 22:2)

Abraham is our model of obedience and maturity.

Abraham was willing to "let go" of the familiar to be obedient to God's command to "go." Abraham could trust God because He knew His nature was good. Abraham's obedience and desire to fulfill the call God placed on his life is refreshing, especially in a world where so many are disobedient.

Like Abraham, we must determine to be obedient to God and ***let go*** of our stagnant beliefs and comfort zones. Then we must ask God to impart newness to us with a fresh word. Listen carefully to how He answers and be sure to obey, not sometime later, or when you feel like it, but immediately.

God will not continue to show us new things until we're obedient to what He's already instructed us to do. If we think we don't know what He wants, we merely need to read the Word He left us. His instructions to us are on the pages of both the Old and New Testament.

Many believe that they must hear from God verbally. But God speaks to us when we read His Word, when we're in prayer with Him, and when we worship Him. Our obedience brings us His continual fresh and living water, which renews the very essence of our soul.

Why should we be obedient to God's will?

So that Christ may receive all the glory and honor due Him.

- "You are worthy, our Lord and God, to receive glory and honor and power, for you created all things, and by your will they were created and have their being." (Revelation 4:11)

We get so accustomed to *asking* from God, that we don't stop and think that He might be looking for something from us in return. He desires and deserves honor from us, simply **because He's God**. There's an additional benefit for us from glorifying God: when we apprehend the greatness of Christ, we too will be blessed.

Four words often seen in Scripture remind us that God alone deserves our praise.

1. *Glory* is the sum total of all that God is and does. Everything about Him is glorious! The glory of human beings, in contrast, fades and withers as grass.

2. *Majesty* means greatness or magnificence. Only God is great, and He alone deserves our unrestrained praise.

3. *Dominion* has to do with God's sovereignty, control, and rule over *all* things. The Greek word means *strength* or *might*.

4. *Power* means not only *strength,* but also *authority*, and that too resides only with God (Matthew 28:18). Jesus' authority extends over the powers of darkness (Ephesians 1:19-23). By obediently yielding ourselves to Him, we share in that authority and can with the Holy Spirit's help accomplish His will for our lives.

Jesus is our best role model of obedience to the Father.

1. Our Lord was never bad-tempered,

2. always calm;

3. never rebellious,

4. always obedient;

5. never fearful,

6. always courageous;

7. never hesitant or indecisive,

8. always resolute;

9. never pessimistic,

10. always cheerful;

11. never subtle,

12. always sincere;

13. never grasping (greedy, materialistic),

14. always generous;

15. never acting from self-interest, but always from principle (belief, standard).

Jesus is our perfect model of spiritual maturity.

The Christian life isn't about ***doing***; it's about ***being***. We're to be a part of Christ by imitating Him. We can grow up only when we understand what it is we're to grow into, and in whose likeness. That's what *being* is all about. Doing keeps us busy, but not necessarily in His presence.

Self-preservation or submission?

Some people recoil at the word submission. Their independent and rebellious nature resists self-sacrifice. The natural human condition is to preserve the self. We naturally seek to save our lives no matter what the cost. This tendency to protect ourselves, although good in one sense, often carries over into our spiritual lives. This is why the Word tells us we must be *conformed* to Christ's likeness by the *renewing of our minds*.

> Jesus said to his disciples, "If anyone would come after me, he must deny himself and take up his cross and follow me. For whoever wants to save his life will lose it, but whoever loses his life for me will find it." (Matthew 16:24–25)

God is in need of dead people—dead to themselves, that is! Only in being willing to die to ourselves can we gain eternal life. Abraham was able to see himself clearly based on his intimate relationship with his Lord. He understood that he was weak and failure prone.

This was his secret to success. When we come to see ourselves in reality and truth, we begin to see God's true nature and long to be like Him.

Change doesn't need to be excessively difficult. If we'll submit to God and allow Him to make the necessary changes within us, we'll experience "effortless change" to which we can willingly surrender. Then and only then are we freed from that futile felt need to *work* at self-preservation!

The nature of change.

We can learn much about change from Abraham for whom God's very first command would require radical change:

> "The LORD had said to Abram, 'Leave your country, your people and your father's household and go to the land I will show you.'" (Genesis 12:1)

Houses, family, jobs and possessions all represent security to us. A house represents something permanent, immovable. As much as we love our homes and what they represent, though, there's danger in staying put.

Many of us are creatures of habit who love returning to familiar things and places. The greatest fear for some is being compelled to leave behind friends and family. But if God calls us to move, this resistance to change will keep us from experiencing His many blessings. Many choose to be disobedient by choosing their own comfort over Christ's requests.

The book of Hebrews tells us that Abraham's life was one of continual change. He was a sojourner.

> "By faith he made his home in the promised land like a stranger in a foreign country; he lived in tents, as did Isaac and Jacob, who were heirs with him of the same promise." (Hebrews 11:9–10)

Abraham didn't live in a permanent, immovable home. He lived in a tent and it was movable, allowing him to transition from place to place. Ironic as this may sound, this was actually freedom. Ease of movement gave him a nature that was always seeking and searching. God wants to build this same vibrancy and willing compliance in us. Frequently this requires uprooting.

Too much sameness can make us apathetic and lethargic. When we have no desire for more of God, no longing to be used in a greater capacity by and for Him, we start languishing. There's danger in settling for stagnation, where no living water flows.

It's easy for us to become complacent, not only in our personal lives but in our churches as well. We like our comfortable theology and predictable services. Yet greater intimacy with the Father requires moving from the natural into the supernatural, where God resides.

God looks for people who yearn for and seek more—more living, more excitement, more ministry, more desire to worship and serve Him. These people gain increased vitality and continuously expect more.

What change will do for you.

Researchers have identified seven major stressors in life, of which moving is considered one. For some, in fact, this one is the most stressful aside from losing a loved one. Change, whether it's moving to a new location, a new job, or even a new relationship, is challenging. Scores of Christians say no to God because they'd rather stay put, than experience the stretching He so frequently calls us to. This is one of the major reasons many Christians don't finish strong in their life's journey.

One distinctive I've noticed in many military people is the desire to move on. Like Abraham, they look forward to their next assignment, the next place of discovery, new people to experience, and foreign lands to investigate. Many get antsy if they're in one place too long as they've grown accustomed to change and crave it.

One of the Church's biggest handicaps today is its resistance to change. I have personally met many who have grown accustomed to settling in one place, one home, one church, and with the same circles of friends; consequently, they can't imagine having to start over again. In fact, some don't wish to invest the time needed to develop a friendship when they learn you won't be staying long. The fear of losing someone they may get close to is too great for them, so they resist reaching out to avoid eventual sorrow.

With God, we too tend to focus more on what we perceive is loss, rather than on what we will gain. God sees the end from the beginning. He knows the plans He has for us. But it takes our willingness to trust Him to see it to completion. Many of us get into a rut, but since we're with other people in similar ruts, we don't readily see it. It often takes force to pull us away. We won't experience freshness until we're willing to let new people and experiences into our circle.

It's only after we perceive how we've changed following the new experiences or location that we can look back and realize how limited our former life really was. We must proactively look for new friends, opportunities to grow, and ways to expand our horizons. When we embrace new relationships, we're exposing ourselves to others' interesting life experiences, which invigorate us. When we don't seek new opportunities to grow as a person, we limit our personal growth and compromise our ability to bless others.

If we want God's blessings, we must be willing to do what He asks, even if whatever that might be is outside our comfort zone. When that opportunity for change does come, be sure to embrace it as Abraham did. God reckoned Abraham's obedience as righteousness, and He views ours the same.

If you feel you're in need of reinvigoration, ask God for a new start in one area or another, as well as for a renewed sense of curiosity.

The Christian life is lived "within."

Scores of individuals try to live the Christian life on their own, only to feel the sting of disappointment, dissatisfaction, and eventual disillusion-ment. Behavior modification (what we do or don't do) is ***not*** the goal of the Christian life.

The secret is to know that this life is lived within. Many focus on changing the outward self, but God has little interest in our outward appearance. We can fool ourselves into thinking we're spiritual by changing our vocabulary, the amount of time we spend in Bible study or small groups, or our church attendance habits. But these outward alterations don't indicate our true heart nature. And we have no power to change our heart apart from the Holy Spirit working in us.

God has a different and better way to get you to the good things He has for you. Everything good starts with God, and that includes your life. If you're going to have a successful, fruitful life, God will have to be your sole source.

Growing in faith and maturity starts when we understand that we don't create anything within ourselves. Only God can give us the mind to think, the emotion to feel, and the ability to produce. We didn't create ourselves, and we don't determine the nature or length of our days.

Our journey to spiritual maturity must be the all-consuming goal of our life. Each stage of this journey has its own duration, unique problems, expectations, and outcome. If we're willing to do our part, God will reveal His purposes for us.

The goal of the Christian life—reach for more!

Many never reach this mature place because they don't realize there's anything to reach for beyond the salvation experience.

Christ is our example of obedience and maturity. He knew His purpose—to do the will of His Father. He knew why He had been sent to earth and born of a woman. He also understood that His time on earth would be extremely short and limited. Since Jesus came with His purpose already set before Him, He understood the importance of time management, setting priorities (what He was called to do and *not* to do), spending time with His Father, and making disciples. He understood that pouring His life into the disciples would enable the "good news" to be carried throughout the world after His departure.

Jesus never became part of the world. Earth was merely a place through which He was passing. His sojourn here was part of His journey—not His final destination. He had been given a job to do—to redeem man back to His Father. Upon its completion, He proclaimed "It is finished." During His time on earth He didn't work in His own strength, of His own accord, by His own methods, or for His own gain.

We could stay on track and not waste so much time wavering in our faith if we would keep our eyes on Jesus and follow His methods.

We fail to reach maturity because we too often look to others for leadership and success principles. They may be able to stretch our natural abilities to some degree, but they can't grow our character or intimacy with the Father. Other methods distract and get us off track. No wonder we're prone to losing whatever it is we construct on our own? No one can take from us what the Father gives. When we learn to despise the world, we stay focused on our reason for being.

Jesus reached maturity because He listened to **no one** but the Father. Yes, He listened to people's pain and sorrow, and with compassion He healed them physically, but He also freed them from their inner demons so they might be made whole and clean. Jesus is about "rest," not just healing and salvation. As long as we hold on to the demons that enslave us, we'll find no rest.

> "Dear friends, now we are children of God, and what we will be has not yet been made known. But we know that when Christ appears, we shall be like him, for we shall see him as he is." (1 John 3:2, NIV)

From what source are you drinking?

Seeking living water that is fresh provides exhilaration and vibrancy. Sluggish lives happen when we've been drinking from stagnant water sources. The polluted, shallow streams of the world will not quench our parched throats.

It's only by extending ourselves to reach deeper, as we do when we seek water from a well, into the things of God that He brings forth in us His "living water." Jesus is the living water and He alone quenches our persistent thirst. It's accomplished in His presence, Word, power, and pro-vision.

> "On the last and greatest day of the Feast, Jesus stood and said in a loud voice, 'If anyone is thirsty, let him come to me and drink.'" (John 7:37)

> "Whoever believes in me, as the Scripture has said, streams of living water will flow from within him." (John 7:38)

Jesus is offering the Holy Spirit, who will satisfy people's thirst for God (John 7:39). The cries of the psalmists have been answered.

> David prayed, "O God, you are my God, earnestly I seek you; my soul thirsts for you, my body longs for you, in a dry and weary land where there is no water." (Psalm 63:1)

This invitation to come and drink is the climax of a series of references to water in the book of John:

1. The water *turned* into wine (chapter 2)

2. The water of the *new birth* (chapter 3)

3. The *living* water (chapter 4)

4. The *cleansing* water of Bethesda (chapter 5)

5. And the *calming* of the waters (chapter 6).

All of these have revealed Jesus as the agent of God who brings God's gracious offer of life.

Cisterns and wells.

A cistern and a well are not the same. A cistern has to be filled with water from the outside. It isn't self-renewing and it can run dry. A well, in contrast, is fed by flowing water from within.

The same difference exists between a person trying to be spiritual and a *Spirit-filled* person. When we become Christians we're given the Holy Spirit, whose presence and power in our lives make all the difference. He's the living water that flows from within. He is part of us. We just need to acknowledge His presence and listen to Him to receive His freshness. It's His living water within us that renews, refreshes, and empowers us.

Living for Jesus is more than just a spiritual commitment on our part requiring our effort; it's the gift and blessing of Jesus enabled by the Holy Spirit.

Maturity requires a teachable spirit and a desire to reproduce.

A fertile heart, like fertile soil, must be cultivated, protected, watered, pruned, and fed. Many don't devote the necessary time and attention, nor do they value highly enough God's written Word for the treasure it holds. They approach it casually, with indifference. It isn't special to them, so they grow cold toward it. But it's the master key to understanding God and to reaching maturity.

Correctly understanding scriptural truth and the Holy Spirit's power to transform our lives brings us to maturity.

It isn't enough to simply read what's written on its pages. We must drink of it deeply, *receiving* it into our being. It must be planted and take root in order to produce a harvest. That's moving beyond knowledge to allowing its words to transform us from within. If we take the Word of God and plant it deeply in our heart, we can be sure that a beautiful, strong oak will sprout and grow from it.

Most people want to know what's in it for them before they comply with something they're asked to do. They aren't interested in knowing that they should do something, particular something "religious." Your flesh doesn't want the things of the Lord, and Satan certainly doesn't want you in the Word. That's because he knows it holds God's truth and that truth will set you free!

Be sure to add virtue to your faith.

Our Savior purchased for us salvation in His once-for-all-time, supreme sacrifice on the cross. Yet in another, individual sense, our salvation isn't a once-for-all-time process. It's true that we ask for and receive it (are converted) only one time, but we must throughout our lives ask for guidance to continue into maturity lest we fall backward into our old habits.

> "For this very reason, make every effort to add to your faith goodness; and to goodness, knowledge; and to knowledge, self-control; and to self-control, perseverance; and to perseverance, godliness; and to godliness, brotherly kindness;

and to brotherly kindness, love. For if you possess these qualities in increasing measure, they will keep you from being ineffective and unproductive in your knowledge of our Lord Jesus Christ. But if anyone does not have them, he is nearsighted and blind, and has forgotten that he has been cleansed from his past sins." (2 Peter 1:5–9)

Jesus sternly warned that not all who pray "Lord, Lord" will enter the kingdom of heaven. He cautioned his listeners not to make false assumptions about their spiritual reward. Even though they could point to things they had done in His name, such as prophesying, casting out demons, and performing miracles, they might still hear the dreadful pronouncement, "Away from me, I never knew you" (Matthew 7:21–23).

We need to be extremely careful about the criteria we choose for assessing our assurance of salvation and level of spiritual maturity. It's a grievous mistake to assume that prayer, Bible study, or active participation in worship guarantees us a spiritual inheritance. All of these activities can, and often are, performed in a perfunctory manner *without faith*. And without faith, as the writer to the Hebrews makes clear in Hebrews 11:6, it's impossible to please God. It's by faith that we ask for forgiveness of sin, and it's through repentance that we become joined with Jesus.

The ***fruit of the Spirit***, as listed by Paul in Galatians 5:22–23, are ***love, joy, peace, patience, kindness, goodness, faithfulness,***

gentleness, and self-control. Each of these is a natural, invariable outcome of the process of maturing. If "good fruit" isn't evident in your life, you must ask yourself whether you've truly been born-again and spiritually transformed.

Spiritual growth is transformational. Lives are changed from unbelief to belief, from ungodliness to godliness. Although your transformation won't be complete until the glory of heaven is realized, there's a recognizable change in you that began with your conversion and will continue throughout your life.

True, you may have ups and downs, spurts and slower times of nearly imperceptible improvement, but throughout it all you are living a new and different life, empowered and directed by the Holy Spirit. What you were becomes more and more distant, as the new you becomes more and more like the Lord you have come to love and serve. These are the marks of spiritual maturity.

BEWARE OF PITFALLS THAT WILL KEEP YOU FROM MATURING SPIRITUALLY

The devil knows the Scriptures too.

Think about it! Satan persuasively quoted the Bible when tempting Jesus (Matthew 4:1–10). Unbelieving persons can be biblical scholars and quote Scripture as well. Any topic can be studied and repeated. Religion and the Bible are no exception. In addition, many people profess to be Christians but know nothing of Jesus Christ and what He came to give us.

The cults use a measure of truth, but they mix it liberally with untruth. That's precisely what makes them alluring to so many. Unless we know the truth of the Word of God for ourselves, we may be inclined to follow a religious belief that leads to our very death. Satan is cunning, and he's the great imitator. We must always be on guard against allowing him to fool us by mimicking the teachings of Jesus.

Cultists are usually very religious people, yet Jesus was anything but religious. Many are inclined to confuse religion with Christianity. Religion is man-made. It's humanity's misguided attempt to reach God.

In contrast, God created man for His own good pleasure; to have us for Himself. God reaches out to His creation and asks us to *receive* Him. Jesus asks us to *receive*, but religion asks us to *do*.

God will not accept man's attempts at making himself acceptable. God has provided His method and person for attaining salvation and it won't come by man devising his own system and terms.

How easy it is for us to trust in our own strength and resources. Despite our innate desire for God, we're naturally inclined to seek independence from Him. Only when we desire to overrule our independent nature, by adopting humility and dependence on the Lord, can we rid ourselves of this tendency.

The Pharisees of Jesus' day had hearts that were far from the Lord. Nevertheless, they set an example of disciplined devotion and devout obedience to the law according to their erroneous interpretation.

We must guard our heart so we can identify untruth when we see, hear, and confront it.

- Paul wrote that "We must grow up in every way into him who is the head, into Christ" (Ephesians 4:15) and

"Brothers, stop thinking like children. In regard to evil be infants, but in your thinking be adults." (1 Corinthians 14:20)

Humility is the secret ingredient that keeps us from being deceived and keeps us safely in God's care. Arrogance brings our sure and swift ruin. For this reason God's Word has many warnings to us. If we'll heed them, we're sure to receive our just reward.

Jesus said, "I tell you the truth, unless you change and become like little children, you will never enter the kingdom of heaven. Therefore, whoever humbles himself like this child is the greatest in the kingdom of heaven." (Matthew 18:2–4)

Pitfalls of the flesh.

The following list reveals the requirements set up for Old Testament kings. I have chosen to include them here because they hold principles for our own spiritual growth and awareness.

1. ***Despise the flesh; beware of pride!*** Pride is an inherent part of the human condition; nothing within our control can protect us from it. The prophet Samuel revealed that Saul was the Lord's chosen leader who was to follow God's instruction in carrying out his role.

    First Samuel 9:2 describes Saul as "an impressive young man without equal among the Israelites."

    God promised Him that the power of the Holy Spirit would come upon him and help him (1 Samuel 10:6–7).

Our Heavenly Father does the same for us. He has chosen us. We didn't initiate the relationship process by choosing Him. He has specified an assignment for each of our lives. The Holy Spirit dwells in us to guide and empower us to carry out His divine plan. Our part is to discover that plan and then to follow it.

Saul needed to remember one important point to be successful: *that his authority came from the Lord*. His responsibilities included executing God's commands and leading the people by example. But like so many of us, Saul had an inflated sense of his own importance. He acted independently of God by breaking God's law and exercising priestly responsibilities that weren't rightly his.

Kingly requirements from God included:

1. The king was to be chosen from among the Israelites (he wasn't to be a foreigner).

2. The king was forbidden to acquire great numbers of horses for himself or to make the people return to Egypt to get more.

3. The king was commanded not to take many wives.

4. The king was forbidden to accumulate large amounts of silver and gold.

5. The king was to write his own personal copy of God's law, read it all the days of his life, and follow it carefully.

By all accounts Saul was disobedient to God's commands and prohibitions. Pride was his downfall.

Every good thing we have, every spiritual gift we receive to enable us to carry out the duties of our assignment, come from God.

We become prideful when we forget that it's God who enables us to perform. He alone is the giver of power, intellect, and ability.

2. ***Abandon self-sufficiency and independence.*** In the Old Testament, horses represented power and self-reliance. By not permitting Israel's kings to acquire great numbers of horses, God was putting a limit on the temptation for them to become self-reliant.

- David said, "Some trust in chariots, and some in horses; but we will remember the name of the Lord our God." (Psalm 20:7)

> "Woe to those who go down to Egypt for help, who rely on horses, who trust in the multitude of their chariots and in the great strength of their horsemen, but do not look to the Holy One of Israel, or seek help from the LORD. Yet he too is wise and can bring disaster; he does not take back his words. He will rise up against that wicked nation, against those who help evildoers. But the Egyptians are mere mortals and not God; their horses are flesh and not spirit. When the LORD stretches out his hand, those who help will stumble, those who are helped will fall; all will perish together." (Isaiah 31:1–3)

Egypt symbolized for God's people human methods, resources, and wisdom, as well as reliance on the flesh for prosperity. Why do we rely on our weak attempts at self-sufficiency? Because of pride!

3. ***Avoid self-indulgence.*** God requires us to rule over our passions—not our passions to rule us. David looked too long at Bathsheba bathing on the rooftop. She probably felt comfortable doing so because she thought all the men had gone to battle. But David had stayed behind in the palace; having more time on his hands than usual, he wandered out onto the palace balcony. That wasn't wrong in itself, but instead of turning away from temptation he lingered there, relishing the sight of an unsuspecting naked woman and thereby igniting lust for another man's wife. Losing control over his desires set in motion a series of sins that increasingly, incrementally estranged him from God. Where once he had been intimate with the Lord, he became alienated. His sins not only caused him to lie, but cost Uriah, Bathsheba's husband, his life. His sin also cost the life of the baby conceived in the adulterous affair.

David's son through Bathsheba, Solomon, serves as a tragic example of another king who arrogantly ignored this command from God. Instead of just having numerous wives like his father David, Solomon acquired a harem.

> "King Solomon, however, loved many foreign women besides Pharaoh's daughter—Moabites, Ammonites, Edomites, Sidonians and Hittites. They were from nations about which the LORD had told the Israelites, 'You must not intermarry with them, because they will surely turn your hearts after their gods.' Nevertheless, Solomon held fast to them in love. He

had seven hundred wives of royal birth and three hundred concubines, and his wives led him astray. As Solomon grew old, his wives turned his heart after other gods, and his heart was not fully devoted to the LORD his God, as the heart of David his father had been." (1 Kings 11:1–4)

This was willful disobedience, for Solomon wasn't ignorant of God's commands. In fact, he was intimately acquainted with the Lord, who had appeared to him at least twice. His flagrant disobedience brought irreparable loss and suffering upon his family and upon the nation he ruled.

How many of God's servants have been destroyed by self-indulgence and sexual immorality? Many lack the self-control to manage their appetites, instead allowing those appetites to manage them. They have neither mastered restraint nor learned to delay gratification. Self-indulgence is the mark of an immature babe, not a trademark of maturity.

A self-indulgent, sexually immoral society is ripe for a fall. God is protecting us when He calls us to control our appetites.

- "Put to death, therefore, whatever belongs to your earthly nature: sexual immorality, impurity, lust, evil desires and greed, which is idolatry." (Colossians 3:5)

4. ***Avoid the love of money.*** The fourth area over which God required self-restraint on the part of the king involved his personal finances. God didn't want the king to continually acquire more wealth. God's Word warns us not about money, but about the *love of* money.

> "People who want to get rich fall into temptation and a trap and into many foolish and harmful desires that plunge men into ruin and destruction. For the ***love of money*** is a root of all kinds of evil. Some people, eager for money, have wandered from the faith and pierced themselves with many griefs." (1 Timothy 6:9–10)

If we're determined to get wealth in any way, and if we make it our "god," it will lead to our ruin. There's blessing and honor, on the other hand, when we choose God's way, which often requires great patience. Impatience signifies our refusal to wait upon the Lord, His timing, or His ways.

5. ***Know God's Word and adhere to His commands.*** This is the fail-proof secret to reigning in life. God required for a reason that Israel's king thoroughly acquaint himself with God's law and hold fast to its commands.

> "It is to be with him, and he is to read it all the days of his life so that he may learn to revere the LORD his God and follow carefully all the words of this law and these decrees and not

consider himself better than his brothers and turn from the law to the right or to the left. Then he and his descendants will reign a long time over his kingdom in Israel." (Deuteronomy 17:19–20)

Leaders who see no value in God's Word, nor heed its teachings, soon become easy targets for sin. They quickly excuse their behavior and rationalize away their shortcomings for their hearts are cold and hard. It wasn't long before Saul thought nothing of taking many wives, of buying great amounts of silver and gold, or of neglecting to spend time in God's Word.

Determine to give God the time He desires. He'll make your paths straight and your way prosperous. We can be blessed financially and reign as kings when we decide there's value in God's instructions.

Consider what your "work" is producing for you.

Anyone can work in the Church. Even well-meaning religious folks who haven't accepted Christ personally as their Savior do so. But work based on a love response to Christ's overwhelming love for us, is different in nature. When our heart is filled to overflowing with the love of God and the transformation process that happens as a result, it's hard not to do for others.

The spiritually mature Christian is able to function contentedly in any circumstance. Reacting negatively to every situation that comes our way, means fighting battles the Lord has not given us to fight.

Acting first, inquiring of the Lord later, will create problems for us, as it so often did for Peter. Sulking, blaming others and God, losing heart, running away, indulging in self-pity, being self-indulgent, responding with motives of anger, malice, revenge, or throwing tantrums, all thwart our progress in sanctification.

Signs of an underdeveloped, immature Christian.

All difficulties, whether personal, relational, physical, or financial can be reversed when we acknowledge that God is the source of all good things. Satan's most effective scheme is trying to convince us that God is our problem. A ***spirit of offense*** is one sign of spiritual immaturity.

> "Brothers and sisters, I could not address you as people who live by the Spirit but as people who are still worldly—mere infants in Christ." (1 Corinthians 3:1)

The apostle Paul was addressing the Corinthian church, a church that had been enriched with much knowledge and many spiritual gifts. Yet in spite of these many blessings and graces, its members remained babes in Christ. They couldn't digest the deeper matters of faith or understand the profound mysteries or higher truths of the gospel. Why couldn't they digest the "meat" of the Word?

Frequently such people choose to remain infants in Christ not bothering to explore the simplest doctrines of Christianity, let alone the weightier matters involved with holiness and sanctified living. This is evidenced by their lack of discernment when they adhere to the teachings of false teachers who offer them a license to sin.

The Bible tells us that many will fall away in the end times. Sadly, we see denominations that are wholesale casualties of a refusal to hold to the truths upon which they were founded, leading multitudes away from saving grace through faith in Christ.

Signs of spiritual immaturity in the church.

Too often we hear of spiritual leaders who must step down because of marital unfaithfulness or ethical, moral, and/or financial failings. Why? They lack the character to fulfill their calling.

Without the necessary discernment and spiritual maturity, we may accept the negative influence of underdeveloped and carnal spiritual leaders. Those in the church will call the underdeveloped into leadership when they value natural abilities, and even spiritual gifts above godly character. The Church has grown worldly, and worldly people naturally gravitate toward secular methods for growing the Church. When godly character isn't our first priority, we end up choosing leaders with appalling character and morals.

> "For a time is coming when people will no longer listen to right teaching. They will follow their own desires and will look for teachers who will tell them whatever they want to hear. They will reject the truth and follow strange myths." (2 Timothy 4:3–4, NLT)

Many of God's chosen leaders lacked suitable character at the time He chose them. God often revealed to them in their youth the plans He had for their lives. But He didn't put them in their places of authority until many years later. Why? Because there was progress to be made before they could be completely usable.

God had to take *out* of them the obstacles that would hinder them from fulfilling their calling, and He had to instill *into* them the traits that define godly character. Often this comes through hardships and trials. These "testings" are meant to reveal to us problems in our character that may be hidden even from ourselves. We frequently fail to perceive our deficiencies until it's too late—until we're already deeply in trouble.

Even when we're aware of having less than godly character we frequently chose to push through, even ahead of God's *perfect* timing. We fall because we become impatient with God's *conforming process*. We think we know better. But what we may not see is that we're full of pride. Only God-built humility keeps us in the position God has for us.

God knows when we're ready. His timing is always flawless. Until the world is taken out of us, we'll continue to have an appetite for it. As long as we desire it, we'll remain spiritually immature and susceptible to all kinds of deception. Signs of immaturity always include a weak character and a lack of wisdom, as well as a tendency to be easily misled and an inability or unwillingness to distinguish right from wrong.

We must allow God to build our character. The word *die*—as in minting—carries the idea of image, coinage, copy, or likeness. God is always scrupulous about whom He chooses. He looks for men and women willing to *die* to self. This means we willingly submit to Christ's "minting" process…to put pressure on us so we'll bear His image. When He's finished, we gleam, as a new coin is polished and bears the image intended by its designer.

This is beauty of character to God. God isn't looking for charisma or talent as people do. He's concerned with the essence of a person. A rebellious individual won't submit to God's conforming process. The result: they can't be used for kingdom purposes.

Character flaws are what trip most people up, not lack of ability or talent, as some believe. An immature or weak character will keep us from enjoying quality relationships, a strong marriage, or the ability to significantly impact the next generation.

When it comes to our spiritual leaders, we're to look for men and women whose sole focus is feeding the flock and making disciples, not just growing a large church. Too much attention on an abundance of programs, even well-intentioned outreach programs, is no substitute for solid meat. We in the Church have become accustomed to being entertained and consuming diet-food messages. We've taken out the bulk, the heart of the message of the cross to appeal to the masses.

Junk-food Christianity leaves us sick and anemic. Instead of growing in our faith and knowledge of Christ, we're settled for *Christianity Light*. This is the reason so many Christians are weak— weak in their relationships, finances, ethics, morality, and certainly in their faith, soul, and spirit. They often know little of healing, spiritual authority, or putting Satan under their feet.

Why does nourishing, substantive food, rather than the microwave diet plate always taste better? Because the fat holds the flavor, it satisfies. It keeps us from continuous hunger. Foods touted as "no-fat" have little flavor or ability to satisfy.

God's Word is the real deal. It's food that satisfies completely. It holds the substance and sustenance we need for life. It fills us and satiates our spirit. It was given to be consumed. We must chew on it long enough to be *nourished* by it. When we do, we revive. We have hope and confidence. We understand why we were created and for what purpose. We understand why Jesus died for us—to have us as His own.

Putting away childish things.

What prevents generations from growing up? During the sixties and seventies, the generation we know as baby boomers, saw a great resurgence of spiritual awakening. They witnessed a great harvest of souls as God moved powerfully. Thousands of churches came into existence to accommodate new converts, and thousands more experienced dramatic changes as churches became less a place to meet on Sundays and more dynamic gatherings for genuine worship. The exercise of spiritual gifts to include healing and prophecy increased, as well as the revival of prayer.

But spiritual maturity was not the mark of this generation. The Church didn't rise to become the powerful instrument the Lord requires to transform nations. Many of these converts never matured into adulthood and remained stunted because of their own choice to remain selfish, immoral, and worldly.

This carnality brought spiritual imbalance. Individuals lacked direction and purpose. America hadn't experienced war in its homeland in decades. We didn't understand extreme poverty or hunger. Discipline at home was often slack or nonexistent, making for a self-indulgent generation intent on living the "good life."

The Church is now filled with believers who began in the faith, who professed knowing the saving knowledge of Christ, but ceased growing in Christ likeness.

Many believers ignored or avoided the command *to go into all the world and make disciples*—to the point that many failed to teach their own children well. Members of this generation who fit this pattern represent some of the Church's present leaders, as well as the parents of America's younger pastors.

What does spiritual immaturity produce? Spiritually stunted churches! This self-perpetuating pattern will continue until a generation feels the compulsion to move beyond spiritual infancy. [2]

We're indeed living in perilous times. Christ's church must be mature and equipped to overcome this evil world. Until we seek God's face and cry out for the direction and passion He alone gives, we'll remain underdeveloped and ineffective.

God gives His Holy Spirit to believers to equip them for this work. He's looking for particular believers, those who are serious about making disciples and carrying His Word to the ends of this earth. Spiritual maturity marks the believer who can handle rightly the responsibility God places on them for service to others.

Think what an incredible gift our life represents. Surely one we don't want to waste. Unless we learn to value God's Word as instruction from which to profit, we'll end up spending it on empty things with no lasting value.

In an increasingly shallow world, it becomes more and more difficult to make sound, responsible, and mature decisions. We're tempted to follow the familiar gods of success, materialism, fame, or title. We follow them when we fail to reach maturity, and we won't see maturity until it becomes the all-consuming goal for our life. Just wanting it doesn't make it happen. Pouring ourselves into the Word and praying rightly, transform us. This is what God looks for in those He calls.

Signs of spiritual immaturity as outlined in the Word of God.

1. ***Spiritual babes can't chew meat.*** Such Christians aren't sufficiently advanced in the teachings of the Word of God. They're still majoring on the simplest biblical truths. Those who refuse to spend time with God with the intent of deeply knowing Him will see Him as one-dimensional, perhaps as a God of love but not of judgment. God is infinitely complex and creative. It stands to reason that He is at least as complex as the world He created?

> "I gave you milk, not solid food, for you were not yet ready for it. Indeed, you are still not ready." (1 Corinthians 3:2)

2. *They have not forsaken the foolish.* Proverbs is full of warnings by Solomon and others about keeping bad company. When we refuse to walk away from those who would take us down with them, we're choosing to disobey God. Presuming to know best, we believe we can maintain these relationships and still cling to our relationship with the Lord. Yet God's Word tells us that we'll eventually conform to the darkness around us. Uncertainty, anxiety, torment, and anguish are all signs of a disobedient spiritual life. Darkness produces unfruitful works, and unfruitful people live for pleasure. They have no goals, no gentleness, and certainly no love or joy. What they set their heart on doing, they do. They are…

> "…blown here and there by every wind of teaching and by the cunning and craftiness of people in their deceitful scheming." (Ephesians 4:14, NIV)

> "Leave your simple ways and you will live; walk in the way of insight." (Proverbs 9:6)

Because they have not settled the course for their lives, such believers bounce around from one place to another, seemingly unable to find a toehold in their Christian life. Not motivated to search the Scriptures for themselves, they are continuously looking for a "word" from someone else who may appear spiritual.

3. *They're carnal.* It's easy to lose sight of the fact that God's original intent was to keep people safe from harm. Carnal man believes instead, that God wants to keep him from having fun. Most adherents to this view obviously believe that sin is fun, which indeed at first it may be. But it isn't long before the realization comes that Satan has placed a hook in our jaw and that he's yanking hard on it. That hook is what addiction, pain, darkness, and loss are all about. Satan doesn't have any fun to offer. Quite the contrary, he has only pain and death in mind. The moment we try to elude his influence, he yanks hard on that hook. God knew what He was protecting man from. But man, with his limited knowledge, didn't understand that the desire to go his own way would result in his demise. God chooses not to tell us everything up front. We don't have the ability to handle the whole truth. But He tells us everything we need to know. We owe it to Him to trust His intentions to give us what's best. Obeying Him keeps us from harm. Disobedience opens us up to all sorts of evil.

Significant spiritual "disqualifications" for the believer.

(As listed in Leviticus 21)

Jesus was sent to redeem us from the curse, the law. The Old Testament contains the law which we're no longer under. But the Old Testament is full of illustrations of spiritual principles, and God frequently uses Old Testament types and symbols to convey spiritual truth to His Church today. Although these disqualifications pertained to the priesthood, we're priests by virtue of our relationship with Christ and can learn from the "whole" of God's Word.

Like Aarons sons, we can be excluded from higher, honored ministries for the Lord by not taking seriously His requirements. Although we operate under the new covenant, the old one is for our admonishment and it's written for us to learn from. The new covenant, therefore, has two basic characteristics:

First, it describes an internal spiritual transformation resulting in a new relationship with God and a new possibility of obedience.

Second, the new covenant results in the forgiveness of sins for those in covenant with the Father, Jesus, and the Holy Spirit. Note that the Holy Spirit is given to us to enhance our ability to remain faithful, pure, and holy. When we walk closely with Him, He enables us to walk away from the wickedness that would disqualify us for continued service.

Disqualifications:

1. ***Lack of revelation/spiritual blindness.*** In this context the Bible was talking about physical blindness; one couldn't perform certain priestly duties without sight. The Bible often speaks about spiritual blindness. Our priestly calling requires that we have a clear understanding of spiritual matters. One reason for Jesus' anointing was to restore sight to the blind, both physically

and spiritually. How desperately we need the Lord to open our eyes, minds, and hearts that we might see Him afresh and understand the Scriptures more fully.

> Jesus said, "For judgment I came into this world, that those who do not see may see, and those who see may become blind." (John 9:39, ESV)

> "But blessed are your eyes, for they see, and your ears, for they hear." (Matthew 13:16, ESV)

2. ***Lack of consistency/lameness.*** In Moses' day, someone who was lame couldn't qualify for the priesthood. Why is this significant today? The word lame means to hop, hesitate, or limp. This implies that someone who is inconsistent and whose spiritual life tends to ebb and flow might be swayed by circumstances or feelings. We're to walk as Jesus walked, steadfastly and uprightly.

3. ***Lack of discrimination/disfigured face.*** A disfigurement, such as a broken nose, could disqualify a son of Aaron from the priesthood. Even before the eyes detect a certain problem, the nose can discern that something is wrong. Since one of the functions of the priest was to discern between the clean and the unclean, he needed a keen sense of smell. We're in greater need of discernment today than ever before. The Bible tells us to examine everything carefully, to hold fast to the good and to

judge all things. Jesus clearly taught that in the last days, deception will be one of the major problems Christians face.

> "For false Christ's and false prophets will appear and perform great signs and miracles to deceive even the elect—if that were possible." (Matthew 24:24)

Only by calling upon the Lord for discernment can we be saved from Satan and his deceiving tactics. Earnestly ask for the gift of "discerning of spirits," as well as for wisdom and understanding.

4. ***Lack of proportion/deformed limb.*** Many of us prefer sweets over vegetables. We gravitate toward what we like, not necessarily what we need. Many Christians suffer from "tangent" Christianity—an overemphasis on one aspect of truth to the detriment of others. When this happens we major on extremes and become unbalanced in our faith. We're to be complete in Christ. Are you balanced? Is your walk with Christ proportioned? Are you spiritually nourished and well adjusted?

> "Instead, speaking the truth in love, we will in all things grow up into him who is the Head, that is, Christ." (Ephesians 4:15)

> "You have been given fullness in Christ, who is the head over every power and authority." (Colossians 2:10)

5. ***Lack of dominion/broken foot.*** Throughout Scripture dominion is symbolized by the foot. In Genesis God instructed man to "subdue," literally "to tread down." Jesus told His disciples that He was giving them the authority to subdue the enemy.

> "I have given you authority to trample on snakes and scorpions and to overcome all the power of the enemy; nothing will harm you." (Luke 10:19)

Believers are failing to take their rightful places in the kingdom. We must "accept" and "take back" our authority, learn how to overcome the evil one and seize our victory! Defeat and discouragement bring unnecessary suffering. We wrongly believe that God is sending this suffering to teach us lessons, but the culprit may be ignorance of our dominion over all things.

We must comprehend that authority has already been given to us by Christ (past tense), that it's only through Him that we overcome. If we fail to appreciate that we already have something to which He has entitled us by His death, it sadly remains for many a rusted, unloaded weapon.

6. ***Lack of impartation/broken hand.*** Those with a broken hand would have been unable to minister to others; rather, they needed to be ministered to. The laying on of hands, called "impartation," occurs throughout the Bible. Jesus often laid hands on people for healing or blessing, as in the case of little children. Laying on of

hands was also for those set apart by the Holy Spirit for ministry. God has called us to be imparters of life through ministering to others.

7. ***Lack of liberation/hunchback.*** I remember a time, when my husband and I were stationed in Korea, when I saw an old woman out in the field who was so bent over that she couldn't look up. In a similar way, spiritual "hunchbacks" are destined to focus on their feet, unable to lift their gaze toward heaven. In the memorable words of a hymn, Jesus longs for us to turn our "eyes upon Jesus, look full in His wonderful face." If we're prevented from doing so, we continually focus on our own faults, failures, and insecurities. We are forever looking downward and inward, not upward and outward at Jesus, and those around us He calls us to serve.

> "When Jesus saw her, he called her forward and said to her, 'Woman, you are set free from your infirmity.' Then he put his hands on her, and immediately she straightened up and praised God." (Luke 13:12–13)

8. ***Lack of maturation/spiritual dwarfism.*** The dwarf in this context symbolically represents someone who has never grown up or reached his/her full potential in Christ. Not reaching full stature, the person remains a spiritual babe. Paul told the Corinthians that they were immature, that he had to feed them milk, not meat. The writer to the Hebrews reminds the immature

that although they've had time to grow up and should already be teachers, they were still in need of being taught the basics.

The Christian life is meant to be progressive. The intent is to move from one faith milestone to another, from faith to faith and from victory to victory. Determine to press on to maturity. Nourish your faith and spirit on God's Word every day. Begin a new discipline by spending 15 minutes or more of each day learning God's Word. Ask the Holy Spirit for understanding, as understanding ignites appreciation, interest, and eventually passion. Be sure to walk in obedience when you learn and understand new truth.

9. ***Lack of clarification/defective eyes.*** Imperfect eyesight represents the believer who lacks unclouded vision or a clear sense of direction. The reference isn't to a sightless person (see #1) but to one who is unable to focus properly.

Many are nearsighted, with limited long-range vision. A shortsighted person is taken up with everyday life, bogged down by the cares of this world. They see no future, because they fail to see God. Others are farsighted, unable to see things close up. Their faith may have an otherworldly, impractical, intangible focus.

"…fixing our eyes on Jesus, the pioneer and perfecter of faith. For the joy set before him he endured the cross, scorning its shame, and sat down at the right hand of the throne of God." (Hebrews 12:2)

"Your word is a lamp for my feet, a light on my path." (Psalm 119:105)

10. ***Lack of purification/eczema, scabs.*** Skin conditions are often contagious. Sin can be "infectious" too. It was the requirement In Old Testament Israel for spiritual leaders to be holy, without blemish, set apart. In a similar way our leaders today are to be above reproach. Upon His return, Christ will be looking for a Church that is without spot, wrinkle, or any such defect.

"They must be holy to their God and must not profane the name of their God. Because they present the offerings made to the LORD by fire, the food of their God, they are to be holy." (Leviticus 21:6)

11. ***Lack of reproduction capability/crushed stones.*** In Old Testament times, barrenness, the inability to produce offspring, bore a terrible stigma, producing shame and guilt. (Note that the reference to crushed stones is interpreted variously in different commentaries. Some suggest that it signifies either no or only one testicle; others that the testicles have been in some way damaged; still others that the reference is to a hernia or rupture.) God desires that His children reproduce themselves by leading others to Christ and by reflecting the Christ who is in that sense

"reproduced" in them. If we don't willingly and joyfully share with others the "good news" that brings healing, salvation, and freedom, our refusal signifies a lack of love. God commands us to love because He first loved us; love demands to be reproduced by being given away.[3]

Reconsider what the covenant of grace teaches us.

Malachi 2:1–17 contains by extension warnings for us regarding our own priesthood as believers. The prophet reproved the priests of his day for neglecting their covenant with God.

The Bible is written in types and shadows. What was true of the covenant of the priesthood, is equally true of the covenant of grace made with all true Christians today.

God *chooses us* for service, a sacred calling we're to consider an honor. Just as the lips of the old covenant priest were not to keep knowledge from the people, neither may ours. We're to read God's Word and seek from the Holy Spirit the gift of understanding so we can minister sound doctrine that converts the lost and dying. Departing from God's holy living to which He calls us, will result in leading others astray.

Those who walk with God are called to do so in peace and righteousness; to turn from their sin and honor God with their lives. God will honor us only when we honor His name in the presence of others. We're never to hold in high esteem those who despise the God we love.

We were "born" of the resurrection.

We're called to be reborn, to start over as new creations in Christ. As we learn to surrender our will to the work of the Holy Spirit, who in turn goes to work renewing our mind, we gradually become transformed and spiritually mature. Those who knew us before no longer *recognize* us. We've gained a Father—a heavenly Father—and with it a whole new forever family, inheritance, eternal destination, and identity.

Who's in charge?

God's purpose for humanity was to reconcile us to Himself for His own reasons, benefit, and glory. Because time is irrelevant to an eternal God (time and space are both temporary concessions He has made for us), both Father and Son will always be greater than the other sons and daughters born into the family of God.

1. Jesus sits at the right hand of God (Hebrews 8:1)

2. As the "King of kings" (Revelation 19:16)

3. And our eternal high priest (Hebrews 6:20).

The true Christian yields her life to Christ, understanding fully her place in the whole of creation. David expresses in awe and wonder to God, "What is man that you are mindful of him?" Yet, incredibly, God is more than mindful. He takes great delight in you.

> "The Lord your God is with you, the Mighty Warrior who saves. ***He will take great delight in you***; in his love he will no longer rebuke you, but will rejoice over you with singing." (Zephaniah 3:17)

You can be on your way to an amazing new life in Christ, ready to receive and appropriate all His richest blessings and favor.

Day by day, as you learn to walk with God in total surrender, you'll become increasingly like Him. This is what spiritual maturity looks like.

6

SHE UNDERSTANDS TRUTH

"Lead me in your truth and teach me, for you are the God of my salvation;

for you I wait all the day long." (Psalm 25:5)

Will Rogers once said, "Everybody is ignorant, only on different subjects." If this is true we must ask ourselves, "On what subject might I be ignorant?"

No matter what the subject matter, nothing is more important than knowing the truth especially about something that affects us not only today but through eternity. Consequently, the ability to distinguish truth from falsehood is a matter of life and death for us.

Knowledge isn't the same as wisdom, for it takes wisdom to discern truth when we hear it. For that reason, the Bible has much to say about truth, wisdom, and deception.

The Bible speaks of gaining wisdom, but people typically prefer to gain knowledge. People desire to be brilliantly educated, but God's Word says He gives wisdom even to the simple. It's clear that man's ways are not God's way.

> "If any of you lacks wisdom, he should ask God, who gives generously to all without finding fault, and it will be given to him." (James 1:5)

> "The law of the LORD is perfect, reviving the soul. The statutes of the LORD are trustworthy, making wise the simple." (Psalm 19:7)

What is truth? Do any of us really know it?

Ignorance comes in many forms: a lack of knowledge or education, unawareness, or the refusal to accept instruction. Ignorance is most often a matter of choice. Some are ignorant because they may lack opportunity or ability.

Yet some choose to remain "willingly ignorant," and are happy to keep it that way.

The prophet, Hosea, warns of the consequence of *deliberate* ignorance, which constitutes **rebellion**.

> "My people are destroyed from lack of knowledge. "Because you have rejected knowledge, I also reject you as my priests; because you have ignored the law of your God, I also will ignore your children." (Hosea 4:6)

The ***rejection of truth***, not unintentional ignorance, always has serious consequences. God never rejects us because of our lack of knowledge. The real danger for us is failing to recognize, assimilate, or internalize God's truth when we hear it.

Have we rejected God's wisdom?

The Old Testament Israelites didn't want to hear the truth. Some things don't change. When people reject God's truth to pursue their own limited, worldly knowledge, there's always danger.

America is going through a time of testing. Could this be the result of rejecting God's clear direction in favor of our own *truth*? God's Word calls that foolishness. Have we forgotten God, who has tremendously blessed America? Do we trust more in ourselves and in our wealth as a nation than we do in God? Have His many blessings caused us to become self-indulgent and complacent?

Because you have rejected knowledge . . .

We're all spiritually ignorant until we come to know the Lord personally. Conscious rejection of God's truth comes in many forms. When all our sources for information are secular, we're inclined to accept, or at least become accustomed to, a distorted world view.

Christians are called to be "set apart." The world will never have a God-centered view of decency and principled living because the world is at enmity with God. When we think and act like those around us, we're rejecting God's wisdom and His ways.

Multitudes are being deceived today.

If we're indeed living in the last days, truth has never been more important. In a spiritually "dumbed downed" world, Christians now more than ever before need to understand God's clear truth. Deception is actually our most dangerous adversary.

> Jesus declared, "Watch out that no one deceives you." (Matthew 24:4)

> "Watch out that you are not deceived. For many will come in my name, claiming, 'I am he,' and, 'The time is near.' Do not follow them." (Luke 21:8)

Many professing Christians have become incredibly ignorant of the realities of the Christian faith. They may attend church, engage in Bible study or fellowship with other Christians, yet remain ignorant of spiritual truth. They may know little about spiritual warfare and be unaware that a battle is raging. The only answer is to be constantly on guard. This can't be overstated.

The lies of Satan and his demons surround us in many forms. Witchcraft is everywhere. Never have so many scoffed at the Bible; relevant truth; or the concepts of hell, judgment, and Christ's certain return. And never have people been so tormented. Satan continually accuses believers to keep them in shame and bondage, never fully experiencing the liberation that's rightfully theirs.

The book of Revelation gives us an account of Satan, the accuser of Christ's followers.

> "The great dragon was hurled down—that ancient serpent called the devil, or Satan, who leads the whole world astray. He was hurled to the earth, and his angels with him. Then I heard a loud voice in heaven say: 'Now have come the salvation and the power and the kingdom of our God, and the authority of his Messiah. For the accuser of our brothers and sisters, who

accuses them before our God day and night, has been hurled down.'" (Revelation 12:9–10)

Truth in parables.

The disciples didn't like Jesus using parables, for neither they nor the multitudes could grasp their underlying meaning. So, they came right out and asked Jesus why he resorted to this teaching method (see Matthew 13:10).

Jesus' response must have been mystifying. He used parables to confuse the people and keep them from understanding. He didn't want them to be converted.

> "He [Jesus] replied, 'Because the knowledge of the secrets of the kingdom of heaven has been given to you, but not to them. Whoever has will be given more, and they will have an abundance. Whoever does not have, even what they have will be taken from them. This is why I speak to them in parables: "Though seeing, they do not see; though hearing, they do not hear or understand. In them is fulfilled the prophecy of Isaiah: 'You will be ever hearing but never understanding; you will be ever seeing but never perceiving. For this people's heart has become calloused; they hardly hear with their ears, and they have closed their eyes. Otherwise they might see with their eyes, hear with their ears, understand with their hearts and turn, and I would heal them.'" (Matthew 13:11–15

Jesus used parables to keep the *hardhearted* from receiving the "good news." God never keeps His truth from those who want to know it and who will *with faith* reach out to Him. God knows who will accept Him, and it's those whose hearts are open to Him to whom He reveals more of Himself.

Did the disciples' concern cause Jesus to stop using parables? Not at all! Matthew tells us He used them exclusively from that point on.

> "Jesus spoke all these things to the crowd in parables; he did not say anything to them without using a parable." (Matthew 13:34)

Truth is a blessing to be greatly treasured.

People spend little time pondering the vastness of God's power, strength, intelligence, creativity, and capacity to love. Although we were created with intelligence and tremendous potential, that aptitude falls infinitely short of God's all-encompassing knowledge and wisdom.

Without truth, we're doomed. Our glorious Lord has concealed His truth from those who believe themselves to be wise by worldly standards. God considers such people foolish and ignorant.

> "Brothers and sisters, think of what you were when you were called. Not many of you were wise by human standards; not

many were influential; not many were of noble birth. But God chose the foolish things of the world to shame the wise; God chose the weak things of the world to shame the strong." (1 Corinthians 1:26–27)

"At that time Jesus said, 'I praise you, Father, Lord of heaven and earth, because you have hidden these things from the wise and learned, and revealed them to little children. Yes, Father, for this is what you were pleased to do. All things have been committed to me by my Father. No one knows the Son except the Father, and no one knows the Father except the Son and those to whom the Son chooses to reveal him.'" (Matthew 11:25–27)

God will reveal to us the truth contained in His Word if we will but ask Him (Psalm 119:1–16; 1 Corinthians 1:22–24).

After a certain point in his ministry, Jesus always spoke to the crowds in parables.

- "I will open my mouth in parables: That it might be fulfilled which was spoken by the prophet, saying, I will open my mouth in parables; I will utter things which have been kept secret from the foundation of the world." (Matthew 13:35, KJV)

Those who proudly believe they know God but aren't interested in learning about Him in truth, are arrogant.

Our present darkness.

The battle for truth is fought not only in the heart and home, but also in the workplace, the Church, and state. The Church, like the family, is always only one generation from extinction. We must guard the truth and pass it along to our children.

In the past, thousands of saints were martyred for their faith. They willingly suffered to the point of death so that we might receive the truth of God. Many fail to realize that this is still happening in many parts of our world today. Sadly, though, modern-day martyrs are glaringly absent in the West. We aren't accustomed to "contending for our faith" (the Greek word rendered "contend" is an athletic term meaning "*agonize*").

The period of the Dark Ages seems unrelated to us today. The tumult of the era, its religious conflict and debatable time period seems irrelevant. Yet, the irony is that our 21st-century world is in many ways no less dark. But it's a darkness that begins with individuals, only to expand as those who reject God come together to dominate politics, education, and society. Our age is characterized by seemingly endless intellectual and technological advances, but our morality is going in the opposite direction. Paul describes the characteristics of real darkness:

> "But mark this: There will be terrible times in the last days. People will be lovers of themselves, lovers of money, boastful, proud,

abusive, disobedient to their parents, ungrateful, unholy, without love, unforgiving, slanderous, without self-control, brutal, not lovers of the good, treacherous, rash, conceited, lovers of pleasure rather than lovers of God—having a form of godliness but denying its power. Have nothing to do with them." (2 Timothy 3:1–5)

It's crucial that we understand the difference between fact and opinion. While identifying the true from its counterfeit is often difficult, it isn't impossible.

1. ***Opinion*** is a belief not based on absolute certainty or positive knowledge, but on what *seems true,* valid, or probable in one's own mind.

2. ***Fact***, in contrast, is the state of something *that is*; it's the *reality*, the actuality, the truth.

Why people accept opinion as fact.

People often accept opinion as fact simply because they fail to examine their own thinking or that of other people, blindly accepting whatever they're told. When people want to persuade others, they rarely express that what they're saying is a personal belief or opinion, as opposed to a documented fact.

Granted, this issue is confusing, since what is accepted as truth can change based on newly discovered facts. As a result, what was once accepted as true becomes untrue.

Consider how and why "truth" may change.

Prior to the 15th century people believed that the earth was flat. Religious leaders, academicians, and the majority of early scientists stated it as fact, and stories based on the "reality" of a flat earth had been passed down from generation to generation.

Today we know differently. Truth changed when scientists demonstrated the round earth by studying the heavens. Adventurers like Columbus and Magellan proved that the earth is round by navigating its oceans.

Applying Scriptural truth.

When God's people know truth but refuse to apply it continually, they fall into doubt and disobedience.

Charles Spurgeon once stated that "the new views are not the old truth in a better dress, but deadly errors with which we can have no fellowship."

Error must be revealed. We must speak up against falsehoods with truth, but we must learn to do so in love.

Our weapons must be spiritual. We aren't fighting personal enemies but the enemies of the Lord. We must stand our ground for the sake of the faith. This stand may offend some, but the honor and glory of Jesus are at stake. Timothy reminded us to "fight the good fight of faith" (1 Timothy 6:12).

- "Your righteousness is an everlasting righteousness, and your law is truth." (Psalm 119:142)

"To the Jews who had believed him, Jesus said, "*If* you hold to my teaching, you are really my disciples. Then you will know the truth, and the truth will set you free." (John 8:31–32)

"Jesus said, I am the way, the truth, and the life. No one comes to the Father except through me.'" (John 14:1)

"This is He who came by water and blood—Jesus Christ; not only by water, but by water and blood. And it is the Spirit who bears witness, because the Spirit is truth." (1 John 5:6)

"However, when He, the Spirit of truth, has come, He will guide you into all truth; for He will not speak on His own authority, but whatever he hears He will speak; and He will tell you things to come." (John 16:13)

God delivered the Israelites from Egypt and led them to the Promised Land. Yet for all they witnessed of the good things of

God—deliverance, sustenance, protection, and guidance—they continued to lack the trust to stay faithful to Him.

Their lack of faith produced such fear in them, that they expressed a desire to return to Egypt, the land of their enslavement. They preferred familiar bondage to the prospect of stepping out in faith and believing God (Numbers 13–14).

Moses, Joshua, and Caleb encouraged this ungrateful and obstinate mass to obey God in faith, but they were met with stalwart refusal. This refusal constituted rebellion against their benevolent God who had chosen them to be His own people.

People have a chronic rebellion problem!

In direct defiance against God's divine rule, people want to be in charge. God is a Spirit, and since we can't see Him, we're prone to act as though He doesn't exist, or is uninvolved with His creation. We know from His Word that neither is true. Not surprisingly, God refused to tolerate such presumption in His people Israel. Consequently, everyone twenty years of age and older (with the two exceptions of the faithful Joshua and Caleb) was destined to die over the next forty years in the desert.

Although the whole Jewish nation had received deliverance from Egypt, not every individual possessed personal faith in the Lord. God corporately granted His chosen people freedom based on His grace and mercy. But with privilege came responsibility. God wouldn't treat the rebellion of His people lightly. Jude would later warn that if any of his readers dared follow false teachers, they too would face the discipline of the Lord (Jude 3-19).

"So, if you think you are standing firm, be careful that you don't fall!" (1 Corinthians 10:12)

The sin of Israel was rebellious unbelief—the same situation as today.

Unbelief, rebellion against authority, and sensuous indulgence were rampant in the Old Testament, just as they are now. Our generation, believed by many to be the last, will see an increase in false teaching (apostasy). Our world is growing increasingly dark. Perversion, and the appetite for it, continues to expand.

Both Peter and Jude knew that God's judgment of Sodom, Gomorrah, and their surrounding cities was an example to warn the ungodly. These cities engaged in ungodly behavior, specifically in sexually depravity. The occupants of these cities were engaged in ***excessive, habitual, chronic immorality*** and God's judgment was swift.

God will judge sin! Although He is indeed longsuffering and no longer deals with us as He did His Old Testament people, He will not ignore our bent toward sin

They gave themselves over to "strange" flesh.

The Bible uses Sodom and Gomorrah as an example to us of how God views this bent toward unnatural sexual sin. Homosexuality and bestiality are both treated scripturally as unnatural or relating to a "different flesh."

> "Therefore God gave them over in the sinful desires of their hearts to sexual impurity for the degrading of their bodies with one another. They exchanged the truth about God for a lie, and worshiped and served created things rather than the Creator—who is forever praised. Amen. Because of this, God gave them over to shameful lusts. Even their women exchanged natural sexual relations for unnatural ones. In the same way the men also abandoned natural relations with women and were inflamed with lust for one another. Men committed shameful acts with other men, and received in themselves the due penalty for their error. Furthermore, just as they did not think it worthwhile to retain the knowledge of God, so God gave them over to a depraved mind, so that they do what ought not to be done. They have become filled with every kind of wickedness, evil, greed and depravity." (Romans 1:24–28)

God gave the people of Sodom and Gomorrah over to what was already in their hearts to do. We're warned not to surrender to these desires or to the degrading of our bodies. God didn't fashion us to be dishonored. We're made in God's image, an assurance that there's nothing about us that doesn't bear His glory, honor, and excellence.

God is the only "perfect" designer. He's the One who fashioned people with their temperaments, desires, and abilities. He designed woman to complement man. God was absolutely deliberate in His intention for humans, male and female, to function together. Yet people choose to go their own way.

God intended for people to be free, not tormented. We're His crowning achievement, His "glory," exalted by Him because He loves us.

Satan, in contrast, wants to degrade us, to makes our lives miserable. He wants to take our very life from us . . . to steal, kill, and destroy us (John 10:10). When we willingly give ourselves over to such defilement, our hearts are appallingly hardened, to the point that our every inclination is to go against our Creator and His ways.

God gives everyone everywhere the opportunity to receive or reject His truth. His grace and mercy abound until we see that our own ways have deceived us.

- "They exchanged the truth of God for a lie, and worshiped and served created things rather than the Creator—who is forever praised. Amen." (Romans 1:25)

- "…by loving the LORD, your God, obeying his voice, and holding fast to him. For that will mean life for you, a long life for you to live on the land which the LORD swore to your ancestors, to Abraham, Isaac, and Jacob, to give to them." (Deuteronomy 30:20)

Ignorance is no excuse.

The power and deity of God are observable by all. The willful refusal to glorify God and be thankful toward Him has dire consequences. In the case of the Israelites, "their foolish hearts were darkened." Once our heart is darkened, we can no longer perceive the light God gives.

> "For the wrath of God is revealed from heaven against all ungodliness and unrighteousness of men, who suppress the truth in unrighteousness, because what may be known of God is manifest in them, for God has shown it to them. For since the creation of the world His invisible attributes are clearly seen, being understood by the things that are made, even His eternal power and Godhead, so that they are without excuse, because, although they knew God, they did not glorify Him as God, nor were thankful, but became futile in their thoughts, and their foolish hearts were darkened." (Romans 1:18–21)

At any time, the unbeliever can turn from her unbelief and ask God to reveal Himself to her. In response He'll shed His truth and light, and she will see that God is indeed real. At no time does God wish to keep Himself from anyone who desires to know Him. God has already disclosed Himself in two ways as part of His revealed will to us.

1. Through His *creation*.

2. Through the *conscience* He has implanted within us.

Israel was told that even in captivity her people could find God if they diligently sought Him.

- "But from there you will seek the LORD your God, and you will find Him if you seek Him with all your heart and with all your soul." (Deuteronomy 4:29)

- God has promised, "I love those who love me, and those who seek me diligently will find me." (Proverbs 8:17)

- Jesus said, "Ask and it will be given to you; seek, and you will find; knock, and it will be opened to you. For everyone who asks receives, and he who seeks finds, and to him who knocks it will be opened." (Matthew 7:7–8)

Satan wants to keep you defeated and from God's very best. He entices us to believe He's telling us the truth, that it's God who deliberately lies.

Believing that what is good, is actually bad, and vice versa is a sign of the end times in which Jesus warned. A heart that's been hardened by rebellion against God, has God's Spirit removed from them by their own invitation.

Hell is hell precisely because it's a place where God is not present. Anytime God is *not* with us, we're living a hellish existence.

King Saul experienced torment when God's Spirit left him.

- "Now the Spirit of the LORD had left Saul, and the LORD sent a tormenting spirit that filled him with depression and fear." (1 Samuel 16:14, NLT)

Ensuring that the Holy Spirit remains close to us requires our sincere desire to turn from our sin, toward God and His truth. Humility keeps our heart from becoming rebellious.

It's our responsibility to pursue truth.

Every Christian woman has within her a still, small voice—the voice of the Holy Spirit. He continually draws us back from the enemy. Our present world is noisy and distracting, and many don't perceive that He's there trying to get our attention.

Much of our unhappiness comes as a result of *continual rebellion* against what we know to be displeasing to God, yet we continue to do it. God has placed our conscience that we might instinctively know right from wrong. It's a gift from God and a source of wisdom for us.

The Holy Spirit's job is to convict—not to condemn.

The Holy Spirit brings gentle conviction *to turn us from our sin.* If you're feeling *conviction*, it's coming from God. *Condemnation*, on the other hand, comes from Satan. Satan would have you believe that you're a complete failure who can't possibly turn to God after all you've done. Don't believe it!

Jesus Himself encourages us to watch and pray. The enemy is busy, targeting every person with his sinister messages and suggestions. We can't afford to become indifferent or we'll accept false teaching and doctrine.

We must separate ourselves from those who deny Jesus and the fundamentals of what He taught. There's no need for us to segregate ourselves based on minor doctrinal differences. Instead, we must stand together as believers for God's truth. If we don't know what that truth is, we'll have no clear idea what to stand for or what to turn from.

- "I urge you, brothers and sisters, to watch out for those who cause divisions and put obstacles in your way that are contrary to the teaching you have learned. Keep away from them. For such people are not serving our Lord Christ, but their own appetites. By smooth talk and flattery they deceive the minds of naïve people. Everyone has heard about your obedience, so I rejoice because of you; but I want you to be wise about what is good, and innocent about what is evil. The God of peace will soon crush Satan under your feet. The grace of our Lord Jesus be with you." (Romans 16:17–20)

- "Do your best to present yourself to God as one approved, a worker who does not need to be ashamed and who correctly handles the word of truth." (2 Timothy 2:15)

- "And this is love: that we walk in obedience to his commands. As you have heard from the beginning, his command is that you walk in love. I say this because many deceivers, who do not acknowledge Jesus Christ as coming in the flesh, have gone out into the world. Any such person is the deceiver and the antichrist. Watch out that you do not lose what we have worked for, but that you may be rewarded fully. Anyone who runs ahead and does not continue in the teaching of Christ does not have God; whoever continues in the teaching has both the Father and the Son. If anyone comes to you and does not bring this teaching, do not take them into your house or welcome them. Anyone who welcomes them shares in their wicked work." (2 John 6–11)

Just as children need constant reinforcement and repetition to learn how to be safe, we need it too, especially in important spiritual matters.

Beware of "another gospel."

As many churches modify their beliefs about doctrine and relevant truth to appeal to a changing society, members no longer hear the truth of the gospel.

- "But I am afraid that just as Eve was deceived by the serpent's cunning, your minds may somehow be led astray from your sincere and pure devotion to Christ. For if someone comes to you and preaches a Jesus other than the Jesus we preached, or if you receive a different spirit from the Spirit you received, or a different gospel from the one you accepted, you put up with it easily enough." (2 Corinthians 11:3–4)

1. *Another Jesus*—The Greek *allos* "else" or "different" is the active word here. The name (Jesus) is the same, but the reference is not to the Jesus of the Bible, despite some surface similarities.

2. *Another (different) Spirit*—*Heteros* means the "other" of "two." One that's different in the sense of not being of the same nature, form, class, or kind.

3. *Another Gospel*—As above, *heteros* suggests "another," in this case in the sense of being of uncertain affinity, different, altered, or strange. The gospel isn't the same message Paul preached, but has a qualitative difference.

Alterations to the Christian message have been around since the earliest beginnings of the Church but seem today to be more rampant and outrageous. Paul warns,

- "I am astonished that you are so quickly deserting the one who called you to live in the grace of Christ and are turning to a different gospel—which is really no gospel at all. Evidently some people are throwing you into confusion and are trying to pervert the gospel of Christ. But even if we or an angel from heaven should preach a gospel other than the one we preached to you, let them be under God's curse! As we have already said, so now I say again: If anybody is preaching to you a gospel other than what you accepted, let them be under God's curse!" (Galatians 1:6–9)

The gospel is the only "good news" in a world gone bad, yet countless are being deceived into believing that "another gospel" is actually the enlightened truth.

We must never lose sight of the fact that God's Word holds ***all truth***. Churches that have left behind the preaching of God's Word in favor of pop-psychology and trendy topics are modern apostates. They're interested in rallies, seminars on popular topics, the arts, and culture—anything but, it would appear, the truth contained in God's Word.

"Now, brothers and sisters, I want to remind you of the gospel I preached to you, which you received and on which you have taken your stand. By this gospel you are saved, if you hold firmly to the word I preached to you. Otherwise, you have believed in vain. For what I received I passed on to you as of first importance: that Christ died for our sins according to the Scriptures, that he was buried, that he was raised on the third day according to the Scriptures." (1 Corinthians15:1–3)

The gospel proclaims three central truths.

1. Christ died for our sins.

2. He was buried (thereby proving His death).

3. He rose again (taking up the same body in which He had come to earth). It was Jesus' resurrection, not His crucifixion alone that ultimately conquered sin and death.

The four Gospel accounts constitute a record of Jesus and His finished work on the cross. The gospel which is the "good news" is a message of pure love. That love was manifested through Jesus' death and resurrection that made possible the removal of our sin. When we accept Jesus' finished work, we're restored to the Father.

If what's being preached focuses on anything other than Christ's triumph on our behalf, it isn't the pure gospel of Christ and can't lead to salvation.

> "And we have seen and testify that the Father has sent his Son to be the Savior of the world." (1 John 4:14)

> "For it is by grace you have been saved, through faith—and this is not from yourselves, it is the gift of God—not by works, so that no one can boast." (Ephesians 2:8–9)

We work *from* salvation (it's our starting point as Christians), not *toward* it. God makes us partners in His finished work by appointing us to preach the good news and to make disciples for Him.

No alternative or "other" gospel holds the power to transform darkness into light. You and I as Christian women must be absolutely sure we're building our lives on God's foundation of truth and salvation.

Reflections for the thinking woman.

Josh McDowell, author of *Evidence That Demands a Verdict*, stated that most evangelical Christian youth in the United States no longer believe in absolute truth:

> "In 1991, 52 percent of our born-again church kids said there is no absolute truth. In 1994, 62 percent said there is no absolute truth. In 1999, 78 percent of born-again church kids said there is no absolute truth. In 2002, 91 percent of church kids said there's no absolute truth."

Anugrah Kumar of the *Christian Post Contributor* commented on McDowell's words as follows:

"Atheists and skeptics now have equal access to our children as we have, which is why the number of Christian youths who believe in the fundamentals of Christianity is decreasing and sexual immorality is growing, apologist Josh McDowell said. 'What has changed everything?' asked the apologist from Campus Crusade for Christ International as he spoke on 'Unshakable Truth, Relevant Faith' at the Billy Graham Center in Asheville, N.C., Friday evening. His answer was, the Internet."

Before the internet and since the 1960s, a major contributor to this problem was the influence of secular education and media. This adverse effect on moral authority is also reflected in the beliefs and attitudes of those teens' parents.

Until recent years, Christians throughout history accepted the classic evangelical doctrine of the absolute authority of God's Word. The Bible is the Word of God and that as such it is *infallible* and *inerrant*. Jesus taught the authority and complete reliability of the Bible in everything it teaches.

Whether or not our generation accepts or rejects it, the Bible is still God's Word and is inerrant (without error) in every detail relevant to our salvation. Jesus affirmed the Bible's inspiration, inerrancy, and indestructibility, stating that the Scripture cannot be broken (John 10:35).

There are teachers in our day who foolishly play Jesus against the inspiration and infallibility of the Word of God. When people reject the unique, divine character of the Bible, they throw out its authority too. God stands behind His Word. But for the past half century many in the Church have bought wholesale into the world's system of beliefs.

Jesus is central to the biblical message. He perfectly fulfills the Law and the Prophets, which point to and are fulfilled in Him (Luke 24:25–27, 44–47). Jesus fulfilled the moral laws by His obedience and fulfilled prophecy by specific events in His life, centering on His once-for-all, atoning death on the cross.

Second Peter 1:21 tells us that the men whom the Holy Spirit chose to record the Scriptures were carried or borne along as they wrote, ensuring that they would produce (although in their own words) the truth God intended for them to record.

The word in the original text meaning "carried" or "borne along" was used of a ship being carried along by the wind (see Acts 27:15, 17). Metaphorically, the prophets raised their sails and the Holy Spirit filled them and carried their craft along in His intended direction.

These men wrote as men, yes, but as men inspired by the Holy Spirit. They relied on their individual literary styles, vocabularies, and personalities, but the Holy Spirit guided them, guaranteeing the accuracy of the original manuscripts. This has until recently been the unanimous view of the Church.

- "No prophecy ever came by the impulse of man, but men moved by the Holy Spirit spoke from God." (2 Peter 1:21)

John Calvin put it this way: "This is the principle that distinguishes our religion from all others, that we know that God has spoken to us and are fully convinced that the prophets did not speak of themselves but as organs of the Holy Spirit uttered only that which they had been commissioned from heaven to declare—all those who wish to profit from the Scriptures must first accept this as a settled principle, that the law and the prophets are not teachings handed on at pleasure of men or produced by men's minds as their source, but are dictated by the Holy Spirit. We owe to the Scriptures the same reverence as we owe to God, since it has its only source in Him and has nothing of human origin mixed with it." [1]

John Wesley concurred, proclaiming that "In all cases, the church is to be judged by the Scriptures, not the Scriptures by the church. The Bible is still the supreme authority for the Christians in all matters. It's not what we think Jesus would do or how we feel He would interpret the Scriptures, but, 'Thus says the Lord.'"

What we need to know about false teachers (apostates).

1. *The cause of their rebellion: They reject divine authority.* All authority comes from God. He is the originator and possessor of it. Authority in the home, the Church, the workplace, or the state, is authored by Him. Those who exercise authority are themselves under His authority whether or not they're willing to acknowledge this dependence.

2. *The rebellious are so because they believe Satan's lie.*

    - "You will be like God" (Genesis 3:5).

    As a result, their world is filled with futility and delusions. Having turned from God's truth, they feed upon false doctrine that inflates their egos and encourages their rebellion.

    - "In the very same way, on the strength of their dreams these ungodly people pollute their own bodies, reject authority and heap abuse on celestial beings." (Jude 8:10)

    - "Likewise also these filthy dreamers defile the flesh, despise dominion, and speak evil of dignities." (Jude 8:8–10)

    Animals, not people, were created to live by instinct. We were created to live by the Spirit of God.

3. ***The "course" of their rebellion—they defile the flesh.*** Living to satisfy beastly lusts is a consequence of rebellion and pride. When a person despises God's authority, they feel free to disobey God's laws and live as they please. But God will not be mocked. It's easy to forget, or to fail to acknowledge in the first place, that God attaches penalties to broken laws. There's no escaping these consequences.

4. ***Their tongues are used to express their rebellion against God.***

   - "…those who say, "By our tongues we will prevail; our own lips will defend us—who is lord over us?" (Psalm 12:4)

   The King James Version states that such people "speak evil," which means "blaspheme." Blasphemy involves much more than taking God's name in vain. We blaspheme God when we take His Word lightly or joke about it. We blaspheme Him when we deliberately defy His ability or intention to judge us.

   The mouths of blasphemers lay claim to heaven, and their tongues presume to take possession of the earth. They say,

   - "How would God know? Does the Most High know anything?" (Psalm 73:9–11)

5. ***The consequences of their rebellion: They destroy themselves.***

- "Yet these people slander whatever they do not understand, and the very things they do understand by instinct—as irrational animals do—will destroy them." (Jude 10)

- "When the sentence for a crime is not quickly carried out, people's hearts are filled with schemes to do wrong." (Ecclesiastes 8:11)

These people corrupt and defile themselves, bringing about their own destruction while all the while believing they're promoting themselves. Despising authority and speaking arrogantly against the authority God has established, is dangerous. Satan in his rebellion said, "I will be like the Most High" (see Isaiah 14:14). His bait to us is along the same line: "You will be like God" (Genesis 3:5). When we proclaim in our ignorance that we will be like God, we're falling in step with Satan.

The horror and consequence of sin... "Woe unto them!"

Jude 11 cites examples from the Old Testament to illustrate the enormity of three men's sins and the consequences they suffered for rebelling against God's authority.

Cain rebelled against God's way of salvation (Genesis 4; 1 John 3:11–12). God made it clear to Adam and Eve when He clothed them in animal skins that the way of forgiveness is through the shedding of blood (Genesis 3:21). This is the way of faith, not good works (Ephesians 2:8–10). But Cain rejected God's authority and His authorized way of doing things and decided to approach God's altar with the fruits of his own labor.

God rejected Cain's offering most likely not due to any defect in the offering itself, but because He was rejecting Cain, whose heart was not right before Him.

God isn't interested in the nature of our sacrifice as much as He is in the *disposition* of our heart and the *attitude* we hold toward Him and His requirements.

The "way of Cain" is the way of religion.

Religion is man-made, and as such, devoid of faith. People follow in Cain's way by trying to achieve righteousness based on their own character, merits, and ledger of good works. This way is the way of pride—of people establishing their own way and relying on their own righteousness. The individual following the "way of Cain" pridefully rejects the righteousness of God that comes to us by faith in Christ. (Romans 10:1–4, Philippians 3:3–12)

Three acts of rebellion; three sets of consequences.

1. *Cain* became a fugitive who tried to overcome his wretchedness by building a city and developing a civilization (see Genesis

4:9). He ended up with everything man could want—except God!

Satan came to deceive the whole world. Those who are worldly, to the last person, reject God's way of salvation. Many live the lives of fugitives, but they're fugitives by choice, having opted against accepting God's redemption plan. Left in their sin and alienated from God such men and women believe, as Satan prompts them, that they can become like god. When people choose the way of rebellion, they choose the consequences of living without God too. Man chooses to go his own way when he forgets that he's the *created* and not the Creator!

God is the only One who determines the way and the method for He alone is God.

2. ***Balaam*** rebelled against God and believed he could get away with it.

> The ***"way of Balaam"*** is that of merchandising one's gifts and ministry for the sole purpose of making money. It's using the spiritual to gain the material (1 Thessalonians 2:5–6; 1Timothy 6:3–21). False teachers are greedy for material gain and, like Balaam, will do just about anything for it.

The *"error of Balaam"* is to believe we can get away with this kind of rebellion. Balaam, a true prophet of God, prostituted his gifts and sought to destroy God's people.

The *"doctrine of Balaam"* (Revelation 2:14) is that you can violate your separated position and get away with it. God personally chose each one of us and requires us to live as a separated people. We aren't to defile ourselves as pagans do.

Balaam had thought this through and he told King Balak that the fastest way to destroy Israel would be to corrupt the nation by having the people defile themselves with the pagan nations around them. Balaam's suggestion was to turn "the grace of God" into lasciviousness by provoking lust (see Jude 4).

3. *Korah* is a prime example of blatant rebellion against authority. In Numbers 16, we find Korah and his followers resenting the leadership of Moses and daring God to do something about their insurgence. In speaking against Moses, they were speaking against the Lord who had given Moses his authority. This story serves as a warning to us today; how many of us don't fall into the trap of speaking ill against spiritual or governmental leaders (Titus 3:1–2)?

Apostates resort to deliberate hypocrisy (Jude 12–13, 16).

It's a serious responsibility to be a shepherd over God's flock. Our prime example of such is Jesus, the "good shepherd," who gave His life for the sheep. False shepherds use and abuse people to get what they want. Ironically, too often the people endure it. Paul marveled at this, remarking,

- "In fact, you even put up with anyone who enslaves you or exploits you or takes advantage of you or puts on airs or slaps you in the face." (2 Corinthians 11:20)

Such shepherds are selfish and arrogant. There's a great qualitative difference between a true shepherd and an imposter. The true shepherd cares for the flock, while in too many cases the imposter cares only for himself.

- "Son of man, prophesy against the shepherds of Israel; prophesy and say to them: 'This is what the Sovereign LORD says: Woe to you shepherds of Israel who only take care of yourselves! Should not shepherds take care of the flock?'" (Ezekiel 34:2)

We're called to be alert, to guard against stumbling, and to remember God's Word.

From the very beginning Satan has attacked, attempted to detract from, and insinuated against the Word of God: "Did God really say?" (Genesis 3:1). Once we begin to question God's Word and authority, we open ourselves up and become vulnerable to Satan's other tactics. Only the truth in God's Word can protect us from the enemy's deception.

It's possible that Eve, at the moment of temptation, forgot God and believed what the serpent said was true. One way or another, she desired the ability to be like God—knowing good and evil. Instead of immediately rebuking Satan, she *considered* what he said. At that moment her pride entered into the equation, being equal with God was indeed desirable to her.

On our own we'll never have all the information needed to make truly wise decisions. Some information is withheld from us because God knows we aren't yet equipped to handle it. While, it may be true that, as the saying goes, "A little information is a dangerous thing," too much information can be downright devastating.

God doesn't restrict us to hinder us, but to protect us. Satan consistently implies that God isn't a good God. To know otherwise requires a study on our part about the real nature and intent of God toward us.

- "Consult God's instruction and the testimony of warning. If anyone does not speak according to this word, they have no light of dawn." (Isaiah 8:20)

Remember who gave the Word.

Wherever there's the authentic, there's also a counterfeit. False apostles, teachers, and prophets will always be with us. We can ask the Holy Spirit to give us wisdom to discern these wolves in sheep's clothing. Being so equipped will help us avoid the deceptions they preach. Being a student of God's Word will help protect you from false teachers. When you hear new teaching, check it out by going to God's Word.

The last days will be filled with false teachings. It's also prophesied that in those days' mockers will deny the Word of God. Ask yourself whether a given teacher is walking after his or her own lusts. In many cases you'll be able to discern for yourself whether they're true or an apostate.

Discerning truth.

In distinguishing truth from falsehood, ask yourself why you believe something to be true. Is it simply because someone has told you so? We must examine what we accept as fact, by going through the following steps:

1. Consider the evidence provided in support of the alleged fact.

2. Ask yourself whether the evidence is credible or biased.

3. Ask whether the evidence is distorted, prejudicial, or based on personal perception.

4. Ask whether the statement was once considered true but has since been proven false.

We can learn to identify fact (truth) as opposed to opinion, when we take the time to examine the basis of our own beliefs. We must always be prepared to face the possibility that what we have always believed to be true—is in reality *opinion*.

Satan has already been conquered.

And it was Jesus who conquered him! No other religion deals with the sin issue or with Satan and his demons. Jesus' death and resurrection conquered Satan and his fallen angels *once for all*. Past tense.

Accepting Jesus always brings healing and restoration. Accepting Satan always brings deceit, torment, and death. Satan understands that his rule will one day end and he knows that the day is getting closer. Already defeated he vengefully desires that none be left for God to have as His own.

Why would God have allowed Satan temporary power on the earth? The answer may surprise you—because it serves His purposes.

The doctrine of demons.

Satan has been a liar and murderer from the beginning. The worship of "gods" is the worship of demons. Satan's organized kingdom afflicts and antagonizes the human race at every level of personal and social life. Demons aren't heavenly beings; they're associated with death and the underworld and are in reality unholy, banished, evil angels. Evil angels curse God just as Satan does.

Traits of those who accept and operate by the doctrine of demons.

Some common traits are:

They lie about God: They misrepresent and malign His person and character; make false accusations against Him; ridicule, libel, and blaspheme God

They lie about God's Word: They distort or deny what God has said, including promises to his people and His Word of prophecy.

They lie about God's people: The reference here is both to the nation of Israel (blood descendants of Abraham) and to the kingdom of Israel (descendants by adoption and thereby sons and daughters by promise).

We should not be surprised that one of the end-times signals we see today is the expression and manifestation of the "doctrines of demons." Satan's mocking words of deception and lies come at us like they came at Eve. He twists and makes obscure God's promises, warnings, and commandments. "Did God really say that?" "Can God be trusted?"

The troubling truth is that many, including some in the church, have fallen away and question the goodness of God. They have believed the serpent's doctrine of evil.

- "The Spirit clearly says that in later times some will abandon the faith and follow deceiving spirits and things taught by demons." (1Timothy 4:1, NIV).

Good angels in contrast, are holy and work to bring God all glory and honor. Praise is always on their lips.

False doctrines and doctrines of demons.

There are numerous religions and beliefs. Many call themselves Christian, but they are far from the basic doctrines of Christianity. Some pervert, twist, or dilute God's Word. They destroy access to truth by adding to grace.

- As Jesus said about the Pharisees of His day, "A little yeast works through the whole batch of dough." (Galatians 5:9)

Jesus was pointing out that just a little false doctrine in our church or in our personal belief system, will lead us far astray. We must ask God on a continuing basis for the wisdom to discern evil from good and error from truth.

- "Trust in the LORD with all your heart and lean not on your own understanding." (Proverb 3:5)

- "Above all, you must understand that no prophecy of Scripture came about by the prophet's own interpretation of things." (2 Peter 1:20)

- "…pay no attention to Jewish myths or to the merely human commands of those who reject the truth." (Titus 1:14)

- "The Spirit clearly says that in later times some will abandon the faith and follow deceiving spirits and things taught by demons. Such teachings come through hypocritical liars, whose consciences have been seared as with a hot iron." (1 Timothy 4:1–2)

Every doctrine of demons is a contradiction of God's Word by Satan. People are easily seduced when they're willing to depart from the faith prompted by their own lusts or fears. Paul describes the people who will be deceived by lies:

- "For the time will come when people will not put up with sound doctrine. Instead, to suit their own desires, they will gather around them a great number of teachers to say what their itching ears want to hear." (2 Timothy 4:3)

Paul defines this false doctrine as lies and hypocrisy. Then he describes teachers of such doctrines as having no conscience or of being incapable of having a guilty conscience.

- "For such people are false apostles, deceitful workers, masquerading as apostles of Christ. And no wonder, for Satan himself masquerades as an angel of light. It is not surprising, then, if his servants also masquerade as servants of righteousness. Their end will be what their actions deserve." (2 Corinthians 11:13–15)

These false teachers and prophets can, and do, pretend to be ministers of light or apostles of Christ, but they are in fact servants of hell. When these false teachers begin to lie about God, they lie by extension about His Word and His people.

It takes spiritual discernment and the love of truth to expose their lies. Jesus warned that these false prophets would come and that they would attempt to deceive the elect (Matthew 24:5, 11, 24; Revelation 13:14).

- "For this reason God sends them a powerful delusion so that they will believe the lie. Those who believe false doctrines have believed a lie." (2 Thessalonians 2:11)

- "Let no one deceive you with empty words, for because of such things God's wrath comes on those who are disobedient. Those who teach lies and false doctrine will receive God's wrath in full measure." (Ephesians 5:6)

To distinguish a lie, you must first be able to distinguish truth. If you can't or won't believe the truth, you'll believe the lie!

Those who love truth will search for it; those who don't won't (Acts 17:11a–12).

Jesus said that there would "arise in the last days many false prophets and false teachers" (Matthew 24:11). This is dealing with those who profess to be Christians but who are deceptive and manipulative within the true flock. This isn't speaking about cults, which clearly have nothing to do with true Christianity. The Bible says of such people that

- "They have a form of Godliness, but deny the power thereof." (2 Timothy 3:5)

LEARN HOW TO AVOID DECEPTION

There are common excuses we may make unknowingly that lead to our being deceived. The Bible warns that many things keep us preoccupied but they hold no real value. We must become aware of these pitfalls to avoid deception.

1. ***STOP making excuses.***

Adam blamed Eve, and Eve, in turn, blamed the serpent. But God had given them clear instructions. When God reveals His will to us we have no excuse for disobeying.

- Jesus said: "If I had not come and spoken to them, they would have no sin, but now they have no excuse for their sin." (John 15:22)

2. ***Preoccupation is no excuse.***

Many people who believe in God are so occupied with their daily activities that they neglect to serve Him.

- 'A certain man was preparing a great banquet and invited many guests. At the time of the banquet he sent his servant to tell those who had been invited, "Come, for everything is now ready."' But they all alike began to make excuses. The first said, "I have just bought a field, and I must go and see it. Please excuse me." Another said, "I have just bought five yoke of oxen, and I'm on my way to try them out. Please excuse me." Still another said, "I just got married, so I can't come." The servant came back and reported this to his master. Then the owner of the house became angry and ordered his servant, "Go out quickly into the streets and alleys of the town and bring in the poor, the crippled, the blind and the lame." "Sir," the servant said, "what you ordered has been done, but there is still room." Then the master told his servant, "Go out to the roads and country lanes and compel them to come in, so that my house will be full. I tell you, not one of those who were invited will get a taste of my banquet'" (Luke 14:16–24)

The man who hosted the great supper represents God.

The supper represents the spiritual blessings God has prepared for us. The people invited to the wedding banquet of the Son decline the invitation (Matthew 22:1–3). Here and elsewhere Jesus uses the same idea to warn people not to refuse His invitation to come to Him or to be found unprepared for the coming of the Bridegroom (Christ's second coming).

1. The kingdom of heaven is like a wedding banquet (verses 1–2).

2. The specially invited guests refuse to come, meaning that they *persistently* refuse (verse 3).

God gave advance invitations to the people of Israel through the Old Testament prophets and Scriptures. The kingdom of heaven is compared to a wedding banquet. The parable tells us that some will accept the call to come while others will have excuses. Those that make excuses don't perceive the honor in being asked to attend a very special banquet. What a privilege for each of us to be personally invited to the Lord's banquet.

The parable says the king was hosting a wedding banquet for his son. The presentation of the King's Son, the Messiah, as a bridegroom is not uncommon in the New Testament (see Matthew 9:15; 25:1; John 3:29; Ephesians 5:25–32; Revelation 21:2, 9).

When all was ready, He sent His Son to call His people to gather for the feast. But the religious leaders and scholars of Israel were so preoccupied with their worldly pursuits that they didn't value what was being offered. To such people Jesus said,

- "Truly I tell you, the tax collectors and the prostitutes are entering the kingdom of God ahead of you. For John came to you to show you the way of righteousness, and you did not believe him, but the tax collectors and the prostitutes did. And even after you saw this, you did not repent and believe him." (Matthew 21:31–32)

The three examples of excuses given all indicate:

1. Preoccupation.

2. Self-centeredness.

3. Indifference to the invitation.

It's interesting that different wording is used in the three examples given. In the first case the invitee, referring to his field, indicates that he "must go and see it." In his mind this was of utmost importance, even though it would prevent him from attending the great feast.

This instance represents people who give priority to their possessions. They're so preoccupied with them that they neglect to serve God. This reminds us of the parable of the "Sower."

> "The one who received the seed that fell among the thorns is the man who hears the word, but the worries of this life and the deceitfulness of wealth choke it, making it unfruitful." (Matthew 13:22)

The first man was a proud property owner, while the second, who expressed an urgent need to try out his newly purchased oxen, was a distracted businessman. He informs the messenger that he "must go." No ifs, ands, or buts. In fact, he's already en route. The activities of both of these men could have waited until the next day. Their own affairs were more important in their minds than the affairs of God.

- "But seek first the kingdom of God and His righteousness, and all these things shall be added to you." (Matthew 6:33)

While the first man declared "I must go" and the second "I am going," the third had the audacity to state unapologetically "I can't come!" It was simply out of the question; he had, after all, just been married himself. Once again, this thinly disguised excuse made clear that he simply devalued the invitation. This last individual represents people who let preoccupation with family or other personal considerations prevent them from serving God.

- Jesus warned, "Anyone who loves his father or mother more than me is not worthy of me; anyone who loves his son or daughter more than me is not worthy of me." (Matthew 10:37)

- But our Lord also promised that "everyone who has left houses or brothers or sisters or father or mother or children or fields for my sake will receive a hundred times as much and will inherit eternal life." (Matthew 19:29)

The master of the house was furious at these eleventh-hour excuses. What about today? Are we so preoccupied with worldly affairs that we too neglect to come to the Lord's feast? God will judge us for undervaluing the spiritual blessings and salvation He offers. The prior invitation was given to a select few, the people of Israel. Now the invitation is open for all. [1]

The king extends his gracious invitation again. He sends other messengers out to invite the same list of preferred guests. This is so characteristic of the way the Lord continues again and again to beckon people toward Himself.

What does the wedding banquet have to do with us?

The lesson closes with an explanation, "many are called but few chosen." The word "many" isn't intended to serve as a restricted number; it's used several times in Isaiah 53 to speak of those for whom Christ poured out His blood. The invitation has gone out to all who care to listen. But just as in the days of Noah and again in the times of Isaiah, some refused and others wanted to come, but refused to submit to the requirements of entrance. The result of such refusal: none of these will be present in the kingdom to come. Christ died and rose for all humanity, but only those who accept His gift by faith will be allowed into the Kingdom of God.

Those Jesus refers to as "chosen" are the ones who respond to the invitation and in the proper manner so they can be prepared for entry. Because the Bible refers to the recipients of grace as *chosen*, God isn't surprised by the acceptance by some and the rejection by many.

The *unbelief* of the expected guests depicted in this parable lies behind their *continual refusal*. By refusing the King's free offer of grace, they refuse a share in the banquet and in the world to come. This parable is speaking about an event that's still in the future. It's referring to a spiritual place to which all true believers will go.

The "marriage supper of the lamb" is an event in eternity, a celebration of all who will choose Christ as Savior and Lord. True believers will leave this earth and join Jesus at His second coming.

This climactic event will mark the beginning of a great and glorious future for true Christians as promised in Revelation.

Jesus told us about this when He said, "In my Father's house are many rooms (or mansions); if it were not so, I would have told you. I am going there to prepare a place for you. And if I go and prepare a place for you, I will come back and take you to be with me that you also may be where I am" (John 14:2–3). [2]

What awaits those who refuse to come?

- Jesus told the Jewish leaders who rejected Him, "I say to you that many will come from the east and the west, and will take their places at the feast with Abraham, Isaac and Jacob in the kingdom of heaven. But the subjects of the kingdom will be thrown outside, into the darkness, where there will be weeping and gnashing of teeth." (Matthew 8:11–12)

- "Therefore I say to you, the kingdom of God will be taken from you and given to a nation bearing the fruits of it." (Matthew 21:43)

No one need endure being cast aside. God has put into our spirit an insatiable need to be with Him. He is ever calling us. All we need do is answer in the affirmative and **BELIEVE!**

7

SHE KNOWS THE REVEALED WILL OF GOD FOR HER LIFE

"The secret things belong unto the Lord our God: but those things which are revealed belong unto us and to our children for ever, that we may do all the words of this law." (Deuteronomy 29:29)

How can I know God's will for my life? is a question most Christians eventually ask. God has an aim, a perfect plan and will for His people. His desire is for each person to know Christ intimately and to worship Him with all their mind, heart, and soul.

God's overriding will is to prosper His children. God is a generous and giving Father and He delights in seeing His children thrive. He wants us to enjoy the years He gives us and to use our days wisely and productively.

There are numerous benefits to having God as our Father, yet multitudes go through life oblivious to His blessings or how to appropriate them.

Succeeding at life is a matter of knowing God's method, a method spelled out for us in His Word. God showers us with favor and blessings when we choose to dig deeper to unearth His treasures.

The Bible, God's instruction manual to us, tells us what's important to Him. It tells us both what He delights in and what breaks His heart. It holds instructions for receiving blessings and avoiding curses. It tells us what to flee from and what to seek after.

What does God want from every person?

Scripture makes it abundantly clear that God wants us to know Him. He wants us to bring Him glory by the way we live and by how we relate to Him and others. His purpose is perhaps best summed up in these words of Jesus:

- "Love the Lord your God with all your heart and with all your soul and with all your mind, and love your neighbor as yourself." (Matthew 22:37–39; Mark 12:29–31)

Even those who don't directly accept Him as their Savior will flourish to a degree when they live their lives according to His written Word.

Multitudes are fascinated with end times. They want to know more about the Antichrist and the false prophet, but know, or want to know, next to nothing about the Word, or the God of the Word, which has already been revealed to us.

Jesus' words *"Repent, for the kingdom of heaven is near"* is a call to walk in the opposite direction (Matthew 4:17). The word *repent* simply means to "turn from." In the original Greek, *metanoeo* means to "change one's mind." This basic message from Jesus—a call to turn from our ways toward Him—is the "revealed" Word of God to us.

Change of any kind refers to the process of refusing to remain the same. The change to which Jesus calls us is one that brings both instantaneous and continuing transformation and comes only through Him. It begins when we invite Him into our life and express our willingness to embrace the change He offers—the change that brings wholeness, freedom, and forgiveness.

Jesus says that the "kingdom of heaven" is imminent? Jesus is telling us that this world in its present form is passing away and that a new world, a new realm, a new creation, far superior to the present one, will one day replace it. Our world will be completely destroyed—and *that by fire*. Almighty God Himself will live and dwell with His children in the new creation.

In this new kingdom there'll be no more pain or suffering; no more anguish, sorrow, or shame; no more disease or death; no more fighting, anger, hatred, or war. The old order of things will have passed away, and that means no more sin.

Impossible as it is for our finite minds to wrap themselves around the concept, this will be a kingdom unbound by time: it will be eternal, as in forever, and we'll live endlessly in peace, joy, and tranquility. We'll have new, immortal bodies no longer subject to disease, disability, sickness, or imperfections. God Himself will make us new and will live and walk with us. What a glorious day that will be.

The evil of this world will end.

Jesus taught us that there's nothing more important than entering His eternal kingdom. Citizenship in that kingdom is beyond compare, well worth giving up our life here on earth.

Throngs of men and women have over the course of two millennia suffered torture and execution for their faith and hope in Christ and His kingdom. People have witnessed the deaths of their loved ones for refusal to renounce their faith in the living Christ. They've been put to death in the most unspeakable ways because of their faith. No, their martyrdom didn't secure their entry into glory, but their faith in Jesus did.

We're called to accept God at His Word and to turn from our sinful, self-centered lives. Only then can we live in a new manner with a new mindset—one that's focused not on this world but on Jesus and His eternal world to come.

Based on our love and gratitude, we willingly surrender our lives and will to the Lord who bought us with His own blood—who gave up His own life so that we might live. What we relinquish here on earth will be far surpassed by the eternal life only Jesus Christ can give. What good would it do, Jesus asked his disciples, for a man to gain the whole world yet forfeit his very soul? (Matthew 16:26).

The Scriptures teach that there's a specific path to that kingdom. Jesus warned that many people will try unsuccessfully to gain entrance (Matthew 7:13–14, 21–23).

One of the greatest obstacles will be false teachers. False teachers mislead people and inaccurately present God's plan of salvation (verses 15–20).

Some people are endlessly fascinated by God's secret will. They speculate about when the end will come and becoming fatalistic as a result. God has chosen not to reveal everything to us. The truth is that we're on a need-to-know basis, knowing all we need for salvation, but not more than we can handle, and most definitely not everything He knows.

God's revealed will is the most important knowledge we can possess.

When we insist on knowing what God in His infinite wisdom has chosen to keep secret, we've lost the fear of the Lord. Presuming to know God's *secret will*, while choosing to ignore His *revealed will*, can only lead us in the wrong direction.

Adam and Eve lost everything because they choose knowledge that God was protecting them from. Just because He didn't tell them everything that could be learned about evil, didn't mean they could disregard that which He had chosen to reveal to them.

When we choose to ignore everything, or anything, that Christ has said in His revealed will, to go after what He said belongs to Him, we're being outright defiant.

This is what Jonah did. His story is recorded in Scripture as an example for us. Jonah presumed upon the secret will of God, and in so doing he blatantly disobeyed God's revealed will.

Jonah 1:1–2 tells us the revealed will of God in that situation:

- "The word of the LORD came to Jonah son of Amittai: 'Go to the great city of Nineveh and preach against it, because its wickedness has come up before me.'"

That was God's revealed will. What did Jonah do? He fled!

- "But Jonah ran away from the LORD and headed for Tarshish. He went down to Joppa, where he found a ship bound for that port. After paying the fare, he went aboard and sailed for Tarshish to flee from the LORD," (Jonah 1:3)

The prophet's words to God revealed his rebellion.

- "Isn't this what I said, LORD, when I was still at home? That is what I tried to forestall by fleeing to Tarshish. I knew that you are a gracious and compassionate God, slow to anger and abounding in love, a God who relents from sending calamity." (Jonah 4:2)

Jonah actually presumed to set God straight. That he had foreseen what God had somehow missed. Jonah anticipated that God would show mercy and not destroy Nineveh, the capital city of Israel's sworn enemy, so he didn't go to preach against it.

To disobey God by rationalizing what God will do is presumption at its worst. God will do as He wills, and when He asks us to do something for Him, our only acceptable response is one of obedience.

God has a purpose in withholding His secret will to us. We show God that we trust Him when we don't demand information from which God is protecting us.

- "The secret things belong to the LORD our God, but the things revealed belong to us and to our children forever, that we may follow all the words of this law." (Deuteronomy 29:29)

- "I will lead the blind by ways they have not known, along unfamiliar paths I will guide them; I will turn the darkness into light before them and make the rough places smooth. These are the things I will do; I will not forsake them." (Isaiah 42:16)

What is God's will for my life?

Many needlessly struggle with this issue because they don't understand that God never intended His revealed will to be a mystery. That's why He *revealed* it. We mistakenly think this issue must be clouded in secrecy; that we must wrestle to find the answer.

The reality is that there's no need to plead with God to tell us what we need to do with our lives. It's spelled out for us in His Word. When we read it, it guides us in how to correctly think, live, and serve in obedience.

What I love most about my relationship with the Lord is that, as I indicate a greater desire to know Him, He reveals more and more of Himself to me. It makes me want more, so I keep coming back. This is how He wants us to feel about Him. He wants us to *desire* Him. And that is the essence of intimacy with Him.

Remember that God's ultimate purpose for us is that:

1. He would be ***glorified*** (1 Corinthians 10:31).

2. His Kingdom and gospel message would be ***preached to all the world*** (Genesis 50:20; Philippians 1:12).

    - As Paul wrote, "Now I want you to know, brothers and sisters, that what has happened to me has actually served to advance the gospel." (Philippians 1:12)

Doing God's will.

- "Your kingdom come, your will be done on earth as it is in heaven." (Matthew 6:10)

Many are familiar with these words of Jesus and most sincere Christians have a desire to do the will of God. But we may not be aware that it's our responsibility to find out what God's will is, and then to do it.

When we speak of "knowing the will of God for our lives," we're usually referring to the specifics. Who am I going to marry? What career path should I choose? What church should I attend? What are my gifts and calling?

But many of us have never taken the time to find out what the *general will* of God is for our lives, something we can and need to do by simply familiarizing ourselves with His Word. If we focus on doing God's *revealed will*, specific details will become increasingly apparent as we walk out our faith in obedience and patience. Following are some principles from God's Word that will help you to discern His will for you.

1. ***God has great plans for your life.***

Each one of us was created by God, in His image, for a purpose. Just as God set apart from birth Isaiah (Isaiah 49:1), Jeremiah (Jeremiah 1:5), and Paul (Galatians 1:15), he has a blueprint for your life.

- "'For I know the plans I have for you,' declares the LORD, 'plans to prosper you and not to harm you, plans to give you hope and a future.'" (Jeremiah 29:11)

The Bible declares that God's will is "good, pleasing and perfect." (Romans 12:2)

2. ***God's will is that we have a relationship with Him through His Son, Jesus Christ.***

    - "This is good, and pleases God our Savior, who wants all men to be saved and to come to a knowledge of the truth." (1 Timothy 2:3–4)

3. ***God wants us to be Christ's disciples.***

This means that Christians must be committed to following God's will daily, whatever the cost.

    - "If anyone would come to me, he must deny himself and take up his cross daily and follow me." (Luke 9:23)

4. ***The Bible helps us know God's will.***

    - "Your word is a lamp to my feet and a light for my path." (Psalm 119:105)

God promises to give us wisdom if we ask for it in prayer. Discerning God's will come most often through gleaning His wisdom, so it's essential that we don't operate on our own without it. The Holy Spirit is the person who imparts wisdom to us—so be sure to ask for it by name! In Philippians 4:6 God tells us that we can pray about anything and everything.

- "If any of you lacks wisdom, he should ask God, who gives generously to all without finding fault, and it will be given to him." (James 1:5)

5. **God has given us the Holy Spirit for guidance.**

    - "When he, the Spirit of truth, is come, he will guide you into all truth." (John 16:13a)

6. **We should listen to the advice of godly people whom God has placed in our lives.**

Many times, the advice of a parent, pastor, youth minister, church schoolteacher, or other mature Christian is just what we need to discern what God may want to do through us. These people can often perceive areas in which we're gifted or sense where our passions lie.

- "The way of a fool seems right to him, but a wise man listens to advice." (Proverbs 12:15)

- "Plans fail for lack of counsel, but with many advisors they succeed." (Proverbs 15:22)

7. **The Bible says that there's a peace that comes when we're pleasing God with our lives.**

When deciding between two alternatives that you've been praying about, one of the options may give you a greater sense of peace. That option is probably God's will for you.

- "The fruit of righteousness will be peace; the effect of righteousness will be quietness and confidence forever." (Isaiah 32:17)

8. *We should trust God that He will accomplish His will in our lives.*

- "Trust in the LORD with all your heart and lean not on your own understanding; in all your ways acknowledge him, and he will make your paths straight." (Proverbs 3:5–6)

- "…being confident of this, that he who began a good work in you will carry it on to completion until the day of Christ Jesus." (Philippians 1:6)

9. *God has given each of us gifts and abilities to use in His service.*

When God calls us, He equips us. If you aren't gifted in a certain area, God is probably not calling you to minister in that area. Or, He may want you to step out in faith *first*, then He will equip you with the appropriate spiritual gift. However, by familiarizing ourselves with the various spiritual gifts we can come to see where God has gifted us to minister and serve others. (See Romans 12:6-8, 1 Corinthians 12:1-11, Ephesians 4:11-13).

Seeking God's "perfect" will?

We can see from God's "*general will*" that He has certain universal truths for all Christians.

For those who seek more, God has a "*perfect will*" that is more specific.

This comes to those who desire to go beyond salvation, to seek out the "fullness" of the gospel for their lives. These people aren't content with just the introduction; they want the rest of the story. Reaching for the fullness of God does require something from us, however. It requires that we renew our mind. This must be our dominant focus. Living by God's standards must be our supreme emphasis.

The Bible is full of "if-then" statements: "*if*" we do certain things, "*then*" God will most assuredly do His part. Not everyone is called to be a pastor, teacher, or evangelist, but each of us is called to be a witness for Christ. Remember that the body of Christ is made up of many members and that each part is integral and has an important function.

There are no big and small players in the kingdom of God. In fact, Jesus said that the greatest in the kingdom is the one who humbles himself and becomes the servant of all.

Some Scriptures that confirm God's calling and plan for each of our lives.

The question remains, even after we see that God has a plan for us, "How do I find out what it is?" The obvious but often overlooked answer is: *just ask Him!*

We see in the books of Amos and Genesis why God will reveal His will.

> "Surely the Sovereign LORD does nothing without revealing his plan to his servants the prophets." (Amos 3:7)

> "Then the LORD said, 'Will I hide from Abraham what I am about to do?" (Genesis 18:17)

> "Abraham will surely become a great and powerful nation, and all nations on earth will be blessed through him. For I have chosen him, so that he will direct his children and his household after him to keep the way of the LORD by doing what is right and just, so that the LORD will bring about for Abraham what he has promised him." (Genesis 18:18–19)

There are things God in His infinite wisdom may never reveal to us.

Each of us can rest in the fact that God knows all things and that "all things work together for good *to those who love God*." We also know that God is light and that in Him "there is no darkness" (1 John 1:5) or "shadow of turning." (James 1:17)

There are many things that happen in this evil world that we may never come to understand. Why bad things happen to good people is just one of those proverbial questions.

We remember Job, whom God Himself called a perfect and upright man. In Job's case, the ultimate intent of the adversary was to get Job to blame God for his misfortune. The devil still uses that strategy today. Let's not forget that God was with Job and that He blessed him immensely in the latter part of his life. So, it will be for us.

As recorded in John 16:33, Jesus Himself "assured" us that we would have trouble in this world. But in the next breath our Lord directed us to take heart: for He *has* overcome the world. Whenever we face trouble we must remember this verse in Deuteronomy.

> "The secret things belong unto the LORD our God: but those things which are revealed belong unto us and to our children forever,

> that we may do all the words of this law." (Deuteronomy 29:29)

There are things, including many of the whys and wherefores of our individual lives that God will reveal only when we see Him face to face.

The enemy loves to use those difficult circumstances to get us to doubt God's integrity. Guarding our heart keeps us from believing lies. How then do we "walk out" the will of God in our lives?

How to discern the perfect will of God.

> Paul wrote in Romans, "Do not be conformed to this present world, but be transformed by the renewing of your mind, so that you may test and approve what is the will of God—what is good and well-pleasing and perfect." (Romans 12:2)

This verse reveals to us the secret, the wisdom key, to determining God's perfect will for our lives. We find that will in the process of: ***turning away from the world*** and ***having our minds renewed.*** Here again we see God's dual purpose: His plan for every believer is both *for our good* and *for His glory*. This purpose encompasses all the suffering and tragedy that come to us in life. (See 2 Corinthians 1:3-7, 2 Corinthians 12:7-10)

God doesn't have an imperfect will.

God doesn't have an imperfect will. We don't need to fear that we'll somehow stumble upon the wrong formula and ruin our lives forever. His perfect will takes into account our ignorance, weaknesses, sin, and even the sins of others against us.

The very fact that we're concerned about offending God demonstrates that our hearts are soft and compliant. Only the hard-hearted need fear God's wrath. This lesson is made plain for us in the account of Joseph.

> "You intended to harm me, but God intended it for good to accomplish what is now being done, the saving of many lives." (Genesis 50:20)

Joseph directs his brothers not to fear him, but to fear God; to be humble before the Lord and to seek the divine forgiveness He freely gives.

Joseph was overcome when his brothers appeared on the scene. He saw that despite what they had done to him, God had made sure that the dream he gave him many years earlier came to fruition. Joseph goes on to assure his brothers of his own kindness to them. In declining to seek revenge, Joseph revealed that he had an excellent spirit within him, a spirit produced by years of seemingly pointless suffering. This is just one example of how God will work good from the bad that happens to us if we'll only let Him.

The Bible speaks in different ways of the will of God.

It's important to understand those differences.

1. The decreed will of God.

This is God's eternal, foreordained plan and purpose. It cannot be reversed or thwarted.

This plan includes our salvation:

> "Praise be to the God and Father of our Lord Jesus Christ, who has blessed us in the heavenly realms with every spiritual blessing in Christ. For he chose us in him before the creation of the world to be holy and blameless in his sight. In love he predestined us for adoption to sonship through Jesus Christ, in accordance with his pleasure and will—to the praise of his glorious grace, which he has freely given us in the one he loves." (Ephesians 1:3–6)

It was God's plan and choice to call the people of Israel:

> "I ask then: Did God reject his people? By no means! I am an Israelite myself, a descendant of Abraham, from the tribe of Benjamin. God did not reject his people, whom he foreknew. Don't you know what Scripture says in the passage about Elijah—how he appealed to God against Israel: for God's gifts and his call are irrevocable." (Romans 11:1–2, 29)

God's covenant promises are a part of His decree (His ruling or verdict), and He will not, and cannot, change His mind about these things.

> "Remember your servants Abraham, Isaac and Israel, to whom you swore by your own self: 'I will make your descendants as numerous as the stars in the sky and I will give your descendants all this land I promised them, and it will be their inheritance forever.'" (Exodus 32:13)

2. *The preceptive will of God.*

This is God's will for all people, given to us in the form of *precepts* or *principles* held in His Word. We're commanded not to murder, steal, covet, or have other gods before Him, etc. These are God's laws as spelled out in the Pentateuch and elsewhere, including Paul's epistles. God's written Word to us is His *expressed* will; it's already obvious to us, so there's no need to seek it. God's precepts on the subject of sexual purity, for example, are clear:

> "Marriage should be honored by all, and the marriage bed kept pure, for God will judge the adulterer and all the sexually immoral." (Hebrews 13:4)

> "Or do you not know that wrongdoers will not inherit the kingdom of God? Do not be deceived: Neither the sexually immoral nor idolaters nor adulterers nor men who have sex with men nor thieves nor the greedy nor drunkards nor slanderers nor

swindlers will inherit the kingdom of God. And that is what some of you were. But you were washed, you were sanctified, you were justified in the name of the Lord Jesus Christ and by the Spirit of our God. 'I have the right to do anything,' you say—but not everything is beneficial. 'I have the right to do anything'—but I will not be mastered by anything. You say, 'Food for the stomach and the stomach for food, and God will destroy them both.' The body, however, is not meant for sexual immorality but for the Lord, and the Lord for the body. By his power God raised the Lord from the dead, and he will raise us also. Do you not know that your bodies are members of Christ himself? Shall I then take the members of Christ and unite them with a prostitute? Never! Do you not know that he who unites himself with a prostitute is one with her in body? For it is said, 'The two will become one flesh.' But whoever is united with the Lord is one with him in spirit. Flee from sexual immorality. All other sins a person commits are outside the body, but whoever sins sexually sins against their own body. Do you not know that your bodies are temples of the Holy Spirit, who is in you, whom you have received from God? You are not your own; you were bought at a price. Therefore honor God with your bodies." (1 Corinthians 6:9–20)

3. *God's preferential will.*

God takes pleasure in the salvation of man. This is part of His preferential will as He is privileged to do as He sees fit. Even so, He takes no pleasure in pouring out His wrath on people.

- "In the same way your Father in heaven is not willing that any of these little ones should perish." (Matthew 18:14)

- "This is good, and pleases God our Savior, who wants all people to be saved and to come to a knowledge of the truth." (1 Timothy 2:3–4)

What gives God pleasure and what doesn't? We know that God loves to show mercy but that He will also execute judgment.

Moses and others prayed on behalf of God's obstinate and sinful people that the Lord would show mercy (Nehemiah 9; Daniel 9). When it comes to actions that aren't clearly commanded or prescribed as sin, our desire should be to do that which pleases God.

4. *God's permissive will.*

This is what God allows even though it is sin. God allowed Joseph's brothers to betray him and deceive their father so that He might bring the Israelites to Egypt, where God would spare them and they would greatly multiply (Genesis 50:20). Similarly, God allows people to reject the gospel and His planned order for living. But in all of this God is still in control, still going about accomplishing His larger purposes. His *decreed* or *declared* will often permits people to violate what gives Him pleasure. Yet, God's *permissive* will is never outside His *decreed* will.

5. *God's directive will.*

This is God's personal guidance in our lives. It doesn't violate any of the "wills" described above. There are times when God specifically wants us at a certain place, doing a certain thing. In most instances the Bible doesn't provide us with this kind of direct and personal revelation of His will. God made known His *directive* will in Paul's "Macedonian call" (Acts 16:6–10) and in His *direct* guidance of Philip (Acts 8:26) and of Peter and Ananias (Acts 10:1–23). God does guide us personally and directly, but this is not as common as some think. Often, God allows for more than one way for us to abide by His *general* will for our lives.

6. *God's discerned will.*

This comes by *perception* of God's will for our life, which in turn comes through wisdom. When we ask for wisdom to discern direction from God in the practical use of our spiritual gifts and/or ministry, He'll over time, reveal it to us. We can often perceive it ourselves, given our awareness of our own strengths and weaknesses. Our area of ministry should align with our spiritual gifts. Those spiritual gifts were given to us for the edification of the Church. At times God will give us additional gifts when we need them, or greatly strengthen those we already have, as the situation requires.

> "Do not neglect your gift, which was given you through prophecy when the body of elders laid their hands on you." (1 Timothy 4:14)

This guidance may come as we read His Word, or through the wise counsel of a godly, spiritually mature person or mentor. Or we may have a strong sense that God is speaking to us. Understanding His *discerned* will may take some time. God may use many seemingly unrelated situations to bring us to the place where He wants us to serve—equipped with the attitude of a servant-leader. It takes time for God to mature us into a humble and compliant vessel, less likely to fall before our ministry sees full maturity and growth.

A mature believer doing the will of God for all to see brings God glory. He or she may also be instrumental through their example in bringing others into faith.

Joseph, at the age of seventeen, knew to a degree what God had in store for him, but he didn't have the necessary maturity at the time to bring it about. God had His methods for bringing Joseph to the end of himself and getting him to see His "bigger-picture" purposes.[1]

Knowing and doing the revealed will of God.

1. ***Renew your mind***. First, only the Bible holds the final, decisive authority of God's will. Every time we ask God to forgive us, our mind and heart is renewed. That's truly good news! When

we ask for it, God's grace lavishes on us His mercy and renewal; that's why God tells us to forgive others and ourselves. Every time we're obedient in this area of God's *revealed* will for us, we're getting to start over again fresh.

> "Therefore we do not lose heart. Though outwardly we are wasting away, yet inwardly we are being renewed day by day." (2 Corinthians 4:16)

> "In your relationships with one another, have the same mindset as Christ Jesus." (Philippians 2:5)

2. ***Discerning application of Scripture.*** Another aspect of God's will for us is our application of biblical truth to new situations that may not be explicitly addressed in the Bible. The Bible doesn't tell you which person to marry, where to go to school, or where to live. Many people fixate on minor details, but God is looking at the larger picture. He knows when our inner man has been renewed—we'll see from the *heart*—not just the mind. This is: "*knowing with understanding.*"

This was the problem Jesus continually had while teaching the disciples. Since they didn't see with renewed minds, they couldn't conceive of what He was saying. They often got stuck on the literal, when Jesus was proclaiming the spiritual. They may have walked with Him daily and watched Him do the work of the ministry, but they didn't understand. The Holy Spirit working within us—a gift they had yet to receive—is the inroad to full understanding.

Seeing biblical truth and having the desire to obey comes by way of a renewed mind. A mind that is so shaped and governed by the revealed will of God that we see and assess all relevant factors with the mind of Christ. This enables us to rightly discern what God is calling us to do.

There's a world of difference between praying and laboring for a renewed mind. The believer must not only discern how to rightly apply God's Word, but nurture the habit of asking God for new revelation. (John 8:32; 17:17).

3. ***Reflect in advance regarding your actions.*** The vast majority of people don't reflect much before acting. Most of what we do throughout the course of a day, or a life, isn't premeditated. Our thoughts, attitudes, actions, and beliefs are often spontaneous, a reflection both of what's going on inside us and of what has happened to us in the past.

> Jesus said, "You brood of vipers, how can you who are evil say anything good? For the mouth speaks what the heart is full of. A good man brings good things out of the good stored up in him, and an evil man brings evil things out of the evil stored up in him. But I tell you that everyone will have to give

account on the day of judgment for every empty word they have spoken." (Matthew 12:34–36)

Jesus goes on to say, don't be angry or prideful; don't covet or be anxious or envious. These kinds of actions are certainly not premeditated; they're part of the actions and attitudes of the "natural" man.

We're all born into sin and our sin nature produces these emotions in us. Anger, pride, covetousness, anxiety, and jealousy rise up out of the hearts without conscious reflection or intention. We're all guilty because all of us have them. Yet, they break the clear commands of God.

This is why God places so much emphasis on the one immense and grand task of the Christian life: ***Be transformed by the renewing of your mind.***

We're in such need of a new heart and a new mind . . . to "Make the tree good [so] the fruit will be good" (Matthew 12:33). That's the great challenge: to have the same mindset as Jesus by the renewing of our mind.

That's what God calls us to but we can't do it on our own. We need the power of the Holy Spirit, who leads us into Christ-exalting truth and works in us truth-embracing humility.

Pray that the Spirit of Christ would make you so new that the spillover will be good, acceptable, and perfect—for this is the will of God for you.

8

SHE IS EVER WATCHFUL AND MINDFUL OF THE TIMES

"Watch and pray so that you will not fall into temptation.

The spirit is willing, but the body is weak." (Matthew 26:41)

Jesus encouraged His disciples to be "ever watchful." In fact,. He rebuked them for not being able to stay awake during the one hour prior to his arrest. We too are inclined towards spiritual sleeping. Indeed, it is one of the end times signs. Therefore, the New Testament commands us to "**watch**."

This is the usual English translation of two different Greek words: *gregoreuo* and *aprupneo*, which have the similar meanings of "stay awake" and to "be sleepless." Together these spiritual states:

being vigilant, on guard, fully awake, and alert give us the strength we need to withstand temptations and carnal struggles.

In Matthew 26 the meaning of the word *watch* is primarily physical. The apostle Paul wrote to the Christians in Corinth,

> "Watch, stand fast in the faith, be brave, be strong. (1 Corinthians 16:13, NKJV)

> "And he took with Him Peter and the sons of Zebedee, and he began to be sorrowful and deeply distressed. Then he said to them, 'My soul is exceedingly sorrowful, even to death. Stay here and watch with me.' He went a little farther and fell on his face, and prayed, saying, 'O my Father, if it is possible, let this cup pass from me; nevertheless, not as I will, but as you will.' Then he came to the disciples and found them sleeping, and said to Peter, 'What! Could you not watch with me one hour?'" (Matthew 26:37–40, NKJV)

Jesus was reproaching His disciples for not understanding the time in which they lived. He went on to admonish them personally, telling them that they needed to be watchful for themselves:

> "Watch and pray so that you will not fall into temptation. The spirit is willing, but the body is weak." (Matthew 26:41)

Jesus always knows more of the big picture than we do. Since He was there *in the beginning* with the Father and the Holy Spirit, He has knowledge that we don't.

The disciples had limited knowledge of things to come and often didn't understand what Jesus was teaching them on a day-to-day basis. Spiritual concepts were difficult for them to interpret because Jesus spoke of things they knew nothing about and in parables with veiled meanings. Jesus told them that human willpower alone would not keep them awake or alert. They would need to exercise **spiritual watching** if they hoped to be victorious.

For Christians today, *watching* is done through the power of the Holy Spirit and through prayer. When we desire to fulfill what Jesus has told us is necessary and useful, we can ask Him to help us internalize and understand it.

> "Come back to your senses as you ought, and stop sinning; for there are some who are ignorant of God—I say this to your shame." (1 Corinthians 15:34)

Paul was saying that even true Christians succumb to spiritual sleeping. He was also warning the Church already in that day, that the time of the end was closer than they thought

- "And do this, understanding the present time. The hour has come for you to **wake up from your slumber**, because our salvation is nearer now than when we first believed." (Romans 13:11)

The cost of spiritual ignorance.

Those who won't shake themselves from their stupor to see what's really happening around them will live as in the days of Noah. Those surrounding Noah watched him build the ark, no doubt enjoying the distraction, but chose not to really see or listen. That choice came with a high price tag—it cost them their lives. They couldn't imagine what was coming.

Likewise, in our day, millions are ignorant of what will ensue in the last days. The sad part is that they choose to remain oblivious, deciding not to believe or commit.

It's crucial to believe what God has revealed to us in His Word and to tap into a power source that's greater than our human reasoning.

Noah listened to the Lord. He became accustomed to, and over time, familiar with His voice. He eventually came to trust in God so much that when God instructed him to build the ark he complied without question. Consequently, he and his whole family were spared when the deluge came. Noah was continuously ridiculed by amused crowds, yet He continued to trust God and obey His directives.

What a beautiful place to be when we care less about what other people think and more about what an awesome God thinks and says to us.

Foolish people will abound when Christ returns. As in the days of Noah, they'll be spending their time, energy, and resources on the meaningless. They'll be caught unaware, spiritually sleeping as the disciples were, oblivious to the warning signs of imminent disaster. They'll be no more prepared to enter heaven than the hecklers in Noah's day were to embark on the ark. The harsh reality is that pursuing a worthless agenda brings anguish people will recognize only in hindsight! [1]

The tyranny of the urgent.

Satan has his ways of keeping us on a continuous hamster wheel of worry and urgency. We live our lives as though *everything* is of the utmost importance. Much of what we do is nothing more than those trivial, mundane, repetitive tasks that keep us ever moving but never productive.

Many people naively think they need more time in their day to accomplish all their relentless tasks. But just as new and wider highways soon congest with added traffic, extra time means people will fill their days with more meaningless activity.

Students often believe that when they're finished with their formal education they'll have more time to themselves and will feel less pressure to perform. But all too soon they find that their chosen career requires just as much time and energy expenditure. Climbing the ladder of success has its own set of continual demands.

A young mother might believe that when her little ones are out of diapers the workload will ease. But before she knows it they're teenagers who demand more of her time—and much more of her energy.

At some point on the treadmill we realize that the passage of time doesn't alleviate stress. Indeed, it grows in proportion to the added demands of responsibility. Ask any mother, student, pastor, or CEO whether the stress has lessened as their responsibilities have increased.

What we're likely to discover is that we're working more but enjoying it less. Our dilemma goes deeper than not having "enough time" in our day.

Our problem is one of priorities. Hard work doesn't hurt us. In fact, we discover that the weariness that comes from working long hours on necessary undertakings also comes with a sense of achievement and fulfillment.

It's when we move beyond what we can realistically expect to accomplish, that we begin to experience doubt, misgivings, and anxiety.

When we reflect back on the past and discover that we've spent enormous amounts of time and energy on what holds no lasting value, we begin to lose heart. We become overwhelmed, disillusioned, and depressed when we come to grips with our failure to do what's most important, that a sense of dread pervades our spirit. Acknowledging that yet another year has passed, that we've once again knuckled under to other people and their incessant demands on us, that we find ourselves in the vice grip of dissatisfaction. [2]

Our home should be a place to retreat from the world—our sanctuary. But this isn't always the case as the home is often a place of chaos, clutter, racket, and incessant activity. Homes have become noisier, busier, and lonelier as family members engage more with electronics and social media than they do with each other. Empty and disillusioned, we turn away from family in the direction of work or pleasure hoping to incorporate some meaning into our lives.

What creates this disturbance of spirit? How is it that we succumb to leaving undone those things we ought to do and expending ourselves on those we ought not to involve ourselves with?

Is there any way to escape from these patterns of chaotic living?

The Gospels demonstrate that Jesus worked hard. Mark recounts the following, setting it within the context of the end of a busy day . . .

> "That evening, at sundown, they brought to him all who were sick or possessed with demons. And the whole city was gathered about the door. And he healed many who were sick with various diseases, and cast our many demons." (Mark 1:32–34)

> On another occasion Jesus worked well into the evening meeting the needs of people. In fact, He worked so late the disciples were concerned about His well-being (Mark 3:21). But one day after teaching at length to the gathered crowd, Jesus and His disciples sought refuge in a boat. Jesus was so weary that even a storm didn't arouse Him from His exhausted slumber (Matthew 4:37).

Jesus was never frazzled, and He regularly took the time to impart truth into people's empty lives. He was consistent is offering "living water" to the hurting. He changed a Samaritan woman's life by stopping to talk to her at the well. He led by example, an example that revealed a tremendous sense of balance and timing. But that timing meant that, despite these examples of His selflessness, He didn't ignore His own physical, emotional, and spiritual needs.

Jesus remained focused.

When Jesus' brothers wanted Him to go to Judea, He replied, "My time has not yet come" (John 7:6). Jesus didn't say yes to every request, nor did he teach or heal endlessly, ignoring the physical and spiritual depletion that came as byproducts of His human nature. He often pulled away to spend time with His Father in prayer. This is where He received nourishment to reenergize His body, soul, and spirit.

Jesus had an unwavering sense of purpose that came from spending the necessary time with His Father. He did nothing apart from what the Father told Him to do. He knew His role and what He had come to accomplish. He didn't expend His time and energy on tasks that others could just as easily accomplish. Instead, He wisely focused on mentoring, giving Himself in particular to the disciples to ensure that they would be prepared to carry on the work of the gospel after His death.

Jesus knew His time on earth was limited. And He knew His mission: ***to be about His Father's business.*** People's demands for His time, energy, and ability to heal, deliver, and meet needs didn't distract Him from His primary calling and purpose.

Jesus came to offer us a way out of our meaningless lives. Yet what He offers is so often rejected and ridiculed. Most never view it as worthwhile to study His life, His purposes—or His success and the methods that enabled it.

If we want to experience real success, we must discover the person behind the concept. If we're willing to do it His way, Jesus provides us with innumerable blessings and opportunities.

Jesus possessed inward rest even when His outward world was hectic. He held the secret to dealing with the pain and suffering surrounding Him without being personally depleted by it. He was able to change human misery into supernatural joy when those who heard His message received it by faith with gladness.

Your greatest challenge.

Reprioritizing your life may be the hardest thing you'll do. The process is, and is intended to be, a struggle. It's the necessary struggle of an emerging butterfly, the very struggle that makes it resilient and beautiful. Likewise, the baby bird struggling to break free from its shell emerges the stronger for the effort.

A weak person (one who hasn't achieved strength through application) is susceptible to all of Satan's ploys. It's mandatory for us as Christians to learn to peck and scrabble our way out of the clutches of sin if we hope to gain enduring strength.

Learning what's really important and staying with it long enough to develop spiritual muscle, will prolong your life. Our life on earth is exceedingly short. Imagine that you have so little time that you can't afford to waste a moment. Then pause to reflect on what's "all important"—*doing what the Father has sent you to do.*

For what purpose did He give you life? What does He want you to accomplish while you're on earth? Determine your assignment with the guidance of His Word and the Holy Spirit, by considering the one-of-a-kind you He knit together. Your experiences, gifts and strengths, all reveal how He wants you to operate in this world. If you want to know what your assignment is, *just ask*. Understand that the answer may take some time in coming. He may make you struggle for it. Wrestle with it! Insist on finding out more from the God who created purpose.

Slough off the apprehension that's wasting your life. Discontinue the activities that are keeping you from your heavenly calling. Ask the Holy Spirit to reveal to you what you need to know. It's called wisdom; ask for it by name as Solomon did. It will ensure your success.

Spend time with the Lord. Take time to read His Word, to pray, and to listen to Him. Worship Him in your quiet time. Listening is an art. Develop and treasure it. God speaks to those who wait with expectancy to hear from Him. Be diligent and patient. Quiet yourself before Him and adjust your schedule so this becomes your main focus. Eventually you'll find that you love your quiet time with the Lord. It will become so precious to you, in fact, that you'll drop other things rather than give it up. Steadily you *will* find your purpose. This shared time is the most **urgent** thing on your "to-do" list today . . . and every day.

"Watching" involves using your God-given intellect.

God has given us an amazing mind and He rightly expects us to use it for learning, studying, analyzing, judging, and thinking. Many people are mentally lazy. They devote massive amounts of time to the trivial, the temporal, the mundane, as well as in pursuit of materialistic accumulation.

Even more spend their time idly fixated for countless hours on television, the computer, or electronic gadgets and games. Social networks may keep us distracted from our overly busy and unfulfilling lives, but they do nothing to alleviate either the busyness or the lack of fulfillment.

Readers are becoming rare, even though more books are being written now than at any other time in history. We've grown accustomed to the passivity of pictures and entertainment when we have free time to fill. But in-depth learning requires practical, positive, and personal investment with words and ideas. The Bible holds the words God spoke. They're His words of life to us. Christians are distinguished by knowing His words.

God hates ignorance and indifference. He provided both the Living Word (Jesus) and the written Word (the Bible) for our instruction and guidance.

The Bible is God's divine revelation of absolute truth. It's always relevant—especially today. Let it be the filter through which you perceive and judge all information. Allow it to accurately interpret all worldly events. It will keep you from being deceived. And it will give you the critical clarity you need for the difficult days ahead.

Watching involves knowing the true condition of your heart.

The Bible speaks of two conditions of the human heart.

1. A *true heart* draws near to God.

    "Let us draw near to God with a sincere heart and with the full assurance that faith brings, having our hearts sprinkled to cleanse us from a guilty conscience and having our bodies washed with pure water." (Hebrews 10:22)

2. An *evil heart* departs from God.

    "See to it, brothers and sisters, that none of you has a sinful, unbelieving heart that turns away from the living God." (Hebrews 3:12)

> "The field is the world, and the good seed stands for the people of the kingdom. The weeds are the people of the evil one." (Matthew 13:38)

"Watching" involves being aware of counterfeits.

Counterfeits are everywhere! Counterfeit artwork has been known to show up in some of the finest art galleries and even in private collections. Such pieces are cleverly disguised by those who have been trained to mimic the great masters. The clothing and handbag market has been flooded by replicas, and jewelry and watches are imitated, reproduced, and often sold as the real thing. Almost anything can be stolen for a price and then duplicated and counterfeited.

How can we guard against counterfeits? Only by studying and becoming masters at identifying the ***original***.

Counterfeits are nothing new; in fact, Satan is the consummate counterfeit and imposter. Many fail to study and get to know the real Master—Jesus. Those who don't know Him intimately are sure to be easily swayed by the counterfeit, Satan.

Our world has false Christians, a false gospel, and even false righteousness. And at the end there will be a false Christ.

> "For such people are false apostles, deceitful workers, masquerading as apostles of Christ. And no wonder, for Satan himself masquerades as an angel of light. It is not surprising, then, if his servants also masquerade as servants of righteousness. Their end will be what their actions deserve." (2 Corinthians 11:13–15)

> "You belong to your father, the devil, and you want to carry out your father's desires. He was a murderer from the beginning, not holding to the truth, for there is no truth in him. When he lies, he speaks his native language, for he is a liar and the father of lies." (John 8:44)

We're to accept no other gospel. Only by the earnest study of the true gospel can we recognize a false one.

> "I am astonished that you are so quickly deserting the one who called you to live in the grace of Christ and are turning to a different gospel—which is really no gospel at all. Evidently some people are throwing you into confusion and are trying to pervert the gospel of Christ. But even if we or an angel from heaven should preach a gospel other than the one we preached to you, let them be under God's curse! As we have already said, so now I say again: If anybody is preaching to you a gospel other than what you accepted, let them be under God's curse!" (Galatians 1:6–9)

When we're deceived, we'll accept a different gospel! But this acceptance leads us to rebellion and hard-heartedness towards God.

"Watching" involves remaining true in the midst of evil.

Noah remained true to God in the midst of evil. As a result, he was delivered from the sin of those around him. He and his family were surrounded by people steeped in moral and spiritual darkness. Although he was not shielded from this perversion, God did provide a way of escape from it. God allowed Noah and his family to remain pure in the midst of this corruption.

We can likewise remain pure in a sexually explicit and morally decaying world. Lust, greed, and violence continue to escalate, but we don't have to partake. True, we may at times feel alone and misunderstood, but the reward will be life forever with our Father.

Noah and his family were surrounded by people but were unable to fellowship with other believers, yet God arranged for believing wives for Noah's sons and protected and preserved this family He loved.

Abraham remained true, but Lot was led astray.

Lot was influenced by Abraham's righteousness, but as Lot's wealth increased, he found it necessary to part company with Abraham and his godly influence. Scripture tells us that Lot's degradation happened incrementally. He initially "pitched his tent toward Sodom" (Genesis 12:12) but eventually moved into the city (see Genesis 14:12). God used a local war to get Lot out of the clutches of this wicked city, but he couldn't keep Sodom out of Lot. Lot had allowed his heart to be turned irrevocably in its direction. Peter clearly states that Lot was saved, but we must wonder about the attraction Sodom had held for him.

Genesis 19 gives us the account of Lot and his family living in Sodom. It's possible that Lot had at least four daughters, two of whom had married men of Sodom. We do read that while Lot was living in Sodom his soul was "tortured" and "greatly troubled" by the filthy conduct of the people.

While Lot offered hospitality to two angels (men) in his home, the men of the city surrounded his house and demanded that he send them out so they could have sex with them. How horrifying to have men knocking on your door demanding homosexual relations with your guests.

We can speculate that Lot may have made the grave mistake in believing what so many today assume—that they can influence for good the evil world around them. If that was his plan, he failed miserably. The tragedy of such naiveté is failing to comprehend how great an influence evil can have on us. No matter how pure our intentions the fact is that we *must* flee. We simply can't withstand remaining in the presence of such perversity.

Lot and his family weren't rescued because of any goodness on their part. Lot was saved because he was a believer and because his uncle Abraham had prayed for him.

Abraham had more influence outside of Sodom than Lot did inside. Lot settled. He compromised himself and his family by choosing to remain in Sodom. This resulted in his having a weak witness and no testimony to offer his wife and daughters. His daughters scoffed at his warning, and his wife disobeyed God and was turned into a pillar of salt for taking one last longing look when told to flee without a backward glance. Lot's family didn't take God or His instructions seriously, because they didn't take Lot seriously.

Lot chose to live in Sodom but could have lived elsewhere. It isn't always possible in our world to remove ourselves from sin's pervasive influence, but we can control how much of "Sodom" we allow into our heart and home.

The judgment in Noah's day involved water, and in Lot's case it brought fire. Listen to Peter's warning about the coming judgment of fire:

> "But the day of the Lord will come like a thief. The heavens will disappear with a roar; the elements will be destroyed by fire,

and the earth and everything done in it will be laid bare." (2 Peter 3:10)

Biblical accounts are written to caution us so we don't suffer needlessly. God has duly warned us so we can avoid the terrible destruction that will come to those who rebel in the last days. We can be grateful, as this allows us to adjust our priorities accordingly.

"But even if you should suffer for what is right, you are blessed. Do not fear their threats; do not be frightened." (1 Peter 3:14)

Judgment seems far off because God is…

"long-suffering…not willing that any should perish, but that all should come to repentance." (2 Peter 3:9)

God desires that all those who will be brought in will be gathered in *before* "that day" comes. God's people will be delivered from judgment by God's grace and mercy.

"For God did not appoint us to suffer wrath but to receive salvation through our Lord Jesus Christ. He died for us so that, whether we are awake or asleep, we may live together with him." (1 Thessalonians 5:9–10)

Three accounts of judgment for rebellion against God.

Peter proved that judgment finally does come no matter how secure the sinner might feel. We have numerous accounts recorded in Scripture to let us know that even though judgment is often delayed, it does come most assuredly to the wicked (see Jude 6–8 for three examples):

1. ***Lucifer and the fallen angels:*** Isaiah 14:12–15 describes the fall of Lucifer, the highest of the angels, but the details are shrouded in mystery. Revelation 12:4 suggests that perhaps one third of all the angels fell with Lucifer, who became Satan, the archenemy of God.

   > "How you have fallen from heaven, morning star, son of the dawn! You have been cast down to the earth, you who once laid low the nations! You said in your heart, '***I will*** ascend to the heavens; ***I will*** raise my throne above the stars of God; ***I will*** sit enthroned on the mount of assembly, on the utmost heights of Mount Zaphon. ***I will*** ascend above the tops of the clouds; ***I will*** make myself like the Most High.' But you are brought down to the realm of the dead, to the depths of the pit." (Isaiah 14:12–15, bold italics added)

There are many things we won't know or understand fully until we're united with Christ for all eternity. Until then we have what God has chosen to reveal to us for our caution and protection.

> "His tail drew a third of the stars of heaven and threw them to the earth. And the dragon stood before the woman who was ready to give birth, to devour her Child as soon as it was born." (Revelation 12:4)

Lucifer was probably God's worship leader and most likely in charge of the angelic hosts. He was the most beautiful of all the angels. He didn't possess this great beauty of his own accord, but because God his Creator, had chosen to make him beautiful. Yet on this account he became arrogant to the point of coveting the very throne of God. Such overweening pride kept him from being content with what God had given him to do.

Satan and his fallen, evil angels have been and are defeated. Jesus accomplished this for us with His death and glorious resurrection. This selfless act conquered our sin and death too. However, Satan and his demons are temporarily "free" (by God's concession because they serve His purposes) to continue to work in this world. They're the demonic powers that hinder and bind all people. But if God has already judged the evil angels, who are in many respects higher than people, He'll certainly judge rebellious man.

> "Be alert and of sober mind. Your enemy the devil prowls around like a roaring lion looking for someone to devour." (1 Peter 5:8)

2. *Israel:* Israel was continuously being led astray by false prophets. It was the Jewish false prophets who did the most damage, for they claimed to speak for Yahweh, thereby lowering the people's defenses.

> "The wrath of God is being revealed from heaven against all the godlessness and wickedness of people, who suppress the truth by their wickedness." (Romans 1:18)

Lawlessness, horrendous wickedness, violence, and perversion abounded. Believers in that society were a distinct minority to whom most paid little attention. Nevertheless, the flood destroyed nearly all of them.

Noah ministered for 120 years before God sent the flood. During all that time he served as a messenger of God's righteousness, but nobody believed his message. Jesus made it clear that the people were enjoying their complacent lives up to the very day that Noah and his family entered the ark. (Luke 17:26–27.)

Our current world condition has obvious, alarming parallels. We're to make no mistake about it—God judges His people.

3. ***The sin in Sodom and Gomorrah:*** Many cities were sinful in those days, as in our own, so what was so different about Sodom and Gomorrah? The sin of their residents was *blatant, deliberate,* and *flaunted.*

> "But the men of Sodom were exceedingly wicked and sinful against the LORD." (Genesis 13:13, NKJV)

> "Therefore God gave them over in the sinful desires of their hearts to sexual impurity for the degrading of their bodies with one another. They exchanged the truth about God for a lie, and worshiped and served created things rather than the Creator—who is forever praised. Amen. Because of this, God gave them over to shameful lusts. Even their women exchanged natural sexual relations for unnatural ones. In the same way the men also abandoned natural relations with women and were inflamed with lust for one another. Men committed shameful acts with other men, and received in themselves the due penalty for their error." (Romans 1:24–27)

> "And if he rescued Lot, a righteous man, who was distressed by the depraved conduct of the lawless (for that righteous man, living among them day after day, was tormented in his righteous soul by the lawless deeds he saw and heard) . . . ." (2 Peter 2:7–8)

The overt sin of Sodom was intent on unnatural sex, sodomy, and homosexuality. Such sin is clearly condemned in Scripture (see Romans 1:24–27; 1 Corinthians 6:9; Leviticus 18:22). In spite of Abraham's intercessory prayer (Genesis 18:22) and Lot's last-minute warning, the people inhabiting these "sin cities" perished in fire and brimstone.

> "The men turned away and went toward Sodom, but Abraham remained standing before the LORD." (Genesis 18:22)

Until that moment people went on with their lives confident that all was well. But Scripture shows us that:

1. God did not spare Lucifer or a third of the angels.

2. God did not spare the whole world aside from Noah and his family.

3. God did not spare those in Sodom and Gomorrah.

God won't spare those during our generation either who willfully reject His truth and deny His Son. God has reserved the unjust for special punishment on "that day."

But the children of God will enjoy an inheritance reserved for them in heaven (1 Peter 1:4). Jesus is preparing a home for them there. True believers in Christ will not only inherit mansions in heaven, but a heart that's untroubled by the unspeakable occurrences that will befall the world on that great and terrible day. Jesus gives us peace beyond comprehension.

> "'Do not let your hearts be troubled. You believe in God; believe also in me. My Father's house has many rooms; if that were not so, would I have told you that I am going there to prepare

a place for you? And if I go and prepare a place for you, I will come back and take you to be with me that you also may be where I am. You know the way to the place where I am going.' Thomas said to him, 'Lord, we don't know where you are going, so how can we know the way?' Jesus answered, *'I am the way and the truth and the life. No one comes to the Father except through me.'"* (John 14:1–6, bold italics added)

"For God did not appoint us to suffer wrath but to receive salvation through our Lord Jesus Christ." (1 Thessalonians 5:9)

Will you watch and be ready when Jesus returns?

In Luke 17:20–37 Jesus warns us not to be like Lot's wife, who when told to flee the evil city of Sodom, looked back with longing. God calls believers to a different standard. That standard requires us to live *in* the world, but not to be *of* it. Loving the world means we're drawn to and captivated by it. We come to enjoy and willingly participate in its many lusts and pleasures. But the pleasures of this world are contrary to God. Since we can't give our heart to two passions, we train ourselves to either hate God or hate the world. (See Luke 17:20-37).

When Jesus comes He'll separate the sheep from the goats. Some will be taken into heaven and the others left. "Left where?" the disciples asked, mystified. "Where the body is there will the vultures be gathered together." Not to be gathered to Christ at his second coming is to be left behind for destruction.

All the warnings of Jesus are for our advantage. Jesus came to give us life. His rebukes are to keep us in that life. His admonition to remember Lot's wife is a reminder to keep our heart fixed on Him.

Notice, that Jesus didn't mention sodomy in the list of particular sins that characterized Sodom just before its destruction (see Luke 17:28). In fact, he didn't single out any particular sin, mentioning only the seemingly harmless business of going about a natural life: "They ate, drank, bought, sold, planted, and built."

Judgment didn't come upon Sodom because it had individuals practicing homosexuality, but because all the normal, ordinary activities of life in that city were ***godless***.

Before the day when the fire falls, each of us will need to know whether or not we're ready to go with the Lord. If you're unsure, ask Him to come into your heart and show you the way He wants you to live. Doing so will put to rest any fear of future events from within you.

"Watching" involves protecting yourself against counterfeit religion.

Americans take great pride in their freedom though there are many conflicting definitions of freedom. Nobody is completely free. Every government has laws to maintain order and must prosecutes offenders who disregard the basic standards for decent living. Doing whatever we please is anarchy, not freedom.

Not being aware of the truth that sets one free will lead us to false teachers. They deceive, lie, and make false promises. Freedom is usually one of those. Peter gave three reasons why "false freedom" is false.

1. It's based on *false promises* (2 Peter 2:17–18).

2. It's offered by *false teachers* (2 Peter 2:1–10).

3. It involves a *false experience* (2 Peter 2:21–22).

False teachers make false promises and lead us *away* from the true giver of complete freedom—Christ.

1. **False promises:**

What is offered by false teachers is, not surprisingly, false freedom. These individuals are typically eloquent, impassioned promoters of their *self-proclaimed* doctrines. They *manipulate* and *distort* truth to serve their own interests.

Cult leaders initially offer freedom to their recent converts, but eventually, though, these devotees find out the hard way that, far from delivering on what they had promised, these self-absorbed and often fanatical leaders have delivered them into horrific bondage. Those making false promises know how to impress and entice with their words. Too few in our day of disillusioned seekers have the discernment to differentiate real truth from falsehood.

False teachers *manipulate*, while true teachers *communicate*. False teachers *deceive*; true teachers *liberate*. False teachers are able to appeal to the base appetite of the "old" unregenerate nature of men and women.

Paul delivered the gospel message in a simple, practical fashion. His preaching was intended to *express*, not to *impress*.

- "The acts of the flesh are obvious: sexual immorality, impurity and debauchery; idolatry and witchcraft; hatred, discord, jealousy, fits of rage, selfish ambition, dissensions, factions and envy; drunkenness, orgies, and the like. I warn you, as I did before, that those who live like this will not inherit the kingdom of God." (Galatians 5:19–21)

2. *False teachers:*

False teachers speak *half-truths*, just as Satan did in the garden. Part of what they say may have enough of a ring of truth to disarm the listeners, but it's what they leave out that kills.

False teachers always appeal to our pride. They tell us what our fleshly nature wants to hear. This is the work of a con artist. Their smooth talk is devised to take you in, to catch you unaware and uninformed. What they neglect to mention is that there's a penalty for pride and sin.

False teachers leave out the truth that repentance brings forgiveness for our sins. They present God as one dimensional—as One who is only loving and invariably kind. Again, what they leave out is deadly. They never speak of sin or hell or mention that God is just and is also a judge. They never speak about the fact that one day we'll have to give an accounting of our life before our just judge.

God is completely good and loving, but His goodness and love don't preclude His just and righteous wrath against sin and evil. Tragically, if we become convinced there's no sin in us, we have no need of a Savior. *What, after all, are we in need of being saved from?* If we aren't found lacking, then Jesus has nothing to offer us.

False teachers lead masses of people straight into hell. They themselves have no love for "their" people. They're anything but true shepherds who lovingly lead their flock from harm to safety. Lies always destroy, while truth always heals and sets captives free.

False teachers appeal to immature people and new converts in their faith. New believers (I'm referring here to new Christian converts) are vulnerable to false teachers because they aren't yet grounded in their faith. If Satan can snatch the seed (the Word) that's been received before it's had a chance to take root, his job becomes that much easier.

Many churches fail to disciple their new Christian converts. Young Christians, of any age, are in need of follow-up, reinforcement, encouragement, and grounding. We're called as Christ's followers to make disciples, not just converts. New Christians need protection from a dangerous and predatory world.

3. *False experience:*

In the past 15 years or so, we've seen an increasing number of churches that are "emerging." This trend is often called the "Emergent Church Movement." As explained in Wikipedia, "Participants seek to live their faith in what they believe to be a 'postmodern' society. What those involved in the conversation mostly agree on is their disillusionment with the organized and institutional church and their support for the deconstruction of modern Christian worship, modern evangelism, and the nature of modern Christian community."

Though some of these churches are new, they are for the most part churches that at one time believed and followed the principles of the Christian faith. They've convinced themselves that because our society has changed, they must alter their doctrine and approach to exert any appeal. They're looking for gimmicks and fads to bring in gullible new members. "Doing" has replaced "being." The pastors in this insidious movement are false teachers—apostates from the true faith. Their churches may be quite large, but the teaching is anything but deep. Many make the mistake of believing that large numbers equal successful ministry.

The command to all believers is to go out, to be fruitful, and to multiply. The animal and plant kingdoms reproduce after their own kind; it's a mark of reproduction. In the same way Christians are to reproduce more Christians. Exactly what are we reproducing, though, if we're asking new church members to come and get involved in *activities*, but we have no interest in discipling them? If we're going to reproduce, we must teach new believers the fundamentals of being a Christ-follower.

Many are seeking community, devoid of Christ. Far too many churches are only too glad to jump on the bandwagon of whatever is currently popular. The caveat: that isn't what we've been commanded to do.

Christ, the only true Teacher.

There's great reward for those who seek after truth. God makes Himself known to those who demand the truth. Jesus is the true Teacher, the One sent to show us the "way of truth."

A spring without water is by definition no spring at all. But Jesus told the woman at the well that whoever drinks His water will never thirst again. The water in a well is calm, and Jesus is the calm, the peace, for which we yearn.

The water Christ offers satisfies with only one drink. Christ is the only One who possesses it. False teachers can't make the same offer; they have nothing that compares. They may promise it, but as with many politicians, they fail to deliver on their high-sounding pledges. Jesus delivers on **EVERY** promise He makes to us.

> "Jesus answered, 'Everyone who drinks this water will be thirsty again, but whoever drinks the water I give them will never thirst. Indeed, the water I give them will become in them a spring of water welling up to eternal life.'" (John 4:13–14)

Faith is only as good as its object. A pagan may have great faith in his idol but his fervor is misplaced; his idol can do nothing for him. It has no power in and of itself to produce, let alone reproduce.

Many people put their faith in wealth, power, and possessions, (their idols) yet those things are fleeting and come with no guarantee of long-term, let alone eternal value.

On the other hand, when we put our faith in Christ, that faith accomplishes something, for its object is not only good, powerful, and loving, but altogether dependable.

> "Praise be to the LORD, who has given rest to his people Israel just as he promised. Not one word has failed of all the good promises he gave through his servant Moses." (1 Kings 8:56)

False prophets, pastors, and teachers can't set others free. They aren't even free themselves. Peter makes it clear that even if these individuals have temporarily disentangled themselves from the pollutions of the world, they'll head right back into bondage.

> ***"They promise them freedom, while they themselves are slaves of depravity—for 'people are slaves to whatever has mastered them.'*** *If they have escaped the corruption of the world by knowing our Lord and Savior Jesus Christ and are again entangled in it and are overcome, they are worse off at the end than they were at the beginning." (2 Peter 2:19–20)*

False Christians and false teachers lead others to a false experience.

Jude in his letter describes these same individuals as "sensual, having not the Spirit." Notice that the word "Spirit" is capitalized. This means they do not have the Holy Spirit. (Jude 19). Oh, they do have ample experience with "religion." They'll boldly proclaim that their religious experience has brought them into fellowship with the Lord.

Peter minced no words in describing these apostates.

> "But these, as natural brute beasts, made to be taken and destroyed, speak evil of the things that they understand not; and shall utterly perish in their own corruption." (2 Peter 2:12, KJV)

Peter was not simply expressing his personal contempt for these false teachers, but also teaching a basic spiritual lesson. It's significant to understand that these false teachers aren't, and never were, people who had experienced spiritual rebirth.

We're called to discern false spirits that present themselves as "angels of light" and we're endowed with godly, Holy Spirit wisdom to do so. These people have a way of explaining "the way of righteousness" and using the Word of God to support their teachings. They are like those who produce artwork that mimics the great masters of old. They carefully study each brush stroke, yet have no artistic ability within themselves to produce an original piece. It's *inspiration*, not *imitation* that made the original valuable in the first place.

Because these people so mimic true Christians they're easily able to penetrate the local church. But their experience, like their promises, is false. Only those who study the true Master can spot the imposter.

Peter emphasized the new birth experience. He reminds his readers that they are "partakers of the divine nature" (2 Peter 1:4). There's no indication, as I've mentioned earlier, that the false teachers had ever experienced new birth. They had knowledge of salvation and were fluent in the right rhetoric, but they lacked an authentic salvation experience.

Such people have in fact received the Word of God but turned away from it, evidently before it could take root (2 Peter 2:21). They knew but didn't follow Jesus or become His sheep.

Judas was one of the twelve disciples who followed Jesus. He heard his teachings and observed His ways, just as did the other eleven, but he ultimately turned from Jesus to betray him, hanging himself in utter despair as a result. Scripture tells us simply "that Satan entered into him."

> "Praise be to the God and Father of our Lord Jesus Christ! In his great mercy he has given us new birth into a living hope through the resurrection of Jesus Christ from the dead." (1 Peter 1:3)

> "Now that you have purified yourselves by obeying the truth so that you have sincere love for each other, love one another

deeply, from the heart. For you have been born again, not of perishable seed, but of imperishable, through the living and enduring word of God. For, 'All people are like grass, and all their glory is like the flowers of the field; the grass withers and the flowers fall, but the word of the Lord endures forever.' And this is the word that was preached to you." (1 Peter 1:22–25)

We're living in the last days. Most will be susceptible to false teachers because the Bible warns us that this is one of the signs of the end times.

Gradually, fewer and fewer people know anything about Jesus, His Word or His message to redeem the lost. The ignorant are so because they don't value knowledge. They willingly allow themselves to be drawn away by the trivial. Only those who value substance and seek the Lord with their whole heart will be kept from deception.

"Watching" involves remaining separated in an evil world.

Sin doesn't come roaring in like a flood at the beginning. It seeps into people's lives one drip at a time, slowly and gradually, eventually engulfing a person until there's no way of escape apart from the loving and gracious intervention of the Lord. Even the bondage sin creates is deceitful; the people who are bound actually fancy themselves to be free. Far too late they realize that they're compelled by their own wrong thinking, lusts, and corrupted character.

False teachers bring us bondage by touting lies but Jesus brings us freedom by preaching truth.

> "Then you will know the truth, and the truth will set you free." (John 8:32)

> "But encourage one another daily, as long as it is called 'Today,' so that none of you may be hardened by sin's deceitfulness." (Hebrews 3:13)

Many believe that freedom means "doing your own thing." But that belief is the very essence of sin and bondage. We must become grounded both in terms of what true faith looks like, and whom it resembles—the Lord Jesus Christ! Unless we know the original—not just know of Him, but be intimately acquainted—we'll fall for the counterfeit.

Don't waste your time studying imitators of Christ; that will just make you an expert in the false. Choose instead to study the Master and you'll possess all the wealth and value that comes from owning the original "masterpiece."

Christ is the only real truth. Following Him leads to lasting, eternal freedom. There's no middle ground and no middleman. Make sure you have nothing to do with counterfeit ministries or ministers, no matter how popular and inviting they may seem on the surface.

You must determine what it is you want; there can be no wavering. You either want life or you accept the death that comes by way of deception.

Remember that Jesus, the true Savior and Teacher, brings life and never death. We can and must have within us the assurance of a true salvation experience with Christ.

- "Jesus answered, 'I am the way and the truth and the life. No one comes to the Father except through me.'" (John 14:6)

My sincere desire for you is:

That you'll seize the spiritual wisdom God wants you to enjoy and that you'll become the woman of substance He designed you to be.

As Paul writes in Ephesians 1:15-19:

> "Ever since I first heard of your strong faith in the Lord Jesus and your love for God's people everywhere, I have not stopped thanking God for you. I pray for you constantly, asking God, the glorious Father of our Lord Jesus Christ, to give you *spiritual wisdom and insight so that you might grow in your knowledge of*

God. I pray that your hearts will be flooded with light so that you can understand the *confident hope* he has given to those he called—his holy people who are his rich and glorious inheritance. I also pray that you will understand the incredible greatness of God's power for us who believe him."

****

RECEIVING SALVATION AS A FREE GIFT FROM GOD TO YOU

If you would like to receive Jesus Christ as Lord and Savior of your life, I have included a prayer for salvation below. I've also added additional information so you can fully understand what it means to become a Christian or Christ follower.

****

The surest way to receive the life you were designed to live is to know God personally. It's not enough to know some Scriptures or to know *about* God. You must know Him *personally* by accepting Jesus as your Savior.

This is the only way to receive assurance of your salvation with Jesus at the end of your life. If you have any concerns that you may not be a genuine Christian (verses having religion) you may want to pray this Salvation Prayer and settle this matter once for all in your heart. Your eternal destiny depends on it.

Choose life, dear friend, choose life!

PRAYER FOR SALVATION

The Cornerstone is Christ?

What is the so-called Salvation Prayer? What must I do to receive salvation and eternal life?" At one point or another we all ask ourselves these questions. This is what the Bible tells us:

"That if you confess with your mouth the Lord Jesus and believe in your heart that God has raised Him from the dead, you will be saved." (Romans 10:9)

"Jesus answered and said to him, 'Most assuredly, I say to you, unless one is born again, he cannot see the kingdom of God.'" (John 3:3)

The Basics

The Salvation Prayer is merely a road to rebirth in Jesus Christ. To be born again you must confess Jesus as Lord and believe that He is. When you ask Him into your heart, you're permitting Him to be the Lord of your life.

A. Salvation is the "permission slip" to enter heaven when you leave this world.

B. Salvation takes place when a person hears the salvation message, believes it, and responds by deciding to ask Jesus to come into his or her heart. We can also receive God's message *by faith* through reading the Bible.

The Simple Steps:

1. Acknowledge in your heart that Jesus is Lord.

2. Confess with your mouth that Jesus is Lord.

3. Believe that Jesus died for your sins and was raised three days later.

4. Repent of your sins and be baptized in the name of Jesus.

A Tool to Communicate Our Faith

The Salvation Prayer is not about specific words spoken. It's not the "power of a prayer," but the power of committing our lives to Christ as Savior and Lord. The following is a guideline for a sincere step of faith:

"Dear Lord, I recognize that I've been living for myself and not for You. I acknowledge that I need You, so I am asking you to come into my life now. Change me and mold me into Your likeness. I acknowledge Your completed work on the cross. I ask You to forgive me of my sins as I come to You in repentance. Take up residence in my heart and be my king, my Lord, and my Savior. Help me to live for You and bring You glory with my life as I learn to overcome sin with the Holy Spirit's help. I ask this in Jesus' precious and holy name. Amen."

If you decided to repent of your sins and receive Christ today, welcome to God's family. Now, as a way to grow closer to Him, the Bible tells us to follow up on our commitment.

-Be baptized as commanded by Christ.

-Tell someone about your new faith in Christ.

-Spend time with God each day. It doesn't have to be a long period of time. Just develop the daily habit of praying to Him and reading His Word. Ask God to increase your faith and your understanding of the Bible.

-Seek fellowship with other believers.

-Develop a group of believing friends to answer your questions and support you.

-Find a local church where you can worship God.

~~~

Rejoice, for you are now a new creation in God (a Christian).

"Therefore, if anyone is in Christ, he is a new creation. The old has passed away; behold, the new has come."

-2 Corinthians 5:17, ESV

"If you confess with your mouth that Jesus is Lord and believe in your heart that God raised him from the dead, you will be saved."

-Romans 10:9, NLT

Signed: _____

Date: _____

Before we part I'd like to thank you for purchasing and reading my book. If you found wisdom and help in reading it and believe it will help others too, please take a moment to leave a review on Amazon. Thank you, Lilliet

End Notes

Chapter 3:

1. preacher@sermonnotebook.org.
2. Forerunner Commentary, *The Covenants, Grace, and Law (Part 1)* by John W. Ritenbaugh.

Chapter 4:
1. *The Beginning and the End*, GlobalChristians.org (women).
2. J. C. Wenger, *Introduction to Theology,* copyright 1954, renewal 1980 by Herald Press, Scottsdale, Penn., pp. 90–93. Available from bibleviews.com.
3. http://www.bibletools.org/index.cfm/fuseaction/*Producing-Fruit.*

Chapter 5:
1. Adapted from: *For God's Sake Grow Up*, David Ravenhill, 1997, Destiny Image Publishers, Inc.
2. Ibid.
3. Ibid.

Chapter 6:
1. Calvin's New Testament Commentaries, Vol. 10, p. 330.
2. http://bible.org/seriespage/parable-wedding-banquet.

Chapter 7:
1. http://bible.org/*permissive and perfect will of God.*
   http://bible.org/seriespage/wisdom-and-will-god.
2. John Piper, T*hree Stages of Knowing and Doing the Revealed Will of God*, © Desiring God. Website: desiringGod.org.

Chapter 8:
1. *Be Alert* by Warren Wiersbe, Fourth printing. Wheaton, Ill.: Victor Books, 1988.
2. *The Tyranny of the Urgent* by Charles E. Hummel. Downers Grove, Ill.: Inter Varsity Press, 1967.

LILLIET'S OTHER PAPERBACK BOOKS

1. The Secret Power of Godly Wisdom to Completely Transform   Your Life.

2. A Woman of Grace and Strength – Growing Strong in the Grace and Knowledge of our Lord.

LILLIET'S OTHER BOOKS

http://www.amazon.com/Lilliet-Garrison/e/B004H28MCU

Saying Goodbye to Discouragement-100 Bible Verses About Discouragement
How to Test the Spirits to See if They Are from God-61 Scriptures About Testing the Spirits
Binding the Strongman-How to Keep Satan from Stealing What is Rightfully Yours
How to Know if You Belong to God-54 Scriptures About Knowing God Personally
19 Ways We Grieve the Holy Spirit–100 Scriptures About Grieving the Holy Spirit
How to Resist the Devil-100 Scriptures on Resisting the Devil
Victory without Trying-100 Scriptures About God's Grace
Practicing the Presence of Jesus– 24 Scriptures on the Presence of Jesus
El Shaddai-The God Who is Enough- 67 B.V. on God is Always Enough
How to Die to Self…and receive the life Jesus died to give you
10 Reasons Why the Bible is the Word of God-100 Bible Verses About the Word of God
Recognizing the Antichrist: Bible Signs of the End Times-65 B.V. About the Antichrist
Deliverance from Bondage-100 Bible Verses About Deliverance from Evil
How to be Ready for the Rapture-100 Bible Verses About the Rapture
All of God's Promises are Yes and Amen -65 Bible Verses About Answered Prayers
I Will Not Leave You Comfortless-49 Bible Verses About the Comforter
Satan Wants Your Mind- 85 B.V About Satan & Our Mind -47 B.V. About Having a Sound Mind
How to Pray for the Lost, 100 Bible Verses About Praying for the Lost
Defeating Satan and Evil Spirits-100 Bible Verses About Satan, 58 Bible Verses About Evil Spirits
Don't Let Your Heart Harden- 40 Bible Verses About a Hard Heart
The Most Important Question -7 Benefits to Making the Right Decision about Jesus
How to Have Daily Family Devotions -91 Bible Verses About the Family
How God Guides Us – 96 Bible Verses About God's Guidance
Because Your Heart Was Tender-You Will Not See Evil-100 Scriptures. on the Tender Hearted-98 About Gentleness
A Much-Needed Heart Change- 100 Bible Verses About the Heart
Our Faithful Promiser-100 B.V. About the Promises of God - 67 B.V. About the Faithfulness of God
How to Overcome Sin-100 Bible Verses About Sin
Prayer Puts God to Work – 100 Bible Verses About Prayer
Spiritual Warfare-A Practical & Real Path to Victory over Temptation
Be Filled with the Holy Spirit-Living the Spirit Filled Life
A Faith that Saves-What is Believing Faith?
Choosing to Live One Day at a Time
Nothing Can Separate You from the Love of God
What Does the Bible Say About Satan and the Origin of Evil? 100 Bible Verses About Satan

Satan's Twisted Counterfeits – 100 Bible Verses About Satan
Is Heaven Real? – 100 Bible Verses About Heaven
What God's Love Teaches Us – 100 Bible Verses About God's Love
What Does the Bible Say About God's Mercy and Grace–85 Verses About God's Grace–88 About God's Mercy
What Does the Bible Say About Not Being Fearful–57 Verses About "Do Not Fear"–100 About Fear
What Does the Bible Say About Marriage? – 100 Bible Verses of God's Counsel for a Thriving, God-Centered Marriage
Will God Forgive Me? 100 Bible Verses About God's Forgiveness
What Does the Bible Say About Life After Death – 91 Bibles Verses from God to You
100 Bible Verses About Eternal Life
100 Bible Verses About Money: What God Says About Wealth & Poverty
Scriptures of God's Unfailing Love for You–God's Promises to Love You Forever
100 Bible Verses of God's Healing Power
40 Healing Scriptures That Will Forever Change Your Life
God's Promises to Bless You and Prosper You
Jesus Christ, Our Great Healer
God's Emergency Phone Numbers When You Find Yourself in Need
Prayers in Times of Trouble
The God of All Comfort Devotional
Prayer for Every Circumstance
God's Loving Kindness
The Power of Prayer to Change a Life
How to Be Sure You Are Saved
God's Promises for Your Every Concern
God's Promises to You in the Bible
Considerations for the God Seeker: Gems from Charles Spurgeon
Living Satisfied: Life Lessons from King Solomon and the Book of Ecclesiastes
7 Keys to a Victorious Life
How to Make Good Decisions–Practical Steps to Making God-Glorifying Choices
Secrets to Being a Happy Christian
Absolute Surrender–Surrender What You Can't Keep, To Gain What You Can Never Buy
The Greatest Prayer
How to Develop an Intimate Relationship with God
When God is Silent
How to Gain a Clear Conscience
The Unpardonable Sin – Is This Sin Really Unforgiveable?
A Woman of Powerful Prayer
Don't Be A Worry Wart – Accept God's Peace and Change Your Life
Breaking Free from Guilt and Shame
Getting Unstuck–Moving Beyond What's Holding You Back
The Christian Woman's Guide to Abundant Success
A Woman of Grace and Strength – Growing Strong in the Grace and Knowledge of our Lord
A Woman of Substance–Growing Spiritually Mature in an Immature World (Unabridged, 8 volumes in 1 book)
A Woman of Substance Series (8 individual volumes)

FIND LILLIET'S AUTHOR PAGE ON AMAZON AT:

http://www.amazon.com/Lilliet-Garrison/e/B004H28MCU

Printed in Great Britain
by Amazon